Reading Abbey
A pilgrim church

John Mullaney

With contributions by Kevin Hayward

2023

'Reading Abbey - A pilgrim church'

© John Mullaney

First published xxxx

ISBN 978-0-xxxxxxxxx

Every attempt has been made to contact any holders of copyright for the illustrations used in this book. If we have made any omissions in acknowledging these we would be grateful if you contact us so that this may be rectified in any future reprint.

Jacket design
J.R.Mullaney FSAI

Published by Scallop Shell Press

29 Derby Road,

Caversham,

Reading.

RG4 5HE

Henry I holding Reading Abbey,
from Matthew Paris 'Historia Anglorum'.

Image courtesy of the British Library, Cotton Claudius, D.V1. f 9r

BACKGROUND TO WRITING THIS BOOK

Like many Reading people, I am an incomer. I came to the University of Reading in 1967, and only occasionally ventured into the town. I was vaguely aware of piles of flint, a jumble of ruins, behind the Forbury Gardens. Then there was the Gateway. This had all the appearances of a much restored Victorian reconstruction: very doubtfully medieval.

Some ten years later, married with a small child who was at St James' Church nursery school, I was told by my four year old son that a king was buried under the school playground. A few years on, I was asked by the then Parish Priest, Canon Edward Conway, to write a booklet about the history of St James Church.

Both these events brought me into contact with Reading Abbey and its ruins. I have to admit that what I saw did not impress me. It seemed that there had been a great deal of restoration, much of it poorly executed, to the fabric of the standing remains. It was around this time that Dr Slade was undertaking deep excavations of the apse area; something I look at in the pages of this book.

Leaping forward some twenty five years, having retired, I was asked by another parish priest of St James' Church, Canon John O'Shea (known as Father John), to research and write a more comprehensive book, not just about the church, but about its broader historical context. My wife Lindsay and I delved into the Catholic archives in London and Portsmouth. We produced a book, *Reformation, Revolution and Rebirth*. This traced the origins of St James' parish, from the time of the dissolution of the abbey in 1539, to the design of St James' church by AWN Pugin, and its opening in 1840.

There was an ever increasing public interest in the ancient abbey itself. We received a stream of enquiries as to the whereabouts of the 'king in the playground'. This was stimulated by the discovery of the remains of Richard III. Could Reading too have a 'king under the car park' of the now defunct gaol? It was common knowledge that Henry I had been buried in the church of Reading Abbey, but where exactly?

Lindsay, Father John and I met several times with Phillipa Langley, discoverer of Richard III. I was very doubtful that the king's remains were still *in situ*. Nevertheless, Phillipa had proved herself in Leicester. So we set up a meeting with Reading Borough Council. Sarah Hacker (the Mayor), and Tony Page (Deputy Leader of the Council), were most interested in what we had to say. Together we agreed to create a working group which we called the Hidden Abbey Project (HAP). Richard Stainthorp, who many years had served as a councillor at Reading, and had held the office of Mayor in 2004–5, was Chair. From the start, therefore, as the title indicated, we were not primarily searching for the bones of a long dead monarch. The focus was on discovering more about the abbey itself, especially the parts that were no longer visible, were below ground: were *hidden.*

In the meantime, two important events were taking place. The Government closed the gaol in 2013. They were now seeking to sell it off. As it is an important archaeological site, the Ministry of Justice (MOJ), needed to conduct an archaeological survey. They employed the Museum of London Archaeology. The MOJ joined the HAP group. This now included the Catholic Diocese of Portsmouth, as owners of St James' on whose land the north transept of the abbey lies, and Reading Borough Council, as owners of the main part of the ruins. The enforced closure of the ruins, due to its dangerous state as flints began to fall off the walls, had increased public alarm. Reading Council worked on putting in a bid to get Heritage Lottery Fund money for conservation work. To promote wider interest and support, they created the *Reading Abbey Revealed Project.* This aimed at raising awareness among the public, not just of the existence of the ancient abbey and its ruins, but its importance nationally as well as locally.

In 1984, the Friends of Reading Abbey (FoRA), was founded by a small far-sighted group. The co-founders were Professor Brian Kemp and Janet Bond, with the involvement of Julia Boorman. Its aim was to promote awareness of the abbey's importance, to encourage interest in, and understanding of, its history and architecture, and to support the preservation of the ruins. FoRA was an active supporter of Reading Borough Council's successful *Reading Abbey Revealed Project*, which won Heritage Lottery Funding to conserve the Abbey Ruins and Gate. Completion of this allowed public access to the ruins, once more, from 2018. In June 2021, along with the Council and other local partners, FoRA celebrated *Reading Abbey 900*, the nonocentenary of the abbey's foundation in June 1121, with a summer of public events.

Following on from our researches into the origins of St James' church, Lindsay had looked more closely at the time of the French Revolution, when about 100 French refugee priests came to Reading. One in particular, François Longuet, had founded the first Catholic purpose-built church in Reading since the Reformation: the 'Chapel of the Resurrection'. This was a direct precursor of St James'. In the meantime, I went deeper into the story of the ancient abbey. Between us, we wrote several books, gave talks and published papers about various aspects of the abbey.

Lindsay and I became involved with the production of two plays about Henry I, and his daughter the Empress Matilda. Written by Beth Flintoff, and produced by what is now Rabble Theatre, they were staged at St James' church. This resulted in a book by Lindsay, *Henry I and his Abbey.* I wrote about the largest piece of sculpture found on the abbey site. Probably a pillar capital, it was converted into a baptismal

Reading Abbey - A pilgrim church

font in 1840 for St James' church. It is known as the 'Reading Abbey Stone'. The research for both these publications features in this book.

One of the most intriguing aspects of my researches has been the way stones and carvings from the abbey have been distributed around the town. I met up with Dr Kevin Hayward, a petrologist from the University of Reading and consultant expert, who, among many other projects, contributed to the definitive book about the Cosmati Pavement at Westminster Abbey.

As an offshoot of the HAP, we set up the Hidden Abbey Stones Project (HASP). We found stones that most probably have their origins in Reading Abbey, spread far and wide in Oxfordshire and Hampshire as well as Berkshire. One of the well-documented claims was that some abbey stones had been transported, at the time of Queen Mary Tudor, to Windsor Castle to build the Poor Knights' Lodgings. The results of this investigation are included in this book.

Another fascinating piece of my researches resulted from the publication, by Brian Kemp, of *Reading Abbey records—a new miscellany.* Included in this work is a document Professor Kemp came across in the British Library, where it had been 'misfiled'. It is an account of the liturgy held at the abbey on the first of every month, and, with greater pomp, on the annual anniversary of Henry I's death. It reveals so much, not just about the ceremonial, but also about the structure and use of the abbey, and the daily lives of the monks. In explaining the ritual, I show how the monks and the people of the time viewed the purpose of life, and how this tied into the importance of pilgrimage

Reading Abbey was a Benedictine foundation. Its modern counterpart is Douai Abbey, west of Reading. Lindsay and I worked with the then abbot, Geoffrey Scott, on several projects. In the Douai library you can see some remarkable sculptures from the ancient abbey, including the carved head of a king. We worked on a 17th century book, held at Douai, which tells the story of the Benedictine order in England. Reading figures only a few times, but when it is mentioned, we discovered some important pieces of information with regard to its role as a pilgrim church, and its connection with St James, the apostle of pilgrimage.

The above is an outline of how I came to accumulate information about the abbey. The Friends of Reading Abbey have put many of my research papers on their website. By bringing them all together in printed form, I aim to make my researches more widely available. The book has a unifying theme, and that is the role of Reading Abbey as a pilgrim church. I argue that its art, architecture, music and liturgy, all combine to underpin the importance of pilgrimage.

I ask for a degree of understanding from readers when they approach this work. As each chapter is the result of researches over a period of more than twelve years, there is a degree of repetition across chapters. However, I decided to leave much of this in place, as it means that the reader does not have to refer to details elsewhere in the book. Each chapter stands, to a large extent, on its own.

Likewise, the formats of different chapters differ one from another. For example, some have extensive notes, whereas in others I have included such explanations within the text. Much of the content is factual. But I also include personal, and possibly controversial, opinions. I endeavour to ensure that the reader can distinguish the two. Most of all, I hope this work adds to informed debate and appreciation of Reading's most important relic: its ruined abbey.

John Mullaney, Spring 2023

Reading Abbey - A pilgrim church

The Arms of Reading Abbey
from *Reading Abbey*
Jamieson B Hurry

The Arms of Reading Abbey

The scallop shells represent the apostle St James the Greater.
He is the patron of pilgrimage, whose foremost shrine is at Compostela in Spain, where tradition says he is buried.

The right of the abbots of Reading to wear the mitre, and other vestments proper to episcopal office, was probably granted by the Pope in 1288. The abbots of Reading were not bishops, but 'mitred abbots'. The mitre was an emblem of Divine authority as granted by the Papacy.

The coat of arms therefore represents the twin purposes of the abbey: a place of prayer for the monks, and a place of care for the pilgrim.

CONTENTS

INTRODUCTION   2

1.   THE EAST END OF THE ABBEY CHURCH AND THE BURIAL PLACE OF HENRY I   4

2.   THE ABBEY CHURCH - ITS DESIGN AND PURPOSE   44

3.   MAPS, SURVEYS AND EXCAVATIONS   51

4.   THE CHAPTER HOUSE   65

5.   THE TOWERS   92

6.   NORTH TRANSEPT—MORTAR ANALYSIS (Dr Kevin Hayward and John Mullaney)   112

7.   THE STONES OF READING ABBEY   (Dr Kevin Hayward and John Mullaney)   120

8.   READING ABBEY'S STONES AND WINDSOR CASTLE (Dr Kevin Hayward and John Mullaney)   135

9.   THE 'READING ABBEY STONE'   153

10.   THE STONE OF THE 'CORONATION OF THE VIRGIN'   164

11.   THE COMMEMORATION SERVICE FOR HENRY I   172

12.   THE MUSIC OF A CLUNIAC BENEDICTINE MONASTERY   204

13.   PILGRIMAGE AND RELICS   216

POSTSCRIPT   236

ACKNOWLEDGEMENTS   238

BIBLIOGRAPHY   240

SOME OF THE PRINCIPAL PEOPLE CONNECTED WITH THE STUDY OF READING ABBEY   241

INDEX   243

INTRODUCTION

Reading Abbey - A pilgrim church

The architecture, art, music and spirituality of Reading Abbey, 1121 - 1539.

Henry I founded the monastery at Reading as a place of prayer for the salvation for his eternal soul and for the souls of his ancestors and descendants. It was his mausoleum and was intended to be that of his family ever after.[1]

The first chapters of this work concentrate, not on the abbey's spirituality, but on its physical aspects: its architecture. Like so many writers before me, I start with the magnificence of its ruins. The chapter house itself is a stunning building. Many of those I have taken there cannot believe that this was one large 'room', with a massive single-span barrel vaulted ceiling, and without supporting central pillars.

But then I am asked the inevitable questions, 'Have you found Henry I yet?', or 'Do you know where Henry is buried?'. The answer to the second question is straightforward. We know to within a few yards where he was buried. The answer to the first question could be a simple 'no'. This has led to speculation that his body may still be there, with a call for a search to find it. But the answer I would like to give is 'yes'. And that is what this book is all about.

The answer is 'yes', because, by understanding Reading Abbey, we can indeed find Henry: not his coffin, nor his bones, nor any remnant that may have survived the ravages of a millennium. But we can find the real man, one of the greatest of the kings of England, and we find him in an unexpected way. We find him by going on a journey, a pilgrimage, to the magnificent building that was a testament to his life.

We can also begin to understand the complex system of monasteries and religious orders that were evolving in the 11th and 12th centuries. There was move from independent monasteries, towards congregations or groups. Most, by a long way, followed the rule of the 6th century monk St Benedict of Nursia (Norcia in modern-day Italy). One such group had its main monastery at Cluny in Burgundy, and so known as Cluniacs. Other congregations, also following Benedict's rule of life, such as the Cistercians followed. Reading Abbey was founded by Cluniac monks. There is often confusion over these terms. In short, all 'Cluniacs' were 'Benedictines', but not all 'Benedictines' were 'Cluniacs'.

Today's abbey looks like a dilapidated jumble of stones and mortar. What, if anything, can they teach us? Excavating Reading Abbey, once one of the largest, richest and prestigious in England, not only gives us an insight into Henry, the king and man, but also into the lives of those who lived in, and visited, Reading for a period spanning over 400 years. But it is not a physical excavation, though this may still happen. No, it is an excavation of the ideas and beliefs that created the abbey. It is an excavation where I will use the stones, art and music from the abbey, to reveal a world of profound beauty, deep spirituality, and a space that still offers solace and calm in the heart of a buzzing modern town. It is a place for today's pilgrim, just as it was a place of pilgrimage in medieval times.

The chapters are so arranged that I begin by examining the physical structure of the abbey. I will then show how its magnificence and its opulence reveal a deeper, spiritual meaning, both to those whose home it was, and to its many thousands of visitors for over 400 years.

Finally, I hope to show how its power and influence remain a positive force for good today.

Our journey, or pilgrimage, starts with revealing Henry's burial site. It is the most holy of places, not because Henry was a 'saint', far from it, but because he was flawed and wished to 'put things right'.

Henry I, from Matthew Paris' *Historia Anglorum* c.1253.
Image courtesy of the British Library, Cotton Claudius, D.V1. f 9r

Notes

1.   Foundation Charter: *I, (Henry) therefore, by the advice of my bishops and other faithful subjects have, for the salvation of my soul and that of King William my father, King William my brother, William my son, Queen Matilda my mother, Queen Matilda my wife and all my ancestors and successors, have built at Reading a new monastery in honour of the ever Virgin Mary, Mother of God, and Blessed John the Evangelist.*

Although this charter was clearly written some time after the Abbey's foundation in 1121, it is generally accepted that it reflected Henry's intentions and may be an amended version of the original. (Kemp *Cartularies,* Vol 1 p35*).*

CHAPTER 1

THE EAST END OF THE ABBEY CHURCH AND THE BURIAL PLACE OF HENRY I

CONTENTS   PAGE

PART 1 - ARCHITECTURAL ANALYSIS OF THE EAST END OF READING ABBEY CHURCH   5

PART 2 - DETAILED EXAMINATION OF THE DESIGN AND USE OF THE CHANCEL AT READING   13

PART 3 - THE *READING ABBEY RECORDS* AND THE POSITION OF THE TOMB OF HENRY I   19

PART 4 - THEORIES CONCERNING THE LOCATION OF HENRY I's TOMB   27

PART 5 - OTHER DOCUMENTARY EVIDENCE FOR THE SITING OF HENRY'S TOMB   33

PART 6 - CONCLUSIONS   37

PART 7 -   THE ABBEY SITE TODAY - POSSIBLE LOCATIONS OF THE ABBOT'S SEAT AND OF THE TOMB OF HENRY I,
             SUPERIMPOSED ON THE CURRENT BUILDINGS   40

PART 1 - ARCHITECTURAL ANALYSIS OF THE EAST END OF READING ABBEY CHURCH

1.   The Ambulatory
2.   High Altar
3.   Presbytery
4.   Choir—east end
5.   Choir—west end
6.   North transept
7.   South transept
8.   North aisle
9.   South aisle
10.   East end of the nave

PLAN OF THE EAST END OF READING ABBEY CHURCH

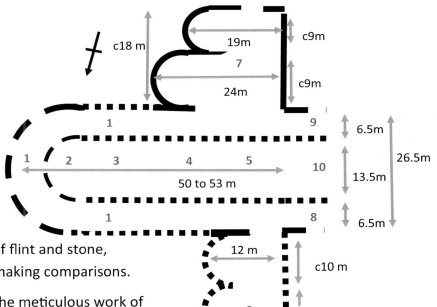

NOTE ABOUT THE MEASUREMENTS

There is a margin of error of one to two metres in these measurements. This is because of differing factors, including the varying thickness of the walls of the standing remains, mostly due to the robbing of flint and stone, and to the lack of any remains elsewhere on the site which would help in making comparisons.

The measurements are based upon Google Earth photographs, and the meticulous work of Dr Baxter, which may be found in his book *The Royal Abbey of Reading,* and on his website, *The Corpus of Romanesque Sculpture in Britain and Ireland.*

DASHES ▬ ▬ ▬ indicate no standing remains but GPR and earlier excavations show their location.

DOTS ■ ■ ■ ■ indicate few, or no, remains or archaeological evidence.

SOLID LINES ▬▬▬ indicate standing ruins.

THE NUMBERING ON THE PLAN

NUMBER 1, and then **NUMBERS 6 TO 10** are merely the standard architectural terms for the areas indicated. I shall look at these areas after examining the chancel - numbers 2 to 5.

Reading Abbey - A pilgrim church

THE CHANCEL: NUMBERS 2 TO 5

The most sacred part of the church was the chancel, where the main liturgical ceremonies took place. In some of the earliest Christian churches this was separated from the rest of the internal space by a low barrier called a templon. In time, this structure became more substantial; the area became screened off and entry was through a gate, or lattice work screen, in Latin *cancellus*. It has been claimed that this gave rise to the term 'chancel'. The area immediately around the altar became known as the 'sanctuary' or 'holy place'. The term 'presbytery', or priests' section, was also applied to the whole area, though sometimes more specifically to the sanctuary or to the open space in front of it. In this work, for the sake of clarity, I am going to distinguish the various parts of the chancel according to their liturgical usage. So on the plan, number 2, where the altar lies, is the sanctuary. To its west come the presbytery, number 3, and, further west still, the choir, numbers 4 and 5. By the 12th century this had become the standard division of most large churches in western Christendom.

St. Clements, Rome. *Templon*

NUMBER 2 The High Altar in the Sanctuary

There has been some debate about the position of the high altar in Reading Abbey. The reason for the discussion is the often repeated statement, by Gervase of Canterbury, that Henry had been buried in front of the high altar *(ante altare sepultum est)*. There has been some suggestion that an archaeological excavation could help identify the altar's exact location. In fact the altar would have been on a raised area, accessed by some steps, usually three, from the presbytery. It would not have had any foundations. There is no evidence at Reading that it stood above a crypt containing the bones of a saint. Some altars were so built. Had this been the case, it would have given an indication of the high altar's position at Reading. It is, therefore, unlikely that any excavation will reveal its location. On the other hand, by comparing the design of Reading with other Romanesque churches, especially those with Cluniac influences, it is possible to come to an informed conclusion about its positioning. Of course, if a crypt were discovered, this would be a most exciting development.

To begin with it is necessary to examine the area of the apse. It is semi-circular, with a width equal to that of the nave of the church: namely about 13.5 metres. Its radius, therefore, is approximately 6.75m. The altar would have been placed on a chord of the semi-circle, within the radius of the apse: the high altar's position in comparable Romanesque monasteries. One possible position would have been close to the rear wall. The altar slab itself would have been at least one metre from front to back, standing somewhat proud of the rear wall of the apse. We shall see that Dr Slade, in his excavations of the 1970s, placed the altar in this position, as did the Ordnance Survey map of the 1870s, which was based on Albury's work in the 19th century. Alternatively, it could have stood further west, within the cord of the apse semi-circle. There is also the possibility that it could have stood even further west, still within the area marked as '2' on the diagram. One reason for postulating these latter two possibilities is that the records of Cluny Abbey say that the monks 'circled' the altar when censing it. This would have required quite a bit of space. It has been suggested that, having located the altar, one could then make a reasonable estimate as to the location of Henry's tomb. I shall examine this theory later.

NUMBERS 3, 4 AND 5
THE CHOIR

It is not possible to be sure as to the exact demarcation points in the chancel for numbers 3 to 5. We can be certain that to the west of the altar there would have been an open space for the liturgical ceremonies, usually referred to as the presbytery, and marked as number 3 on the plan. This would have led onto the choir to its west.

The choir itself may have been divided into segments. There were usually two of these, with access points to the back stalls about half way along. There was a wider space, between the two lines of stalls, where the great lectern could be placed. The stalls were normally in three tiers. Those to the rear were allocated to more senior members of the community. From an early period, these most probably had individual stalls *(stalli),* rather than mere benches

Beverley Minster. Early 16th century choir stalls in three tiers with an access point to the rear stalls in the middle. The back row has elaborate canopies, whilst the front row is a simple bench.

As the centuries passed, the stalls became ever more elaborate, with canopies and highly decorated carvings. The front row was often a simple bench, and was used by the most junior members of the monastic community, such as novices and trainee choristers. The Cluniac customaries, *consuetudines* in Latin, which were the practical rule books for individual monasteries, specifically mention this sort of seating, and warn against intimate contact between the monks, even to the extent of not allowing their habits to touch.

Reading Abbey - A pilgrim church

By allotting a typical 750cm to each monk's stall, we are able to estimate the length of the choir area, with 100 places on both the north and south sides. If there were three rows, then the overall length would have been about 25 metres. With this number of places to fit into the chancel, it is unlikely that there would have been only two rows; if this had been the case, the choir would have impinged on the presbytery and almost reached the altar. This is an unlikely hypothesis.

Two words are used in the *Abbey Records* to describe the seating. These are *forme* (benches), and *sedile* (chair). The words *formae,* or *formulae* (the earlier spelling), can be found in the records of the monastery of St Gall. It is the earliest known monastic plan, dating to the 9th century. These seats had backs, but without divisions. In the 11th century, the introduction of separating arms resulted in stalls (*stalli),* and this term is used in the *Abbey Records* when referring to the abbot's place in the choir. We also read that the abbot had a *sedile.* This is normally just translated as a seat. However, it may refer to a special chair or throne, as described by Daniel DeGreve in his work about clergy seating in the middle ages. [1]

I will be examining the importance of the word *sedile* shortly.

We need to be cautious about being too definitive concerning the uses of these terms. It is possible that some of the seats were just benches. However, in such a prestigious monastery, it is likely that the seating at Reading would have been both highly ornamented and according to the latest designs.

In the plan above the pulpitum is shown with the letter A.

The pulpitum or screen separated the choir from the rest of the church.

Numbering as on page 5.

The Presbytery

This whole chancel area would probably have been raised above the level of the nave and surrounding ambulatory. I have already pointed out that the altar would likewise have been higher than the level of the presbytery, which in turn may have been higher than the choir, though this was not always the case. In the *Abbey Records* there is mention of a pavement. This can be open to various interpretations which I shall look at later. The presbytery was, therefore, a large open space between the altar and the choir where much of the liturgical ceremony would have been enacted.

The principal liturgical act was the Mass. The word 'liturgy' itself comes from the Greek, meaning 'public act'. The Mass at the high altar was the focus of the re-enactment of the suffering, death, and resurrection of Jesus Christ. It consisted of elaborate ceremonial, with readings from the Old and New Testaments, followed by the Eucharist, meaning 'thanksgiving'. The word 'Eucharist' is used in the earliest known Christian liturgies, dating to the first centuries AD.

It should be noted that Slade pointed out a potential position of the high altar. He stated that the area had been destroyed, probably when the gaol was being built in the 1840s. However, the 2016 Ground Penetrating Radar (GPR) survey revealed features not seen by Slade. These include what may be graves near the high altar. There were also anomalous traces which may indicate Abbey remains.

The ceremonial of both the Mass and the Office, at Reading, was so elaborate that it involved many participants. The presiding priest would have been assisted by a deacon and sub-deacon, accompanied by other clergy. As we read in the *Abbey Records,* monks in copes, as many as six of whom are mentioned at one point, would have taken part. There would also have been acolytes, at least two per 'coped' monk, and probably at least two thurifers. There would most likely have been more. For example, though not mentioned in the *Abbey Records*, probably because the readers would have known this, there would have been a nominated candle bearer for each reader. In short, a large open area in front of the altar was an essential element in the church plan.

As in any Benedictine monastery, and especially one following the Cluniac tradition, the ceremonies would have been very elaborate. They would have consisted of complicated and lengthy chants, with incense, candles and processions through the church, many starting from the chapter house, but sometimes from the town. These would have been spectacles to inspire the onlookers. Although the chancel was cut off from the main body of the church, including the ambulatory, the music and perfumes would have pervaded the whole church.

Reading Abbey - A pilgrim church

We read in the *Abbey Records* that, at specified times, bells were rung inside and outside the church. It was not just the material fabric of the church that was built to impress; the whole ceremonial was designed to inspire all-comers with the magnificence of this, the entrance to the New Jerusalem. The presbytery, with its ceremonials, was the beating heart of the liturgy, but it was just one part of it. High Mass would have been sung daily after the Office hour of Sext, at midday. But this has to be placed in the context of the whole liturgy, or *Opus Dei,* the "Work of God", which was dominated by the singing of the Divine Office. This was done mainly in the choir of the church. The exact timings of some of these 'hours' depended on the season of the year, and the length of day. In addition, in Cluniac monasteries, it had become the custom to sing the appropriate 'hour' from the 'Office of the Dead', after each hour of the Office of the day. As devotion towards Mary, mother of Jesus, grew, it was also normal to include the Little Office of the Blessed Virgin Mary. In addition to about eight hours a day in choir, the monks would spend many hours studying, writing and practising the psalms and other texts to be sung. It can be seen that long hours were spent in the choir. For this reason, early on in monastic history, it was agreed that there should be backs to the benches, and eventually seats where the monks, though standing, could rest, half sitting, on the so called 'mercy seats' or misericords.

Just as the chancel served a liturgical purpose, so too did the other areas, such as the transepts and the ambulatory. As with many Cluniac monasteries, Reading was a pilgrim church. Visitation records of Cluniac monasteries consistently report on two areas of primary importance. The first was the correct celebration of the liturgy, and what we may term the internal running of the monastery. This included the saying of Masses, the rule of silence, the proper observation of the liturgy, the *Opus Dei,* comportment at meal times and so on. But, second, and of equal importance, were the requirements of hospitality, almsgiving and general care for the poor. The visitation reports of another Cluniac monastery, Bermondsey, of 1262, supply just one example of how important these were seen to be and how strictly they were enforced. Care for the poor was paramount. We also read about this in the *Reading Records*, as when we see the detailed instructions concerning the distribution of charity, specifically food, known as orts, in connection with the commemoration of Henry's death, which took place not just annually, but every month.

Reading was designed as a pilgrim church. Its large nave welcomed visitors who could circulate round the building. Probably entering by the northerly west end door, groups or individuals would proceed round the church, no doubt stopping to make their devotions at one side altar or another. They would pass through the north transept with its larger altars, where a relic, or at least some saintly or angelic image, may well have been displayed. The sun filtering through the colours of the stained glass windows would mix with the sound of the monks chanting in the chancel, and with the warmth and smoke of the beeswax candles swirling round the church, mingling with the perfume of the incense, rising heavenwards. The pilgrims would then continue their way behind the chancel by way of the ambulatory, and so to the south transept, down the south aisle, to exit onto the garth, or green, in front of the west doors.

In the south transept there are two apsidal chapels, the more northerly being larger than the other. Could it be that this was the chapel which held the shrine to St James? We are fortunate to have a 12th century manuscript, the *Miracles of the Hand of St James,* now in the archives of Gloucester Cathedral, which contains twenty-eight stories which relate to miracles supposedly wrought through the intervention of the apostle, St James the Greater. We read, in Miracle XIII, that there was such an altar and that it had a picture of the saint. If so, most probably, the relic of the Hand of St James would have been brought there on special occasions, such as his feast day, July 25th. The fact that, at least in the 12th century, visitors and pilgrims were not always segregated from the holiest part of the church, the chancel, is amply demonstrated several times in the *Miracles of the Hand of St James*. In other words, the chancel, though reserved for monastic liturgical use during services, was sometimes open for lay pilgrims, including women. Several of the stories tell of monks helping sick pilgrims by bringing them into the chancel.

The ambulatory, which allowed for the circulation of pilgrims round the church, also featured in the ceremonial of the abbey. The Cluniac tradition extolled the spiritual value of processions. These were viewed as mini-pilgrimages which, like all pilgrimages, symbolised the journey through life. Just as the journey of life has an end, so too the processions ended, probably at one of the many shrines in the abbey church, with a concluding ritual promising the forgiveness of sins and eternal joy. 'Salvation', symbolised by this type of ceremonial, was the eschatological purpose of the monastery and of a monk's life.

Right: List of the Office Hours. These would have been sung or chanted. The more solemn the day, the more elaborate would have been the music. The longest by far was Matins. The names, Prime, Terce, Sext and None refer to the 'hour' of the day when said. These were much shorter than Matins, having only three psalms each, though with the addition of hymns and canticles the length was variable.

I suggest the reader interested in more details consults one of the many books or online articles written about the Divine Office.

The Divine Office comprised the following eight 'Hours':
1. Matins—between 2am, or even earlier, and 4 am,
2. Lauds - sunrise
3. Prime - 6 am
4. Terce - 9 am,
5. Sext - Midday,
6. None - 3 pm,
7. Vespers—Sunset,
8. Compline—before bed, anytime time from about 8 pm to 9pm.

NUMBERS 1, 6 AND 7 THE AMBULATORY AND TRANSEPTS

Fig 1 shows how the chancel (numbers 2 to 5) was encircled by a passageway or ambulatory (number 1). This led to the transepts (numbers 6 and 7), and ultimately to the nave and aisles of the church (numbers 8, 9 and 10). Dr Slade excavated part of this area in the 1970s (Fig 2) (*Berkshire Archaeological Journal* - BAJ - Vol 68) and the 2016 Ground Penetrating Survey - GPR - (Fig 3) confirmed aspects of his findings.

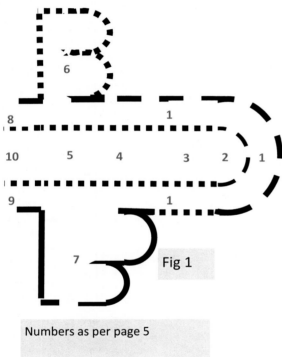

Fig 1

Numbers as per page 5

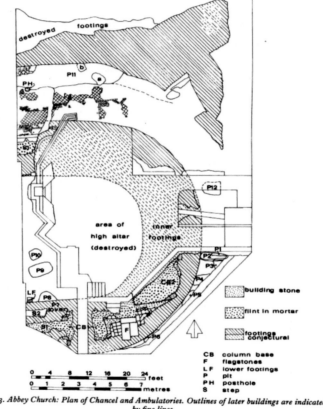

Fig. 3. Abbey Church: Plan of Chancel and Ambulatories. Outlines of later buildings are indicated by fine lines.

35

Fig 2   Dr Slade's excavations 1970s (BAJ Vol 68)

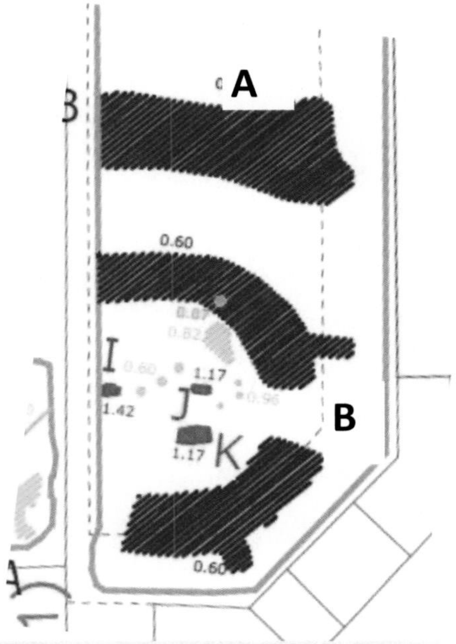

Fig 3

GPR survey

A Outer ambulatory wall.

B Inner wall

I,J,K See pages 9, 24 and 63

PART 2 - DETAILED EXAMINATION OF THE DESIGN AND USE OF THE CHANCEL AT READING

STRUCTURAL AND ARCHAEOLOGICAL EVIDENCE

Before presenting the alternative possibilities regarding the design and use of various parts of the chancel at Reading, I should like to draw attention to the possible existence of a pulpitum in the abbey church. This will help determine the design and positioning of the choir and possibly of the abbot's chair. We shall see how this, in turn, may also help narrow down the location of Henry I's tomb.

The GPR survey revealed the possibility of a pulpitum. When I first saw the findings its very existence was pure speculation on my part, based upon what one might expect to find in a Romanesque monastic church.[2]

I have made frequent reference to Kemp's publication, *Reading Abbey Records a new miscellany.* Among the treasures in this indispensable resource for any serious student of Reading Abbey, is a specific reference to a pulpitum. This architectural feature occurs in one of the *Miracles of the Hand of St James*. It is number XVIII, which Kemp dates to between 1163 and 1187. During the account of this miracle, Kemp's translation says that *the lord Gilbert, bishop of London, went up on to the screen and, as he transferred the hand of the most holy apostle from the old reliquary to the new one, he blessed the people with it.*

What is of interest is the word used in the original Latin for Kemp's English word 'screen'. In the Latin this is *pulpitum.* Here we have probable documentary evidence not just of a screen, but of a particular type of screen, namely a 'pulpitum'. I will describe the full importance of this later. For the moment I should like to point out that this type of screen is always situated at the entrance to the choir area; in fact its primary function was to be the real and symbolic formal entry into the chancel, the most sacred part of the church. (See page 96)

It is possible that the first pulpitum was made of wood, and that the substantial stone screen indicated by the GPR, if indeed this is what the survey is showing, was erected at a later date.

Possible remains of the footings for a pulpitum, as shown on the GPR survey.

It is also possible that the first screen was not sited where the GPR possible footings indicate, but further west in the nave. As we have seen, it is unlikely to have been further east, as the number of choir places required, if there were indeed 200 monks, would have made it difficult, if not impossible, to fit them all into the space available in the chancel.

THE WEST END OF THE CHANCEL

We know, therefore, that some sort of screen, according to the *Abbey Records* a pulpitum, stood in the abbey church by the late 1180s. As this structure was invariably placed at the entrance to the chancel, we may reasonable assume that it was somewhere near to where the nave and crossing met, and this is exactly where the GPR survey shows what could be its footings.

Having also seen the length required to accommodate the number of monks within the chancel, I am taking the liberty of assuming that the pulpitum, be it the original or maybe one built later, is that as shown on the GPR survey, and therefore at the entrance to the crossing, letter A on the plan. I have also inserted choir stalls in areas 4 and 5.

As we have seen, the choir was the area where the monks would have spent most of their time when in church. The *Opus Dei,* the 'work of God', was not just a devotional liturgical act, it was the culmination of the hours spent transcribing, learning and practising the chants. It was considered 'work', and indeed it would have been exhausting labour. For this reason the Cluniacs considered that its observance complied with St Benedict's injunction that the monks should engage in work and prayer. This was summed up in the aphorism 'to work is to pray', *laborare est orare,* which may also be interpreted as 'to pray is to work'. This derives from Benedict's twofold instruction that a monk's life should be one of 'prayer and work', *ora et labora.*

The Cluniac emphasis on elaborate chant was questioned by some. The Cistercians, for instance, stressed the need for manual work, especially in the fields, alongside the duty of prayer in choir.

Numbering as on page 5.
'A' pulpitum, see page 8

Be that as it may, in a Cluniac monastery, the chancel was at the centre of monastic life and the choir area underpinned the liturgy in all its aspects. Just as the ceremonial was ornamented with highly decorated vestments and elaborate liturgy, so too the whole monastery would have been designed to reflect the words of the chants, based on the psalms, canticles and other scriptural readings. In Reading Abbey, as at Cluny, the walls would have been painted with pictures retelling biblical stories. The pillar capitals may well have had sculptured figures representing the struggle between the forces of good and evil, of the vices and virtues, as told in the 5th century allegory, the *Psychomachia*, or *War of the Souls.* Whether or not such existed at Reading, it is certain that Cluniac monks would have been familiar with the images and the morality tales associated with them.

One source and inspiration for art and sculpture was the *Physiologus.* Of unknown authorship, this book was probably compiled in the 5th century, though earlier dates have been suggested, and may be based on ancient Romano-Greek anthropomorphic tales. Unlike some early natural histories, such as Pliny's *Natural History,* the *Physiologus* was never intended to be an accurate account of the animal kingdom. The work does use descriptions of animals found in such earlier works, but its aim was very different. The images were designed to convey a moral tale, representing Christian religious dogma, or warnings as to the consequences of immoral behaviour.

Gloucester cathedral— misericord

They are allegorical figures telling of the virtues and vices which, it was believed, were embedded in nature. This was a metaphysical dimension where moral characteristics transcended the boundaries between the spiritual and physical world. Fantastical hybrid creatures might result, but today's observer should always remember their allegorical and metaphorical intention. Nor is this just a modern interpretation. Origen, writing in the early 3rd century, argued that only someone in danger of 'losing their wits' would believe that 'God planted trees in the garden of Eden like a gardener'. He argued for a metaphorical, moral and spiritual interpretation of scripture. (*De Principiis* IV.IV.1.)

Reading Abbey - A pilgrim church

Misericords and Tiles

Today the most readily visible, and well preserved, examples of these stories and figures, are to found on the misericords of choir seats all over Europe. Whereas many stone sculptures are difficult to see or decipher, as they are either high in the vaults, on top of pillars, or badly weathered from being outdoors, these wooden carved sculptures present us with images of fascinating immediacy and intimacy.

The picture on the previous page shows one such seat from Gloucester cathedral. Like many extant misericords, it dates to the 14th century. The photograph shows the small ledge on which the monk could rest whilst still standing, the misericord. Under this are carved figures, described on the Cathedral's website as 'monsters'.

The one on the left has human hands and a man's face with large protruding ears, under a conical cap, but with three clawed feet. On the right there is a woman's hooded face and four three-clawed feet. Both have lion's tails and appear to have feathered wings. The conical hat was that which, by the 13th century, Jews were obliged to wear to distinguish themselves from Christians. The large ears may denote a monkey. Each of these features is symbolic of some connection with the supposed attributes of the figures portrayed, mythical or real.

There are hundreds such carvings in England, let alone throughout Europe, and this is not the place to make a study of them. However, the design of the choir stalls is an important part in reconstructing an image of the chancel of Reading Abbey. The stalls themselves would have become more elaborate from the 13th to 15th centuries. They may also have been placed in an intricate wooden carved setting covering the bare stonework of the building, as shown in the picture of the choir of Winchester on page eighteen.

Another feature of the chancel would have been the colourful floor tiling. It is unlikely that the remnants we have in our current collections in Reading Museum date from the time of the abbey's foundation. There may have been a tilery at Tilehurst in the 12th century and excavations in Silver Street have confirmed the existence of at least one late 12th century tilery in this area. But, according to Slade, the abbey tiles date to the 13th century and later.

There are two types of tile found at Reading. The earlier used an inlay technique. This involved pressing a wooden stamp embossed with the design into the hardened dark clay, filling this with lighter white clay and scraping away the excess, before firing and glazing. A later technique was to cover the whole of the dark hardened clay with the light soft clay, then press this into the dark clay with the stamp. As this is nearer to the concept of printing, they are often referred to as printed tiles.

Inlaid patterned tile from Reading Abbey

Printed tile from Reading, showing the
three scallop shells of the Abbey crest

A miscellany of floor tiles at Winchester

St James' church. Pre-1926 photograph of
some patterned floor tiles, probably from
Reading Abbey. These were placed next to
the *Reading Abbey Stone* which had been
discovered in 1835, carefully buried in the
chancel of the Abbey church. (See Ch. 9)

The two types are quite different both in appearance and durability. The inlaid tiles have an impression of more than 1/8th of an inch and the pattern lines are clear and sharp, whereas in the case of the printed tiles it is rarely more than 1/16th of an inch deep and the patterns are noticeably less clear cut. Both types were glazed, often with lead, to help resist wear.

There is also a difference in size. The inlaid tiles are normally 6 $^{1/2}$ in. square. with some smaller at half this, 3 $^{1/4}$ in. square; the printed tiles are normally 4 $^{1/2}$ in. square; very few of these are 6 $^{1/2}$ in. square. The inlaid tiles are usually about 1 in. thick, whereas the printed tiles are about $^{3/4}$ in.

One clever and interesting feature, found especially in the smaller inlaid tiles, is that the edges are bevelled inwards from the top, so that the retaining sub-mortar can spread between the tiles to grip them better, but not rise over the surface. Another characteristic is that the earlier inlaid tiles have keying marks on their under-surface; the printed tiles lack these. Keying is more necessary for wall tiles, to prevent slippage during application. Could it be that the tiles had a dual use: floor and wall, or is it that the tile makers were just following a tradition?

Reading Abbey - A pilgrim church

This view of Winchester Cathedral, taken from the presbytery, and looking west down the choir, gives an indication of Reading's possible appearance, certainly by the middle of the 14th century. The presbytery, in the foreground, was an open, and sometimes raised, area where, as we have seen, the rich liturgical ceremonies between the high altar and the choir would have taken place.

We can see the modern tiled flooring and beyond. At the very west end of the choir, the screen leads to the nave of the church. It is possible to make out some seats backing onto the screen. Those who occupied these faced east, and had a clear view of the whole chancel, from the back of the choir right through to the altar. A similar arrangement is to be found at St. George's chapel, Windsor.

Winchester Cathedral choir

The tomb is probably that of Henry of Blois, Bishop of Winchester. It is thought that this is the original site of the tomb of William II (Rufus), whose bones were subsequently moved.

An obvious question is whether this has any bearing, or influence, on where the tomb of William's brother, Henry I, was placed within the chancel of Reading Abbey.

PART 3 - THE *READING ABBEY RECORDS* AND THE POSITION OF THE ABBOT'S CHOIR STALL AND OF THE TOMB OF HENRY I

With the publication of the *Reading Abbey Records,* in 2018, it became clear that there was a close connection between the location of Henry's tomb and that of the abbot's seat in the choir, or maybe one of his places in the chancel. I shall now look at what this information adds to our understanding of the chancel.

According to Kemp, the document concerning the ceremonial surrounding the annual commemoration of Henry's death on the 1st December 1135, is to be found in "a small gathering of additional folios, bound at the end of a 13th century manuscript of the *Summa de Dictamine* or *Summa Dictaminis* by Guido Fava". Originally from Westminster Abbey, it is now in the British Library — (Additional Ms 8167, fo. 200r-v). The ceremonial covers both the day itself and the day before, or vigil. That it was a solemn commemoration, liturgically speaking, is demonstrated by the fact that the *Office of the Dead* was sung with full ceremony. It was, however, also a time of celebration, with extra food and distribution of charity. Thirteen poor people from the town were fed in the monastery's *aula* (hall).

Another manuscript containing the third set of the Annals of Reading Abbey, which is also reproduced in the *Reading Abbey Records,* has a list of feast days and anniversaries observed annually at Reading. It enumerates these special days and how they were to be celebrated, according to their liturgical category. The most lavish, such as Christmas, were known as 'doubles'. Henry's commemoration day is ranked among these.

These two documents provide us with invaluable information. Not only do tell us that the liturgy was to be performed in the most solemn way, but we read that the church was to be lavishly decorated, and that the services were to be accompanied by clergy in what we have to assume to be the best copes. Bells were to be rung both inside and outside the church, and generous portions of special food were to be provided to both the monks and the poor of the town.

The manuscript concerning the ceremonial around Henry's commemoration, is not a full rubric or liturgical text, but rather it consists of specific instructions which read more as clarifications to the full ritual. At times it is written in what best can be described as 'note form'. It comprises instructions for the performance of the liturgy for both the Mass and the Office. Unfortunately, it has suffered from some damage where a hole, on both sides of the folio, makes the meaning of the text uncertain: more about this later.

Reading Abbey - A pilgrim church

Whilst describing, in some detail, the actions and dress of the clergy, the manuscript also gives what we might call 'stage directions'. We read about the roles of certain participants, their number, and where they should stand or sit. Consequently, we also get something of a description of the chancel, and how it was used.

I have written a more complete analysis of the text of *Reading Abbey Records a new miscellany,* in Chapter 11. Here I am going to restrict myself to those sections that make direct reference to aspects of the chancel and how it was used. Using this information, I shall add to it relevant information which I have described earlier, and from what we know more generally about Benedictine monasteries, and specifically their chancels. And so I hope to give a yet clearer understanding of what the chancel at Reading Abbey may have looked like and how it was used.

I shall give sub-headings to draw attention to the features, such as the altar and choir, as they appear in various parts of the *Abbey Records,* and comment on what we can learn from them.

The excerpts are in the order in which they appear in the *Abbey Records* manuscript.

THE CHOIR

To give some idea of the space required for the ceremonials, as found in the manuscript, I am starting with the section which describes the entry to the chancel for the singing of Matins. The English translation is that made by Kemp in the *Reading Abbey Records a new miscellany.*

> At the invitatory, which is 'Circumdederunt', four brethren in (copes) are designated. At the third responsory four,
> at the sixth five, at the ninth six.

The invitatory, or opening prayer, which in this case is Psalm 17, is sung at Matins. This 'hour' is the longest and most complicated of the Offices and is normally divided into three parts, or nocturns. Just occasionally, in Benedictine monasteries, there were four nocturns. We read that, at Reading, by the beginning of the last nocturn, six monks in copes entered the chancel. Their role was to lead the singing of the psalms. These six monks in heavily embroidered copes, no doubt accompanied by their acolytes, two apiece, would have occupied a great deal of space in the chancel. This is but one example of the elaborate ceremonial in Benedictine, especially Cluniac, monasteries and is the reason why the presbytery had to be so spacious.

We then read the following,

> *After Vespers with all bells ringing inside and outside, and the lord Abbot with cope having entered the choir, the*
> *hebdomadary shall begin the antiphon 'Placebo'. The lord Abbot, after the antiphon at 'Magnificat' has begun,*
> *will cense the High Altar and the king's tomb with two in copes assigned for this, who at the end of the third*
> *psalm will enter the choir with censers, and after the censing of the altar and tomb shall proceed to cense the*
> *lord abbot.*

This refers to the beginning of singing the Vespers of the *Office of the Dead*; the *Placebo*, Psalm 114, being the first psalm of this Office. The hebdomadary,[3] whose role was to lead the chant in choir, may have sung this from his place in choir, but most probably from the great lectern in the centre of the choir. The censing of the altar and tomb was an elaborate affair. The abbot would have been accompanied not just by his thurifers (thurible bearers), but by someone carrying the incense boat and most probably at least two other clerics, one most certainly being the precentor. I am speculating that the reference to 'two in copes', means that the abbot would have been flanked by these two other monks in richly embroidered vestments. The precentor directed the whole liturgy. His authority during services exceeded even that of the abbot.

I have no doubt that the procession would also have included at least two acolytes. In other words, we need to imagine a procession consisting of the abbot, two assistant clerics in copes, thurifers, an acolyte carrying the incense boat, and two candle-bearing acolytes. It is most likely that there would also have been a cross bearer who would have led the procession. This adds up to at least eight people who had to manoeuvre around the altar area and then the tomb. It was normal liturgical practice, as it is today, that once the celebrant had finished censing the 'holy objects', such as the Bible, the altar or a tomb, he would hand the thurible to another cleric who then censed him. It would also be usual after this that all those present would also be censed. This is not stated in the manuscript. We must remember that these are additional instructions, or clarifications, and do not represent the whole ceremony.

Consequently, we can be certain that a great deal of space was required for such an elaborate ceremony. It is necessary to consider this when assessing where Henry's tomb may have stood in relation to the altar.

THE TOMB AND THE ALTAR

The tomb and the altar are mentioned in one sentence when describing the Offertory chant during the main Mass of the day.

All are to do the offertory chant, the verse of the offertory 'Redemptor' shall be sung by four between the tomb and the altar.

Four cantors with their attendants require, as shown above, quite a bit of space. I would suggest that, although this action may have taken place at the top of the altar steps, it is much more likely to have been in the more spacious presbytery area. As the text states, these cantors are positioned between the altar and the tomb. The fact that they would have required considerable space, would suggest that the tomb was some distance to the west of the altar.

HOW WAS HENRY I BURIED?

There are three proposals regarding the method of Henry's burial, all of which impact on the nature of the tomb, wherever it may have been.

There is no specific description in the *Abbey Records* of the burial, or the method of burial. In Part 4, I will be looking in more detail at some theories regarding the tomb's location. However, before this I would like to note some comments that have been made about the possible method of Henry's burial.

The following sums up the alternatives.

PROPOSAL ONE: Henry was interred in front of, and possibly very near to, the high altar; then his remains were moved and 're-buried'.

In this case the alternatives are;

1. He was 're-buried' above ground, inside the tomb chest, as in the case of King John at Worcester

2. He was re-interred and the tomb chest with image were placed over this new grave.

As a side note, I should like to draw attention to the use of the words *maius altare.*

All too often, we read the translation 'high altar' for the word *altare.* In these cases it may indeed mean the 'high altar', but it is interesting that here the writer is being very specific. The Latin word *maius* means 'greater', being the neuter comparative form of *magnus* (great). So here we encounter the possibility that there were at least two altars: the 'greater' or 'high' altar and one, or more, lesser altars. This is not unexpected. The high altar was reserved for solemn Masses, whereas lower down in the chancel there was often a simpler altar, the matutinal, for the early morning, or 'morrow' Mass. We know that at Cluny, there were several altars, used for the 'morrow' Masses, behind the high altar. This allowed several monks to say morning Masses. Could this also have been the case at Reading?

THE TOMB

The next directive that mentions the tomb comes after the comments on procedure following the Hour of Sext. This was the liturgical hour of the Office at midday, or the 'sixth hour', and normally preceded the main Mass of the day for the whole monastic community.

> *And immediately after Sext a peal of bells is rung until the abbot and the whole convent are revested. And after the peal of bells the abbot is to proceed to his seat by the tomb upon the pavement to the south side, associated with the prior (if...) or another prelate should not be present. And then after the precentor has started the responsory 'Subvenite', the commendation of the soul will be fully carried out with the customary antiphons, psalms and collects, with the convent revested. Nine rule the choir, the responsory is sung by four, the tract by six.*

This is one of the key passages which may help us determine the location of the abbot's seat and that of the tomb. Unfortunately, it also happens just at the point where there is a hole in the manuscript. This is such an important extract that it is worth quoting the Latin. The relevant text reads i*ngrediatur abbas ad sedile suum iuxta tumbam super pavimentum ex parte australi,* ("the abbot is to proceed to his seat by the tomb upon the pavement to the south side"). This makes it clear that there was a close connection between the location of the tomb and that of the abbot's seat. We shall see, however, that there is some question as to whether this seat refers to one in the choir or whether there was another elsewhere in the chancel. The text categorically states that his seat was 'by the tomb'. The Latin word used is *iuxta* which means 'next to' or 'alongside'. Another important phrase, the significance of which I highlight elsewhere, is that we learn that the tomb is 'upon the pavement', *super pavimentum.* This presents us with the possibility that this refers to the area beyond the choir. However, it may also merely be a reference to the open space of the chancel. It is not possible to come to a definitive answer. This passage both aids us in assessing the appearance of the chancel, and raises some serious problems which I shall address later.

PROPOSAL TWO: Henry was interred in front of, and possibly very near to, the high altar. He was left in this original burial place and the tomb chest and image were erected elsewhere in the chancel at a later date

PROPOSAL THREE: Henry was initially interred ('buried') in the position of the final tomb chest, which was added later.

In this case the alternatives are;

1. He was 'buried' in a sarcophagus which was placed on the pavement, and the chest and image were added later

2. He was initially interred, and the chest and image were added later

COMMENT

The second proposal suggests that, by the time the tomb monument had been completed, the decision had been taken not to move the king's body, so that his monument reflected his burial but, unlike King John's, did not physically contain it. The proponents of this theory claim that it reflects aspects of the GPR survey, such as showing possible graves near the likely location of the high altar. The GPR indicates the possibility that there are two, possibly three, burial sites located within the arc of the apse. These lie within the area of the car park of the former prison.

My opinion is that, as we have seen above, it is not possible to locate exactly the altar's position. There is, therefore, no way of knowing how these possible graves stood in relationship to the high altar.

We should ask whether a dedicated sarcophagus was ready to be installed at Reading. On one hand, Henry had clearly expressed a wish to be buried at Reading, and so it is possible that a sarcophagus had been prepared. On the other hand he died unexpectedly, so we have to ask whether sarcophagus, always assuming his body was placed in one, had already been prepared.

The possibility that Henry's body remained above ground, once the tomb chest was installed, is lessened by the report of 1398 which states that he was 'buried'. The Latin word used, in the genitive singular, is *humati*. This derives from *humare* which means 'to cover with earth', to place in the earth, that is, to inter. This indicates that, by the end of the 14th century, it was believed that Henry was below ground. It is of course possible that the word was being used in a wider sense, but weight needs to be given to the usual meaning of the verb chosen by the writer. The following is the report of 1398, quoted in the *Reading Abbey Cartularies,* where we find this description, followed by my translation.

Tumbam et imaginem Henrici quondam regis Anglie … et fundatoris abbatie predicte (Reading) *in eadem humati …*
honeste facerent reparari. (1398 Richard II - Confirmation of the Abbey's Liberties. Reading Abbey Cartularies 1, 116. p107 ed. Kemp)

"They (the monks) must ensure that the tomb and effigy of Henry, sometime king of England, … and founder of the aforesaid monastery, and who was buried in that same place … are properly repaired".

In my view, it is most unlikely that Henry was initially interred in front of the High Altar and subsequently left in this position, whilst a tomb chest, with image, was erected elsewhere in the chancel; that is further west in the presbytery or even in the choir.

This is the most problematic of all the theories. There are too many alternatives and variations within the proposal. One moves from an unproven assumption, namely that the altar was at the far eastern wall, to assuming that the potential GPR burial sites are positioned directly in front of the High Altar. Moreover, the GPR analysts did not say that these are definitely tombs, only that they give the indications of being tombs. If, however, they are burials, it is just as likely, some would say more than likely, that these would have been behind the high altar. In this case the altar would be further west, although probably still within the chord of the apse.

Furthermore, the documentary evidence of the liturgical instructions in the *Abbey Records,* makes it very clear that the monks in the mid-13th century clearly believed that Henry was buried in the *tumbam* (tomb). They would not have countenanced concentrating the liturgy on the tomb-chest had they believed that Henry was not buried there, but elsewhere, such as near the altar.

The instructions make several references to censing the tomb, having candles burning for the two days of the commemoration around the tomb, and they state that the abbot's seat was next to the tomb. These were theologically-charged ceremonies, linked with the belief in their efficacy in assuring the salvation of Henry's soul: the abbey's *raison d'être.*

It would be very wrong to view these acts, these 'public acts', the liturgy, as symbolic theatre. I also think it is highly unlikely that, only just over 100 years following Henry's burial, the monastic community would somehow have lost track of the burial site of their founder. The abbey was his mausoleum. As the 'Foundation Charter' says, Reading Abbey was built for the salvation of Henry's soul. As such, his place of burial was at the very centre of its existence and purpose.

Reading Abbey - A pilgrim church

Another point to consider is that we read that there was at least one 'morrow' Mass. If we are making architectural comparisons regarding the positioning of altars, it is possible, indeed likely, that there was space, between the high altar and the apse, for the matitudinal altar. At Cluny there were at least three such altars, but in that case they were to the east of the high altar, between it and the rear wall of the sanctuary. The exact positioning of the high altar at Reading is impossible to verify, though it would have been almost certainly within the arc of the apse.

The comparative architectural evidence, therefore, leaves room for significant variations in the location of the altar. These range from the far eastern end of the chancel, within the apse and close to the rear wall, to as far west as the radius of the chord of the apse semi-circle 6.75m (22ft), and potentially even further west than this, a distance of some 10m (over 32ft).*

It is unlikely that Richard II would have been so insistent on the repair of the tomb and its effigy if Henry's remains were elsewhere. We also have the 16th century evidence that the tomb was in the 'midst of the high quire'. Had there been any tradition, or even a burial stone set into the pavement, stating that Henry's remains were not on the same site as the tomb chest, it is unlikely that this would have been noted in such strong terms.

In brief, the mid-13th century liturgical directive clearly indicates the belief that Henry's body was at the site of the tomb chest, and this is supported by two other pieces of documentary evidence.

*Approximate measurements

PART 4 - THEORIES CONCERNING THE LOCATION OF HENRY I's TOMB

In Part 4 I shall use the above information to examine whether it is possible to identify the site of Henry's tomb.

THEORY 1

Abbot's choir stall and tomb at the west end of the choir

In this theory, the abbot's choir stall was immediately to the south on entering the choir from the nave, presumably through the pulpitum.

This description presents us, at the same time, with both an apparent solution and a problem.

There is evidence, from many monasteries, that an abbot's seat was usually positioned immediately on entering the choir area of the chancel, normally through the pulpitum, or a screen of some sort.

We read in the *Abbey Records* that at Reading the abbot's place was in the south side of the choir. By the 12th century, this was the normal side for the presiding cleric's seat or 'throne'. The use of the term 'throne' does not imply that the abbot had the status of a bishop, merely that he presided over the ceremonies. There is a deal of research and commentary about whether the president's seat was on the north or south side, on the Gospel or Epistle side, of the church, and how this came to pass. But for our purposes, as we have an authoritative account of its position at Reading, we need not pursue this further. It is worth mentioning that it is thanks to Kemp's work on the *Abbey Records,* that this area of possible contention has been resolved. If this was the location of the abbot's *sedile,* (seat), then Henry's tomb would have been alongside, or next to, (*iuxta*) his seat near the entrance to the choir, as shown on the plan. However, there is some question concerning the meaning of the word *sedile.* I shall look at this when examining Theory 4.

As seen above, the abbot's seat in choir, or *stallus,* as the *Records* describe it, may have been part of the row with its back to the screen wall at right angles to the choir benches, known as a 'return stall'. In this case, the abbot would have had a commanding position, looking along the rest of the choir with a clear view to the altar. He would also have occupied the traditional orientation of facing east during Mass, even when he was not the presiding priest.

However, we encounter two problems. First of all, the *Abbey Records* tell us that the abbot took an active role in the ceremonial that accompanied the singing of the office. He is described, for example, as exiting the choir to change into a cope; and on re-entering he returns to his seat whilst the tomb is censed.

Does the siting of the tomb in position 'C' allow for such elaborate ritual, demanding quite a deal of space? It should be recalled that the monk censing the tomb would most probably have been accompanied by several others as he encircled it. There would also have been a substantial lectern in the middle of the choir. Would this extra obstacle have made it impossible, or at least difficult, to execute the elaborate ceremonials surrounding the tomb? The answer to both these questions is probably 'no'. The choir area was over 13 metres wide. Allowing for the stalls taking up about 6.7 metres, as at Lincoln, this would leave over 8 metres around the tomb. The tomb itself would have taken up about one metre width, leaving 7 metres around the tomb, or over 3 metres each side between the tomb and the front row of the stalls.

In addition, it is possible that the front row may have been removed at this point, or that there was a gap in the rows of stalls allowing more space around the tomb. We know that the central gap in the choir stalls, apart from allowing access to the back row, also served to give space around the great lectern which would have stood in the centre of the choir. Another problem stems from the text itself. This reads *Ingrediatur abbas ad sedile suum iuxta tumbam super pavimentum.* In other words the Abbot's seat, we read, was not just next to the tomb, but this latter was 'on the pavement'. It is possible that the author may have just been referring to the whole area of the chancel as the 'pavement'. On the other hand, we would normally associate the use of the word 'pavement' with the area of the presbytery, which may have been raised above the level of the choir. It was not unknown for bishop's or abbot's place in choir to be near the altar. This was normally the case in the early days of Christianity but was not so common in the later Middle Ages. I shall look at this when commenting on the 4th theory.

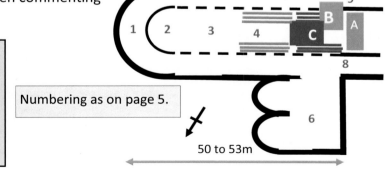

Numbering as on page 5.

50 to 53m

A.	Pulpitum: The GPR survey showed up a feature which is consistent with a pulpitum. The existence of a pulpitum is shown in Miracle XVIII.
B.	Abbot's choir stall: This was on the south side of the choir. The most usual place for the abbot's seat was immediately to the right on entering the choir through the pulpitum.
C.	Possible location of Henry's tomb. (numbering as page 5)

LOCATION OF HENRY I's TOMB

THEORY 2

Abbot's choir stall and tomb at the east end of the choir, near the presbytery 'pavement'

If this theory is correct, then Henry's tomb would have been approximately in the same position in the chancel at Reading as that of King John at Worcester.

In this scenario we overcome the problem of the space required for the ceremonial described in several customaries, as well as in the *Abbey Records.* It would also allow for the Abbot's place in choir to be described as *super pavimentum.*

Tomb of King John, at the east end of the choir in Worcester Cathedral.

A. Pulpitum: The GPR survey showed up a feature which is consistent with a pulpitum. The existence of a pulpitum is shown in Miracle XVIII.

B. Abbot's choir stall: This was on the south side of the choir. It is possible that the Abbot had a 'president's chair' at the east end of the choir

C. If the Abbot's seat was at the east end of the choir then Henry's tomb would have been located as shown.

Numbering as per page 5

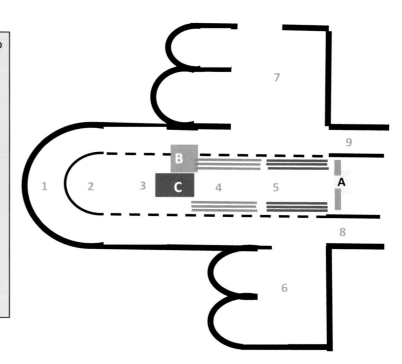

LOCATION OF HENRY I's TOMB

THEORY 3

The abbot's choir seat in the centre of the choir

That this may have occurred sometimes, as on the diagram, is indicated by the existence of elaborate main canopied seats, or thrones, in some choirs.

Apart from this location being rare, one major problem is that it would make the ceremonial requirements very difficult to fulfil.

Another problem is that at Reading we learn that the tomb was next to the Abbot's seat. If this was at this central position, then the tomb would have had to be aligned with the gap in the stalls. Could this be described as being 'next' to the Abbot's seat? Is this a reasonable place for it to be sited?

It also raises the problem of where the great lectern would have stood. The space between the stalls, apart from allowing access to the back rows, also gave room around the lectern for the ceremonial associated with the readings. Nevertheless, it is a possibility.

The great lectern may have been placed elsewhere, such as in the presbytery, or there may have been two breaks in the row of stalls, one for the lectern and another for the tomb.

A. Pulpitum

B. Abbot's chair

C. Henry's tomb

Numbering as on page 5.

LOCATION OF HENRY I's TOMB

THEORY 4

The *sedile* was near the High Altar

This theory would presuppose that the reference to the abbot's *sedile* in the *Abbey Records* is alluding to his place as the officiating priest at Mass. The word *sedile* is in the singular and can mean seat, bench or even stool. Today, it is more usual to find it in its plural form *sedilia*, when referring to the three seats reserved for the celebrant priest, deacon and sub deacon at Mass. These are situated to the south of the altar. An example of this may be seen in the photograph of the *sedilia* at Dorchester Abbey, Oxfordshire (p32). Generally speaking, however, this arrangement appeared in churches later than the time of the manuscript, as permanent recessed stone structures. Moreover, this is late 18th century terminology, so, although the word *sedile* was used in the middle ages, care needs to be taken in the interpretation of both words, *sedile* and *sedilia*.[4]

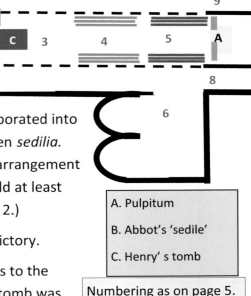

A. Pulpitum

B. Abbot's 'sedile'

C. Henry's tomb

Numbering as on page 5.

This is, therefore, possibly the most difficult of the references to analyse. We have seen that the word used for the abbot's seat, in this context, is *sedile.* As time progressed, *sedilia* were incorporated into the masonry on the south, or epistle, side of the altar. It is also known that there were moveable wooden *sedilia.* If this was the case at Reading, it is conceivable that the reference to the abbot's *sedile* was to such an arrangement and that it was placed next to the tomb, probably below the altar steps and in the presbytery. This would at least allow for the tomb being in the presbytery, as stated in the Lambeth Palace document. (See page 33 no 2.)

There are several considerations associated with this theory, some of which appear to be contradictory.

The first is that it would place Henry's tomb, if alongside the *sedile,* almost certainly near the steps to the altar, and so at the far eastern end of the presbytery. However, in Benolt's *Visitation*, we read that the tomb was in the middle of the choir, which would be at its western end. (See page 35 no 5.)

Reading Abbey - A pilgrim church

Finally, if the word *sedile,* in this context, has its literal meaning of a 'seat', then it could merely be referring to the abbot's seat in the chancel. This would have been his place of honour in the choir.

One other factor is that this key passage in the manuscript is just where there is a hole in the document. It is worth looking at what is written in detail and how Kemp approaches the problem of the missing words.

...ingrediatur abbas ad sedile suum iuxta tumbam super pavimentum ex parte australi, associato sibi priore (si...) [missing section owing to a hole in the ms.] *vel alius prelatus non interfuerit..*

"the abbot is to proceed to his seat by the tomb upon the pavement to the south side, associated with the prior (if...) [missing section owing to a hole in the ms.] or another prelate should not be present".

I think that the key words we should focus on here are *associato sibi priore* ("associated with the prior..."). It is conceivable that although the word *sedile* is in the singular, and does not therefore appear to be referring to *sedilia,* it is possible that we are looking at the description of seats for the presiding priest: in this case the abbot, a deacon (namely the prior who is accompanying him), and another cleric, acting as sub-deacon. Rather speculatively therefore, the passage may have read: "the abbot is to proceed to his seat upon the pavement to the south side, where the prior and sub prior will be seated or, should the latter not be present, another prelate".

This is indeed very hypothetical, but the only way I can see that this passage makes sense is if it is stating that the abbot' seat was in this location.

The diagram opposite illustrates the most likely place for the *sedile* in this theory. However, if the *sedile* was a movable item of furniture and placed next to the tomb, this would be a most unusual place for the presiding priest's chair, which should be next to the altar on the sanctuary, with room for two other clerics.

Dorchester Abbey, sedilia

PART 5 - OTHER DOCUMENTARY EVIDENCE FOR THE SITING OF HENRY'S TOMB

In this section I will look at other historical documentary references to Henry's tomb. I shall examine whether, and if so, how, these may be able to help in identifying the link between the tomb and the abbot's chair or the altar, as seen in Parts 3 and 4.

Apart from those in the *Abbey Records,* there are only a few references to Henry's tomb. However, these do give us clues as to its location.

In chronological order they are:

1. Late 12th, very early 13th century. Gervase of Canterbury (d. circa 1210) - *Opera historica* Rolls series Vol I, page 95 (Quoted in Hurry p 6).
    ante altare sepultum est. ('He is buried in front of the altar') This is often translated as 'the high altar'.

2. 13th century. Lambeth Palace Library ms 371 (For full reference and explanation of this archive follow link below*)

    The tomb is *in medio presbiteri ante altare.* ("In the centre of the presbytery in front of the altar")

The latter is a categorical reference to Henry's tomb being in the centre of the presbytery. As I have commented above, when we read such descriptions, it is necessary to question whether the writer is using terms as defined today in a strictly architectural sense . Nevertheless, taken together with other sources, such descriptions do help build an overall picture.

The reference occurs in an account of how and where Henry's second wife, Adeliza, came to be buried in Reading Abbey. Following Henry's death, Adeliza married William d'Albini, Earl of Lincoln and Earl of Arundel. It is worth quoting the account in full, in translation.

William earl of Lincoln married Queen Adeliza, wife of the founder as is evident in a charter and confirmation of the same William. Accordingly the king's council would not permit her to lie with him (Henry) *in the middle of the presbytery before the altar. She lies buried, however, on the north side of the choir between the columns, apart from King Henry I, our founder and her husband, on whose souls may God have mercy. Amen*

* *https://archives.lambethpalacelibrary.org.uk/CalmView/Record.aspx?src=CalmView.Catalog&id=MSS%2F371*

Reading Abbey - A pilgrim church

3.   13th century. Death and Burial of the infant William of Poitiers. Two chronicles reference this event.

A. *Flores historiarum* - Roger of Wendover, with additions by Matthew Paris.

This concerns the death and burial of William of Poitiers, son of Henry II (grandson of Henry I).

AD 1156 Willelmus quoque primogenitus regis Henrici obiit, et sepultus est apud Radingum

"… also William, firstborn son of King Henry, died and was buried at Reading"

B. *Annales de Waverleia*   (II p237)

For the year 1135:

Anno tertio Henrici secondi regis, obiit Willelmus peror. primogenitus filius Henrici regis, et sepultus est Radingis ad pedes Henrici regis proavi sui.

"In the third year (of the reign) of King Henry II, William of Poitiers, first son of King Henry, died and was buried at Reading at the feet of his grandfather, King Henry (the First)".

Jerpoint Abbey, Ireland

Carving on a 12th century tomb chest

https://commons.wikimedia.org/wiki/File:Jerpoint_Abbey_The_Weepers.jpg

4.   1398 Richard II - Confirmation of the Abbey's Liberties - Cartularies 1, 116 (ed. Kemp)

Tumbam et imaginem Henrici quondam regis Anglie … et fundatoris abbatie predicte (Reading) *in eadem humati … honeste facerunt reparari.*

"They (the monks), must ensure that the tomb and effigy of Henry, sometime king of England, … founder of the aforesaid monastery who is buried in that same place … are properly repaired".

5.   1532 Thomas Benolt Clarenceux (King of Arms)

In 1532 Thomas Benolt made an heraldic visitation when he reported that Henry's tomb was:

in the myddest of the high Quyer (Kemp *Abbey Records* p 102 quoting 'Visitations of Berkshire' ed W H Rylands).

The full record reads:

> King Henry the first iij[d] Sonne to w[m] Conquerour and first founder of the Abbaye of Redding ys buryed in the myddest of the high Quyer w[t]in the sayde place afore rehercyd
> On the right hand of him liethe buryed Ranawd Le fitz parys
> Before our Lady Chappell lyeth buryed Thomas Wood Knight sometyme Justice of the Comune place
> In the bodye of the Churche in our Ladye Chappell lyeth buryed Thomas Prowt

Clarenceux, King of Arms, is the senior of the two provincial kings of arms, and has jurisdiction south of the River Trent. The office almost certainly existed in 1420, and there is a fair degree of probability that there was a *Claroncell rex heraldus armorum* in 1334. The title of Clarenceux is supposedly derived either from the Honour (or estates of dominion) of the Clare family or from the Dukedom of Clarence. (Source Wikipedia)

Reading Abbey - A pilgrim church

COMMENTS

The above extracts confirm the following:

1.   Henry was buried in the chancel of the abbey.

2.   His tomb was 'in front of the altar', which is assumed to be the high altar. However, the word used is *altare.* There is specific reference to a 'high' altar in the *Abbey Records* when the word *maius* or 'greater' is used. Etymologically the word 'altar' has its origin in two Latin words *alta* and *ara,* that is 'high' and '*altar*'. Nevertheless, the word 'altar' was used in the middle ages, as now, for any altar, 'high' or otherwise. The reference to a *maius altare* introduces another element into the debate. I explained above that it was not unknown for large monasteries to have two altars in the chancel. One was the high altar for the main Mass of the day, whereas there was also a lesser, matutinal, altar, sometimes further west, nearer the choir. But, I also pointed out that at Cluny there were altars behind, that is to the east of, the high altar. There were of course many altars around the abbey church, such as those in in the apsidal chapels, in the Lady Chapel, and many others along the aisles.

3.   The exact location of the tomb is mentioned twice. In one case we read it was in the 'presbytery', and in another that it was in the middle of the 'high choir'. This presents us with another clue, but one that also raises as many questions as solutions. The term 'high quire' is ambivalent. The 'superior' or 'high' choir had been used in the early Christian church to refer to a choir behind the high altar. This was clearly not the case at Reading in 1532. It is possible that Benolt was making a distinction between the main choir, in the chancel, and any other choir in the abbey church. It is likely, for instance, that there would have been a choir in the Lady Chapel. This would have been used for the 'Little Office of the Blessed Virgin Mary'. As Daniell points out, the definition of choir is "confused, for as well as the high choir in the east end, the nave itself seems to have been called the 'choir' in some churches". (*Death and Burial in Medieval England,* p.97) It is possible that Benolt was using the word 'quire' in a very loose sense, and that he was referring to the chancel.

4.   There is also the problem of the use of the word 'presbytery'. This could be read as contradicting the observation that the tomb was in the 'myddst of the high Quyre'. As mentioned above, it is possible that the word 'presbytery' is here being used in a more general sense, meaning the whole priests' area, perhaps equivalent to the chancel. However, we cannot ignore the fact that the term has been used, and we need to take note of it.

PART 6 - CONCLUSIONS

Combining the evidence above, to what extent is it possible to locate Henry's tomb and the abbot's place in the choir?

We can categorise the sources as follows

1. General architectural features. These are general principles which we may reasonably assume to be applicable to Reading Abbey. (Part 1)

2. Special features relevant to Reading Abbey, such as the number and size of the choir stalls, the existence of a pulpitum, evidence of tiles and sculpture etc. (Part 2)

3. Evidence from the primary source of the *Reading Abbey Records* which gives strong indications about the possible positions of the abbot's seat and the tomb. (Parts 3 and 4)

4. Other written evidence concerning the appearance of the chancel and the location of Henry's tomb. (Part 5)

EXAMINATION OF THE THEORIES CONCERNING THE LOCATION OF THE ABBOT'S SEAT AND OF THE TOMB OF HENRY I

As I believe the most compelling evidence points to the first and second theories being the most plausible, I am presenting the theories in reverse order.

THEORY 4. (p.31) I think this is the least likely theory. It demands quite a complex set of explanations to make it sit comfortably with the other evidence. This theory works only if the seat mentioned, the *sedile,* is not the abbot's choir stall but part of *sedilia* designated for the celebrants at Mass. However, we should not overlook the fact that this part of the manuscript is indeed talking about Mass, as it refers to the ceremonial after the Office Hour of Sext, which is the normal time for Mass.

There are several problems in siting the tomb in such close proximity to the altar. First of all, for it to be "next to', *iuxta,* the abbot's *sedile*, the tomb would have had to be on the raised area of the sanctuary, up at least three steps, in front of the altar. This would have been virtually impossible without interfering with the ceremonial of the Mass. To place the tomb slightly lower down, below the steps leading to the altar, in the presbytery, would entail removing it from its reported position 'next to' the abbot. One option is that the *sedile* was a movable item and was placed near the tomb, and then moved back nearer the altar during Mass. But, if this was the case, it would not have served in the role of *sedilia,* alongside the altar, begging the question as to its very *raison d'être*. A greater problem is Benolt's statement that the tomb was in the midst of the high choir. If this was the case, it is difficult to see how the word *sedile* referred to the abbot's place as the main celebrant at Mass.

Nevertheless, I have placed this potential location on the aerial view of the abbey chancel area as it appears today. (p. 41).

THEORY 3. (p.30) Although theoretically possible, I think that this is the least likely of the remaining options. The abbot of Reading was not just an observer of the ceremonial: he played a pivotal role in the liturgy. As 'Father' of his community, he had a duty to be present and take an active role in the ceremonies. It would appear that the abbots of Reading took this duty seriously, or at least were instructed to do so, in the liturgical instructions that we find in the *Reading Abbey Records*. As such, if his seat was in this position, it would have been difficult, but not impossible, for him to fulfil such complicated rituals. We have also seen the logistical problems of conducting the elaborate ceremonies, with so many clerics involved, if the tomb and the great lectern were in such close proximity one to another.

THEORY 2. (p.29) I believe this has the edge over Theory 1. It overcomes the problems of Theory 1. Theory 2 does allow for an interpretation that the tomb could have been considered to lie not just in the choir but also in the presbytery. The tomb's position would have been that of his great grandson, King John, at Worcester. This theory does however presuppose that the *sedile* is the abbot's choir seat and not his seat as the celebrant at Mass. If this was the case we must needs revert to Theory 4.

THEORY 1. (p.27) If we were just speculating on the location of the abbot's seat, this would be my preferred option. It allows for two possibilities:

1.   That the tomb was near the abbot's seat in choir.

2.   That there are two seats referred to in the manuscript: one in the choir, the "stall", and the other the "sedile" in the presbytery or sanctuary. We have looked at the problems caused by this latter theory. Once again, we should note that if the seat was on or near the sanctuary, this would appear to contradict Benolt's evidence that the tomb was in the midst of the high quire.

The main problem of Theory 1, is a negative one. The balance of opinion is that the abbot's seat was often, if not normally, placed immediately on entering the choir from the nave, and so to the far west of the chancel. In which case, we have to face both the logistical ceremonial problems and the written evidence which places the tomb in the presbytery. However, the word 'presbytery' could be interpreted in its widest sense, the whole chancel area, which could place the tomb 'in the midst of the choir'.

Having considered the text of the *Reading Abbey Records,* the other documents which reference the tomb, along with the architectural evidence such as at Winchester and Worcester, I am inclined for the moment to believe that the word *sedile* is referring to the abbot's choir seat and that Henry's tomb was at the east end of the choir stalls. The main problem is over the interpretation of one simple word, *sedile.* Was the writer merely using this in its common meaning of 'a seat' or was he talking about a specific liturgical artefact which today we refer to as *sedilia*?

The photograph, right, is of one of the earliest surviving examples of sedilia. It comes from the church of Sant Climent de Taull, Catalonia in Spain, and dates to the 13th or early 14th centuries.

Note that the seats are all at the same level, unlike most other later stone sedilia, such as at Dorchester Abbey.

Sant Climente is best known for its magnificent Romanesque art work, especially that of the 12th century Master of Taull's magnificent frescoes in the apse of the church.

13TH—14TH C Sant Climent de Taull, Catalonia, Spain

PART 7 - THE ABBEY SITE TODAY

POSSIBLE LOCATIONS OF THE ABBOT'S SEAT AND OF THE TOMB OF HENRY I POSITIONED ON THE CURRENT BUILDINGS

The illustration on the page 41 shows the possible sites for the altar, the abbot's seat and Henry's tomb, when superimposed on a modern aerial view of the area. Today, the abbey chancel is occupied by school buildings, its back playground, and, at the time of writing, by the car park of the former prison. The school was built in the 1870s, with additions in the early and mid-20th century. The car park is where the walls and towers of the 1840s Gaol once stood. These were demolished in the 1960s. It was at this time, in the late 1960s and '70s, that Dr Slade undertook his archaeological excavations of the site.

The 1870s OS map, (fig, 1) shows the outer wall of the abbey and, rather more difficult to make out, the wall of the prison and the tower. I have marked with blue dots the remnants of the pillars of the inner apse of the ambulatory as shown on the OS map. I have also highlighted with a yellow rectangle the suggested position of the altar, as marked on the OS map.

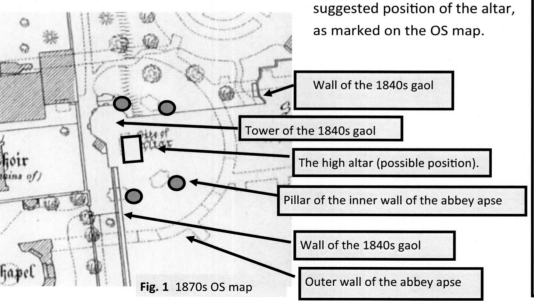

Wall of the 1840s gaol

Tower of the 1840s gaol

The high altar (possible position).

Pillar of the inner wall of the abbey apse

Wall of the 1840s gaol

Outer wall of the abbey apse

Fig. 1 1870s OS map

Key to the aerial photograph on page 41

A   The sanctuary and site of the high altar

B   Possible site of the pulpitum as shown by the GPR survey

THEORY 1.	**T1a** Abbot's seat	**T1b** Henry's tomb
THEORY 2.	**T2a** "	**T2b** "
THEORY 3.	**T3a** "	**T3b** "
THEORY 4.	**T4a** "	**T4b** "

DASHES indicate no standing remains, but GPR and earlier excavations show their location

DOTS indicate few, or no, remains or archaeological evidence

SOLID LINE indicates standing ruins

To simplify the map I have omitted the transepts.

B
T1b
T1a
T3b
T3a
T2b
T2a
T4b
T4a
A
Forbury Gardens
Day Nursery

Outline overlay of abbey footprint ©John Mullaney 2018

10 m

Map data ©2018 Google   United Kingdom

Reading Abbey - A pilgrim church

NOTES

1. https://adoremus.org/2014/08/clergy-seating-through-the-centuries/

2. For my discussion on this topic in 2016 shortly after the GPR results see Chapter 1.

3. Each week a monk was appointed to lead the choir. He would open the chant to be followed by the other monks. After a week this role passed to the other side of the choir, with a new *Hebdomadarius*. The word derives from the Greek meaning seven, or seven days.

4. *'Sedilia in choro sunt fracta': The Medieval Nomenclature of Seating in Churches,* and also *The Englishness od English Sedilia,* British Art Studies, issue 6. James Alexander Cameron. https://www.britishartstudies.ac.uk/issues/issue-index/issue-6/english-sedilia

Primary Sources

From among the primary sources I would like to highlight the following six items. Number 4 is mentioned only out of interest, as the Reading Abbey rubrics are attached to the end of this manuscript.

1. Cluny 'customaries' such as that of Ulrich and Bernard and the *Liber tramitis*. These give us information about Cluny. To what extent they were reflected at Reading is a matter for debate and speculation.

2. *Orderic Vitalis Bk X1   Ch XL111*   https://archive.org/stream/ecclesiasticalhi03orde#page/438/mode/2up   (See especially Henry admitted to the Community of St Evroult 1113 Feb 3, Feast of the Purification of Mary, Candlemas Feb 2.)

3. *Reading Abbey Cartularies,* ed B Kemp

4. *Reading Abbey Records a new miscellany,* B Kemp 2018—commentary and originals

5. *Summa de Dictamine* or *Summa Dictaminis* Guido Fava c 1190-1243 http://www.treccani.it/enciclopedia/guido-fava_%28Dizionario-Biografico%29/ Now BL Add ms 8167

6. *The Visitation of Berkshire in 1532* Thomas Benolt. (British Library Add ms 12479 Oswald Barron)

Secondary Sources

From among the many secondary sources concerning the topics covered, I would like to draw the reader's particular attention to the following:

1. *A Medieval Latin Death Ritual,* Frederick Paxton, which includes in translation the Cluniac customaries of the *Vetus disciplina monastica* and the *Consuetudines*

2. *Clergy Seating through the Centuries Part II — The Enclosed Choir in the Medieval Cathedrals and Abbeys,* Daniel DeGreve

3. *Corpus of Romanesque Sculpture in Britain and Ireland,* (CRSBI) website *https://www.crsbi.ac.uk/.*

4. *From Dead of Night to End of Day: the Medieval Customs of Cluny*, ed. Susan Boynton and Isabelle Cochelin

5. *Monasticism without Frontiers: the extended monastic community of the abbot of Cluny in England and Wales,* C. P. Pearce

6.   *Histoire de l'ordre de Cluny*   Vol 3,   J Henri Pignot

7.   *Reading Abbey (1901),* J B Hurry

8.   *Reading Abbey Records a new miscellany,* B Kemp 2018

9.   *Sedilia* - James Alexander Cameron *http://britishartstudies.ac.uk/issues/issue-index/issue-6/english-sedilia#figure3* and *https://courtauld.ac.uk/wp-content/uploads/2016/11/7.-Cameron-Revisiting-The-Monument-CBO.pdf* (especially page 141)

10.   *The Royal Abbey of Reading,*   R Baxter

11.   *Wood Carvings in English Churches,*   Francis Bond

ABBREVIATIONS

GPR   - Ground Penetrating Radar Survey

Abbey Records   -   *Reading Abbey Records a new miscellany,* B Kemp 2018

CHAPTER 2

THE ABBEY CHURCH - ITS DESIGN AND PURPOSE

INTRODUCTION

Having looked at the abbey chancel, I shall move on to examine the main body of the church: the parts that were generally accessible to the public. I shall show how these developed from the earliest churches, and how the design of Reading was part of an evolving story, with its roots in Cluniac Benedictine ideas concerning the purpose of a church building.

Henry I, intending the abbey to be his mausoleum, would have known that, by asking Cluniacs to build and be in charge of his abbey, he was also engaging with their mission to provide a place of prayer and of refuge for the poor, the traveller and the pilgrim. In short, a Cluniac monastery was a sanctuary of hospitality, both spiritual and physical.

At first sight, today's ruins offer little in the way of information. But by comparing these remains with other Cluniac monasteries, and using the information provided by the Ground Penetrating Radar (GPR) survey that we commissioned in 2016, I hope to present a more complete picture of Reading Abbey than that offered by the skeletal ruins alone.
(Stratascan. Project Title Client Job No. J10003 Reading Borough Council, Reading Hidden Abbey Project)

THE WEST END: Anomalous GPR lines at the west end of the nave of the Abbey church.

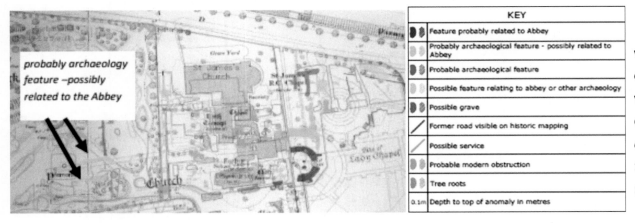

KEY	
▌▐	Feature probably related to Abbey
▌▐	Probably archaeological feature - possibly related to Abbey
▌▐	Probable archaeological feature
▌	Possible feature relating to abbey or other archaeology
▌▐	Possible grave
/	Former road visible on historic mapping
/	Possible service
▌▐	Probable modern obstruction
▌▐	Tree roots
0.1m	Depth to top of anomaly in metres

When we first saw the GPR findings, we were surprised to see the results at the west end of the nave (in the Forbury Gardens), which Stratascan (the group commissioned to do the scan), classified as *probably archaeology feature(s) – possibly related to the Abbey. — light blue on the map*. I have marked these with two black arrows.

First of all, it should be noted that these features may be connected with others totally unrelated to the abbey. For instance, they could be part of the defence system constructed during the 17th century Civil War. They may be footings of one of the walls that we know surrounded the late 18th century school next to the inner gateway (Jane Austen's school). Perhaps they are part of the foundations for some buildings, such as the greenhouses, that were erected in the Forbury botanic gardens during the second half of the 19th century.

I have also looked into the possibility that they may in fact be related to the abbey and that there may be some explanation for their existence as part of the monastery. I must emphasise that any one, or none, of the above may be the explanation, and without archaeology, or the discovery of some documentation relating to them, it is unlikely that we will ever know what they truly represent.

CLUNIAC MONASTERIES FROM THE LATE 10TH TO THE 12TH CENTURIES

Although there are some generalisations that can be made about Cluniac buildings over this period, there is no evidence to believe that they all followed a strict pattern. To some extent, the modern adage that *form should follow function,* would appear to be as true concerning Cluniac Benedictine monasteries in the 10th, 11th and 12th centuries, as it is for some modern architecture today.

We should remember that one of the main functions of a Cluniac Benedictine monastery, unlike its Cistercian counterpart, was to engage with the community. For example, an essential part of the Cluniac rule was to care for the sick, the elderly and the traveller, especially the 'pilgrim'. The monastery was also a place of retreat, prayer and individual contemplation. It was a place to visit, a place of pilgrimage.

The word 'monk' derives from the Greek-Latin word *monachus,* meaning individual or solitary. Apart from caring for the spiritual and temporal needs of the visitor, the main duty of the Cluniac monk was to pray for the salvation of his own soul through the liturgy, the *Opus Dei*. The focus on the 'individual' consisted of prayer, such as the singing of the Divine Office, attending Mass and other services, and the production of copies of books and manuscripts, illuminated or otherwise. But, it was through brotherly, or communal, actions and mutual support, that the monk would gain his eternal reward. This is no more clearly demonstrated than in the detailed instructions concerning the death of one of the community.

Reading Abbey - A pilgrim church

As we have seen, Cluniac monasteries were designed to fulfil the primary aims of prayer and pilgrimage. Examination of the many Cluniac houses throughout France, Spain and even England, arguably shows a degree of homogeneity in iconography and decoration. Is this equally true of their architectural design? It should be noted that there are over 1500 establishments which we can associate with the Cluniac movement. The chronicler Orderic, writing in the 12th century, claimed that there were over 2000.

Pertinent to us is a certain consistency in the ground plan of the houses throughout the whole Cluniac order. I would argue that the houses were designed to fulfil the functions mentioned above, and that form did indeed follow function.

The practices of the reformed Cluniac order in the late 10th century, and subsequently in the 11th and 12th centuries, following the Statutes of Peter the Venerable (Abbot of Cluny 1122-1156) in 1132, demanded a stricter observance of the monastic ideals, of the enclosed life, of prayer and service. But there remained an explicitly conscious aspect: that their mission of service, or apostolate, was to the wider community.

These twin ideals shaped the architecture of Cluniac monasteries and churches. It has been suggested that the design of the buildings followed a sort of 'master plan'. We know of some names of key monks who are credited with playing a leading role in the design and building of the monasteries. One such is Hézelon (Etzelon) of Liège. Peter the Venerable, in a letter to Alberon, Bishop of Liège, says that Hézelon not only gave instructions on the way to build the church, but 'constructed the actual fabric of the new church' of Cluny (*corporalem novae ecclesiae fabricam ... construxit*).

This hands-on interpretation has been questioned, and it has been suggested that Hézelon was more a commissioning agent, raising finance and overseeing the progress of the work. Peter, in his 'Reformed Statutes' of 1132, describes how the workmen at the new church at Cluny were exempt from the rule of silence whilst working. This would indicate that they were associated with the monastery, either as monks or lay-brothers. It is possible that both of these were involved in the construction of the monasteries, but not in all cases. Whatever the truth of this, there certainly appears to be some consistency in the style of the abbeys. Many, if not most of them, were remarkably similar to, if not based upon, the design of Cluny III.

THE DESIGN OF CLUNIAC MONASTERIES

I shall now examine the west end of Reading as revealed by the GPR, and present some possible interpretations of the anomalous lines shown in the GPR survey. I shall show that what we see at Reading conforms to standard Cluniac design. I shall emphasise that the point in making this comparison is that the building's lay-out intrinsically relates to its use.

Following the reforms of the 10th and 11th centuries, Cluniac churches and abbeys were both designed to accommodate the aspects of monastic life we saw above. Fig 1 shows both the diversity and the conformity that may be found in Cluniac buildings. If we look at the west ends, we see a variety of designs.[2] There is, however, an underlying theme: their role both as monastic and as public places.

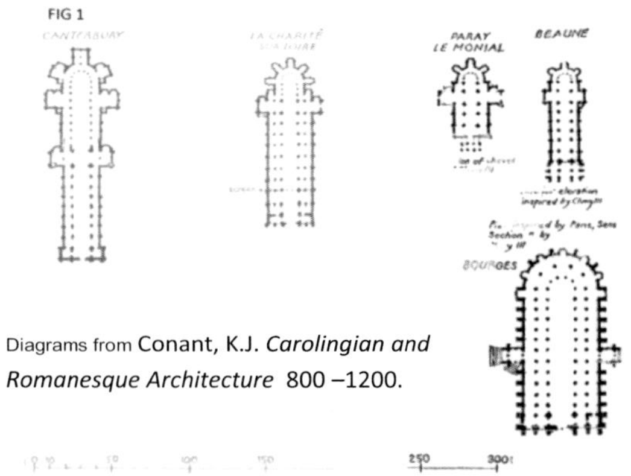

The east end was designed for the monks. Here was to be found the 'choir', an essential element of the *Opus Dei* or singing of the Divine Office at appointed times of the day and night. Here also was the 'high altar', where the daily life of the monastery was focused on

Diagrams from Conant, K.J. *Carolingian and Romanesque Architecture* 800 –1200.

Fig. 1

celebrating Mass. Here were the many chapels and shrines where the monks could make their devotions, and say their own daily Mass. It is interesting to note that in one of the *Consuetudines* ('Customaries' or Rules) of the Cluniac order, monks were reminded not to stay too long in front of any particular altar or shrine, but to be mindful of others who might wish to say their prayers at that place.

The east end of the church, which contained the altar and choir, was, therefore, primarily for the use of the monks. In fact, it was very often part of the enclosure, and so forbidden to laymen and certainly to women. When the number of monks became too great, this section was even extended into the nave. However, we also know that visitors and pilgrims could, on occasion, be allowed to pay their devotions at the various altars and shrines in that part of the church.

Depending on the abbey, there would have been set days when the relics of a particular saint were to be venerated. It was this function of welcoming visitors and pilgrims that accounts for the impressive naves of many abbeys. Their size was based on this aspect of the Cluniac apostolate, namely encouraging lay participation in the life of the abbey. Public celebration of holy days was one way of achieving this.

If we look at the plans, it can be seen that they all follow the basilican pattern of side aisles with rows of pillars. It was along the aisles formed by these pillars, that pilgrims would have been ushered as they went round the church towards the east end chapels, to venerate the relics, and go out down the opposite aisle.

Not all Cluniac churches followed this plan. In smaller country churches , such as Vianne or Mouthiers, where the church was catering to a local community, there was no call to provide such facilities, and consequently these buildings consist of a simple nave, without aisles. Once again, form followed function.

However, most of the Cluniac monasteries were, in one way or another, connected with pilgrimage, and could expect sizeable numbers of visitors. One example is Vézelay, which famously burnt down in 1120 on the feast of St Madeleine, the patron saint of the Abbey. It was reported, probably dittographically, that 1120 people died in the fire. Whatever the true number, clearly the church was crowded for this occasion. Many Cluniac monasteries, such as that at Vézelay, were built to accommodate the needs of pilgrims on their way to Compostela, let alone more local places of pilgrimage.

THE ENTRANCE TO THE ABBEY CHURCH - The Narthex and the Galilee Chapel.

As we have just seen, the design of Cluniac architecture reflected the need to accommodate the large numbers entering the church, either to make the circuitous route around the aisles, or to attend services or other functions that took place in the nave. The solution can be seen in the plans in Fig 1. (page 47).

The western end had a narthex or porch area. In some cases these were named 'Galilees' and designated for a specific use, especially for pilgrims and women. For instance, at Durham it was created specifically for women, who were not allowed near the tomb of St Cuthbert at the east end of the church.

There are several explanations for the term 'Galilee'. One is that it derives from the word 'gallery' (*gallilea*). Another, more liturgical, explanation is that it took its name from the procession at Easter when the main celebrant of the Easter Mass, representing Christ, led the procession into the church, re-enacting Christ's journey after the Resurrection, when he said 'I will go before you into Galilee'. Whatever its origins, its usage was both liturgical, and as a place where visitors could be accommodated prior to entering the church proper. They could even be used for secular activities such as signing legal agreements and contracts. In some cases, as the plans show, they were very distinct parts of the building. As often as not, they had a chapel or rooms above the ground floor. As such, their foundations would have been substantial. It was usual for two towers to be incorporated into any such western extension. These contributed to the aesthetic appearance of the west end, and could be used as belfries, so fulfilling a spiritual role. As Pugin points out, they also served the practical purpose of acting as buttresses.

THE DESIGN OF THE NARTHEX AND GALILEE CHAPEL

In Figure 2 we can see the example of a quite common style of narthex, where it is narrower than the main nave.

Cluny itself had such an addition (Fig 3) and note the existence of towers. The narthex and towers were added over a century after construction of the main church, which began in 1088.

An interesting observation, which may have relevance to Reading and the GPR scan, is that there is evidence that not all additions were necessarily in strict alignment with the rest of the building. This is clearly demonstrated in the plan of Payerne, in Switzerland (Fig 4).

Close examination of the narthex and the towers at Cluny (Fig. 3), likewise shows that they are not in alignment with the nave, or even with each other.

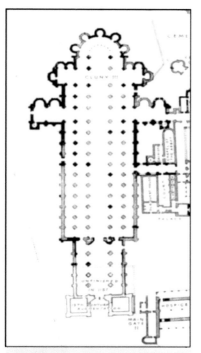

Fig 3 Cluny III,
showing the narthex

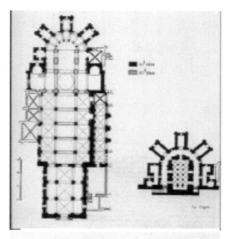

Fig 2. Tournus, Burgundy

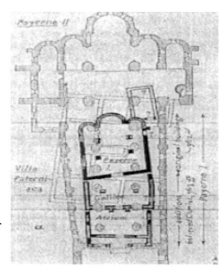

Fig 4. Payerne, Switzerland.
Second half of the 11th century

Reading Abbey - A pilgrim church

At Reading we have two potential examples of walls that were not in alignment with their counterparts. There is the apparent anomaly between the northern wall of the Lady Chapel and its counterpart in the main church. Then on the GPR survey, in the west, there is the northerly blue line which does not run where it might be expected, but rather slightly to its north. (See page 44.)

Does this in fact show some correspondence with the Lady Chapel anomaly? As in the plan shown in Fig 4, the north wall of the larger, newer, nave (fainter on the diagram) is certainly neither straight nor in alignment with the north transept and not parallel with the south wall. Likewise, the dark lines of the older church show much irregularity.

An examination of all the diagrams shows that, within the nave, there was often a physical division between the body of the nave and the 'porch' or narthex. Could this be an explanation for the lines found on the GPR scan at Reading: within the nave yet at quite a distance from its presumed end? Even where a narrower addition to the west end is lacking, there is ample evidence that the rear section of the nave was often separated from its body, and that it served as an entrance lobby or porch.

COMMENTS

1. This is not an exhaustive account of galilees or narthexes as found in Cluniac establishments. For instance, as noted, an important feature is that many had upper chapels. Some of these were substantial structures with pillars and vaulting. They would most probably have required appropriate foundations, which would have to be laid within the nave.

2. The GPR survey at Reading shows traces of possible abbey remains at the west end, which do not fit in with the concept of a symmetrical plan. These do not, following the above observations, mean we have to discount their relevance. In fact, I would say that the above observations give an explanation for stating that these may be possible traces of the abbey. It should be remembered that the exact footprint of the nave is unknown. There has never been any reliable drawing, and certainly no scientific excavation, of the nave in the Forbury. The map on which the GPR scan is superimposed was that of the OS 1879 survey. The outline of the abbey was based upon the work of FW Albury (See Chapter 3).

3. This is only one explanation, and others, some of which I mention at the beginning, are just as feasible.

CHAPTER 3

MAPS, SURVEYS AND EXCAVATIONS

In the previous chapters I looked at the east and west ends of the Abbey, and how the eastern section was the most sacred area, where the monks prayed the Divine Office, attended the daily communal Mass and also where Henry I was buried. In Chapter 2, I showed how the west of the abbey church, including the nave and side aisles, and possibly a narthex, was a space for the public, especially pilgrims.

But with so little of the abbey still standing, how has this been recorded? In this chapter I will look at maps and surveys, starting in 1610, which is the earliest we know about, and ending in the twenty-first century.

1. 1. Speed's Map, 1610.

The earliest extant map of Reading that shows the abbey, is Speed's drawing of c 1610. Although this includes the Forbury and the abbey buildings, it needs to be viewed with some degree of caution.

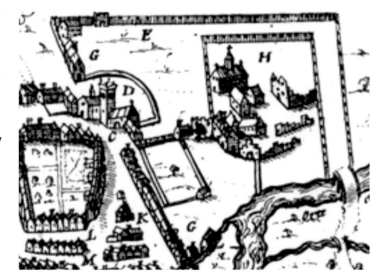

For instance, the abbey church (H) is drawn with a spire. We are fairly certain, from other sources, that this had been removed several years beforehand. Nevertheless, it is a map which tells a story and shows a complex of buildings, many of which are no longer visible.

Legend: C - The Free Schole, D - St Laurence, E - Forbery,
K - Shomakers Row, G - Queens Stables, H - The Abbey   (Spellings as in original).

Reading Abbey - A pilgrim church

2. The English Civil War 1640s

The next map, now in the Bodleian Library, dates from the time of the Civil War in the 1640s. This is a military map showing the defences around Reading, including the abbey and Forbury area. Once again, it would be over-simplistic to read this as an exact piece of cartography.

The abbey buildings are shown as no more than outlines. What is more, the defence wall does not match the line of the Great Ditch that we believe, from other evidence, both written and archaeological, to have been driven through the Forbury. It may of course be that this map was drawn before the Great Ditch was created.

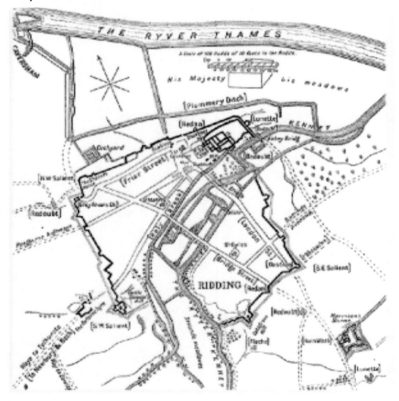

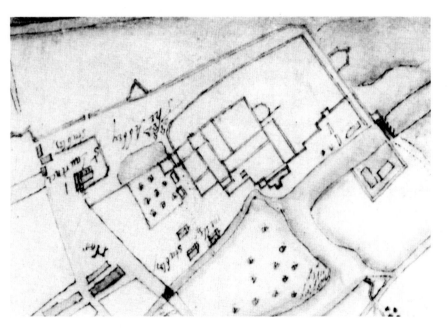

Above: detail of the full map shown on the left

3. Parliamentary Survey, 1650

By 1650, with victory in sight in the Civil War, Parliament ordered a survey of all the former royal properties. This records, in great detail, the land and buildings in the abbey area that had belonged to the Crown. Although there is no map, the information it contains is useful when we try to interpret the site today and match the buildings with existing remains. (See page 71).

4. Englefield's Survey, 1779

The first and only mapped survey of the whole of the abbey was undertaken by Sir Henry Englefield and published in 1779. Shortly after this, in 1786, the first County Gaol was built on the eastern section of the abbey. Its gardens extended westwards over the eastern part of the abbey church, including the 1314 Lady Chapel, and any other buildings which may have existed to its south. Consequently, after this date no survey or excavation of this area was possible. Englefield's work is, therefore, a unique piece of evidence. When I matched it with an aerial photograph, I found that the existing ruins fitted his outline exactly. It should be noted that Englefield's plan does not take us any further west along the nave of the abbey church than its second bay. It shows where he estimated that the Great Ditch, mentioned above (no 2), had sliced through the rest of the nave and the cloisters. Modern archaeological scholarship disputes the siting of 'g' and 'h'.

Key as produced by Sir Henry Englefield

A The Cloister court   148ft sqr

B The Chapter house   78 by 42

C The Refectory   72 by 38

D The South Transept of the church

E The Nave of the church

F The Choir of the church

G The eastern chapel of the church (the Lady Chapel)

H The North transept of the church

I A passage vaulted two stories (sic)

K A passage vaulted

L A wall once enclosing two rooms

M The great gate (the Abbey Gateway)

a The top of the rampart thrown up in the civil wars, which crosses the cloister.

b The ditch of the rampart.

c The spot where the mine was sprung.

d The leaning masses of wall.

e A small house built by the late Lord Fane.

f The remains of a stair-case.

g The lavatory.

h Probable situation of the dormitory.

Key references added by J. Mullaney

X   Site of St James' Church

◆   Approximate site of the abbey's high altar

⊕   Possible site of the tomb of Henry I

5. *The History and Antiquities of Reading,* Charles Coates, 1802. ,

Coates' plan of the area includes the whole of the Forbury and St Lawrence's Church. The outline of the Great Ditch is shown, as is the semi-circle of the Green which also appears in the Civil War map, in the 1842 Post Office map and in the 1853 Board of Health survey. Should any future archaeology take place in the Forbury, it would be interesting to see if there is any trace of this feature. It existed until the mid-19th century, when it was lost with the creation of the Forbury Gardens. There are many written references to it, and illustrations show that it was still present through the first half of the 19th century. It was suggested by Charles Kerry in *A history of the municipal church of St Lawrence ,* that the Green may have been the site of the Danish Viking camp reported in the Anglo-Saxon Chronicle of 870-1, and that the ditch around the Green was in fact the remnants of this fortification. One aim of the GPR, commissioned in 2016, was to ascertain the westerly extent of the 1121 abbey.

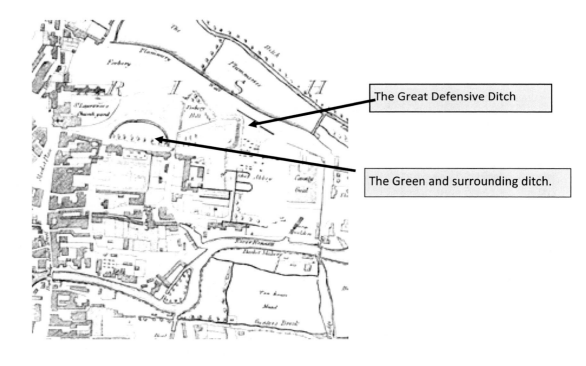

The Great Defensive Ditch

The Green and surrounding ditch.

In his book *The History and Antiquities of Reading,* Coates included an updated and embellished version of Englefield's plan.

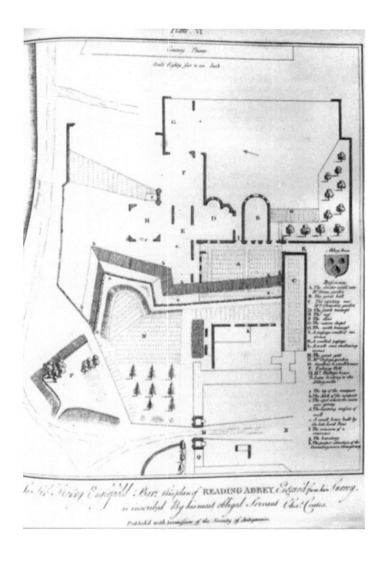

6. 1813 and 1816, John Man

John Man, *The history and antiquities, ancient and modern, of the Borough of Reading, in the county of Berks.* Man published his plan of the area in this work.

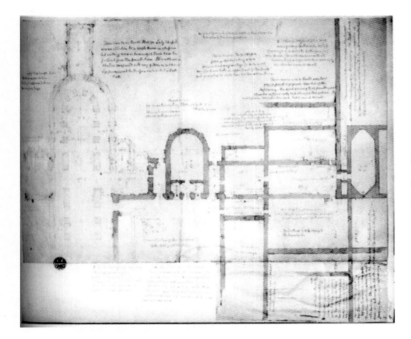

7. 1823, Buckler

C A Buckler, *Survey and Plan*. This is very similar to Englefield's plan, and its likely date is 1823-1824. Once again, nothing is shown further west than the second cell of the nave.

8. 1842 Post Office map (right)

Post Office Map of Reading. This shows little detail of the area.

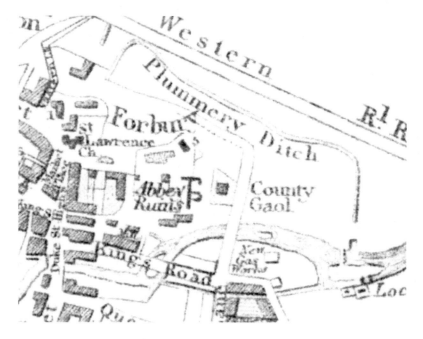

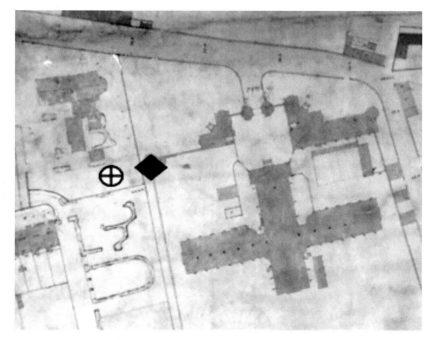

9. 1853 Board of Health Survey (left)

Board of Health Survey. This is one of the most detailed of the maps, showing roads, houses and house numbers and the outline of the standing ruins. It also shows the new Gaol, built in the 1840s

 Approximate site of the Abbey's high altar

 Possible site of the tomb of Henry I

10. 1857 J. Okey Taylor

J Okey Taylor, writing in the quarterly journal of the Berkshire Archaeological and Architectural Society, 1889, reported that in 1857 he and others had been involved in excavating the Forbury area to *a depth of between two to five feet,* and that the topsoil had been removed to create the embankment along the River Kennet to Blake's Bridge, where Chestnut Walk now lies.

11. 1867 John Mellor

The Mayor of Reading gave Mellor permission to excavate in the Forbury Gardens but, according to Slade, *nothing particular was found. He dug twice in the area of the church as mention is made of mortar and flint and portions of the Abbey pavement.*

12. 1879 Ordnance Survey and F.W. Albury

The OS map of 1879 gives us a detailed picture of the area. F W Albury commented that the outline plan of the abbey was inserted following the results of his survey.

Much of the evidence relies on the work of Englefield, Buckler and Albury. Some of this may be speculative, or the cartographers may have had information, based on Albury's original plan, which has been lost to us.

It is possible that Albury did find the foundations of the missing nave pillars. His own report says that he had made a detailed plan, marking in red the positioning of these Abbey remains. This was then incorporated into the OS map.

It was at this time that the eastern section of the Forbury, the part east of the Hill and the Inner Gateway, was being converted into a botanical garden, and much work was therefore taking place here.

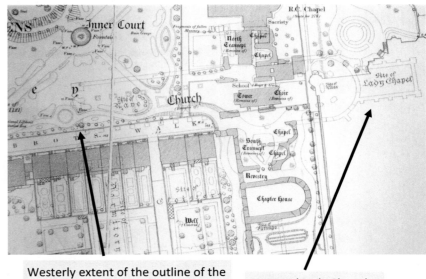

Westerly extent of the outline of the abbey nave on the OS map.

Apse and Lady Chapel

This is the plan on which most, if not all, subsequent maps showing the westward extent of the abbey, have been based. It is likely that Hurry (see 59 opposite) relied on Albury's work.

13. 1900 Dr. J. B. Hurry

Around the turn of the 19th and 20th centuries, Dr. Hurry produced many works about the abbey. These included the detailed plans showing both the standing ruins and the supposed footprint of the abbey buildings, including the church.

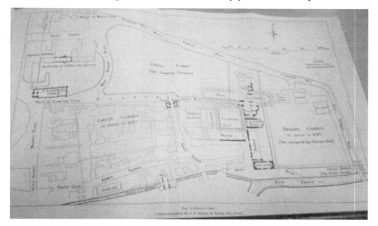 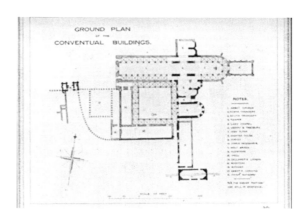

14. 1906 W. Ravenscroft (Berkshire Archaeological Journal 13, 1907)

In 1906, excavations were made for the purposes of laying a drain between Abbots Walk and the Forbury Rd. The drain passed to the west of St James' church, through the Forbury Gardens, to the Forbury Road. About forty skeletons were discovered in the narrow 3ft wide trench. They were all laid out in an east-west orientation with their feet toward the east. This was a Christian custom based on the belief that on the 'Last Day' the bodies of the dead would rise and, by facing east, the first sight of the 'risen' would be towards the direction of Jerusalem, where Christ would be revealed in glory. No cremations or cinerary urns were found; these would have indicated non-Christian funerals. The whole area lies to the north of the abbey's north aisle. Ravenscroft notes that *in the case of the little bit of the aisle wall we ought to have found, the very flint foundations were also removed.*

It was argued, at the time of this discovery, that this supported the opinion expressed by Kerry and others, that this was compelling evidence for a Saxon church in the area. Ravenscroft suggests that the original Saxon church, possibly made of 'wattle and mud' had been destroyed in the 1006 Viking raid, only to be replaced by a more substantial flint building. If so, this could be the one noted by Slade in the 1970s, as described in the next section.

15. 1970s Dr. Cecil Slade

In the 1970s, Cecil Slade excavated the east of the abbey chancel. This is the only deep archaeological dig to have taken place in the abbey church area. It is reported in the Berkshire Archaeological Journal, Vol. 68. In analysing the abbey footings in the prison area adjacent to the land of St James' school, Slade shows sections, depths, soil composition, materials found, and comments about the construction of the 1121 abbey.

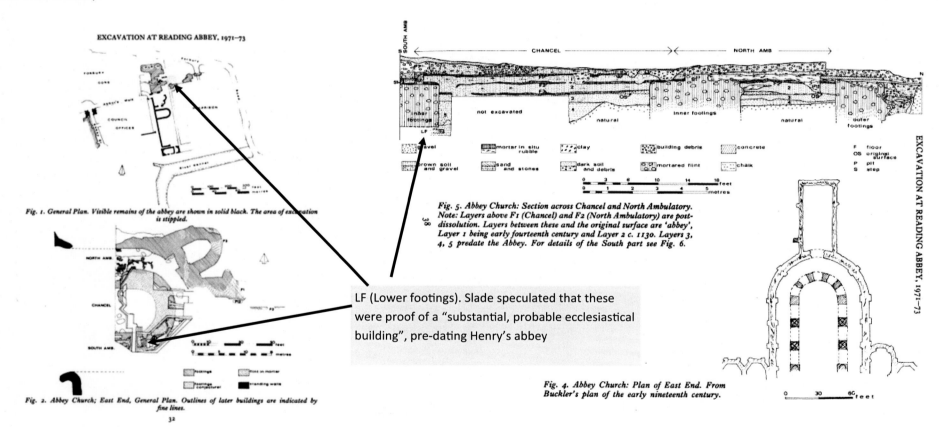

EXCAVATION AT READING ABBEY, 1971–73

Fig. 1. General Plan. Visible remains of the abbey are shown in solid black. The area of excavation is stippled.

Fig. 2. Abbey Church; East End, General Plan. Outlines of later buildings are indicated by fine lines.

32

Fig. 5. Abbey Church: Section across Chancel and North Ambulatory. Note: Layers above F1 (Chancel) and F2 (North Ambulatory) are post-dissolution. Layers between these and the original surface are 'abbey', Layer 1 being early fourteenth century and Layer 2 c. 1130. Layers 3, 4, 5 predate the Abbey. For details of the South part see Fig. 6.

38

LF (Lower footings). Slade speculated that these were proof of a "substantial, probable ecclesiastical building", pre-dating Henry's abbey

Fig. 4. Abbey Church: Plan of East End. From Buckler's plan of the early nineteenth century.

EXCAVATION AT READING ABBEY, 1971–73

Slade wrote that, in the south west corner, he came across what he described as *pre-Abbey footings.* These are marked as 'LF' (lower footings) on his diagrams. Note the different angle and greater depth of the *lower footings.*

Slade also said that the cement and gravel composition differed from the upper layers, which he associated with the 1121 abbey.

His photograph, on the right, shows both these features.

PLATE 13.   *Reading Abbey: Chancel, pre-Abbey footings under Abbey footings.*

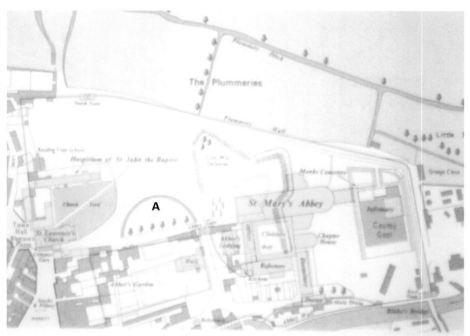

16. 1975 *Atlas of Historic Towns,* C. Slade

Slade not only gave a brief, but intriguing, account of the development of the town, but produced an overlay map showing the various stages of the development of the town, including the Abbey Quarter. He based this on all the evidence seen above.

As noted above, it has been suggested that the semi-circular area known as the 'Green' (marked A), may have been the site of the Danish Viking camp reported in the Anglo-Saxon Chronicle of 870-1, and that the ditch around the Green was in fact the remnants of this fortification.

Reading Abbey - A pilgrim church

17. 2008 Wessex Archaeology

In 2008, Wessex Archaeology published an account of their excavations in the Abbey Quarter. They dug several small trenches in the area, including in the Forbury.

There were very few finds, and no evidence of the missing pier bases of the abbey nave. On the other hand, none of their trenches was in the expected line of the nave.

Note how, even in 2008, the archaeologists were using the OS map, with its suggested outline of the abbey, mentioned above.

Two Second World War air-raid shelters were recorded. These are in the area of the monks' dormitory in the ancient abbey.

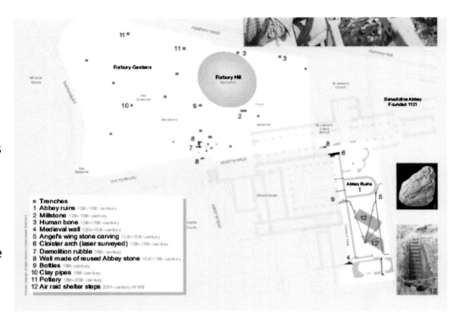

18. Ground Penetrating Radar (GPR) Survey May 2016

In June and August 2016, a geophysics survey by Stratscan Sumo was commissioned by the Hidden Abbey Project group. This consisted of a GPR scan of the area believed to be the main body of the abbey church.

At the west end, the survey did not provide much positive information. The light-blue area, marked **A** on figure 1, page 63, shows the outer wall of the ambulatory, and corresponds approximately to the northern wall of the nave. However, the area marked **B** does not correspond to any known abbey-related feature.

The survey describes these as *probable archaeological features – probably related to the Abbey.*

In the area of the prison car park, at the east end of the abbey church, much more was revealed. The scan appeared to confirm the line of the inner area of the ambulatory (**C**), where Slade had made his excavations.

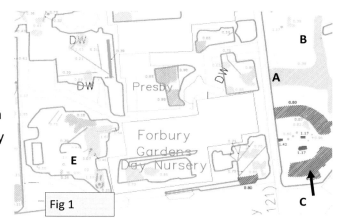

Fig 1

Further north of this still, in the car park area, a red T shaped feature (Fig 2, **D**), with a smaller line to its west, was observed. Once again, no archaeology relating to the abbey is known to exist in this area.

In the apse itself several features were identified (marked in purple), which Stratascan suggested were indicative of graves (Fig 3).

Subsequent analysis of the scan showed up another anomaly at the main entrance into the school. This can be seen in the two light blue lines just to the east of the wording 'Forbury Gardens Day Nursery (Fig 1, **E**).

These may be the remains of 19th century work, but they are in just the right position for a pulpitum at the entrance to the abbey choir. Without excavation to determine their age, this must remain as a speculative hypothesis, but one that would be consistent with later medieval developments in church design. (See Chapter 1)

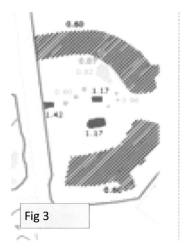

Fig 3

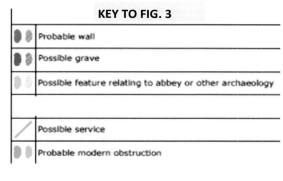

KEY TO FIG. 3	
Probable wall	
Possible grave	
Possible feature relating to abbey or other archaeology	
Possible service	
Probable modern obstruction	

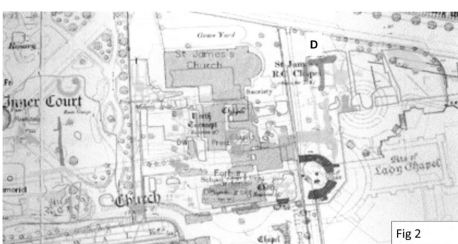

Fig 2

19.   2015 Stuart Harrison.

In 2015, Reading Borough Council (RBC), published the results of the work supervised by Stuart Harrison. This was a comprehensive analysis of the standing ruins. It was commissioned by RBC with a view towards the work which would be required following a successful Heritage Lottery Fund bid for money to conserve the standing ruins. I will be looking at this in more detail, especially when discussing the chapter house, in the next chapter.

20.   Museum of London Archaeology. (MOLA). MOLA carried out a survey in the prison area which include opening trenches. This was carried out on behalf of the Ministry of Justice as part of the process for selling the site.

21.   2020   Reading Libraries, Reading Abbey Quarter Project.

Drome shot of the chapter house and north transept

Accreditation: *Reading Libraries, Reading Abbey Quarter Project*

CHAPTER 4

THE CHAPTER HOUSE

INTRODUCTION AND COMPARISON WITH MAJOR ENGLISH CHAPTER HOUSES

The monks of Reading Abbey belonged to the Benedictine monastic family. That is to say, their way of life was based upon the rule of St Benedict of Nursia (Norcia, near Perugia, Italy), who died in 547 AD. Unlike the eremitic ('of the desert') monks, such as St Anthony of Egypt (d.355 AD), St. Benedict founded a community where all lived communally. Their monasteries are often referred to as 'coenobia', or 'coenobium' in the singular. This is a word that comes from the Greek for 'common' and 'life', (κοινός, koinos and βίος, bios).

It was expected that all the brothers in the community would pray, eat, sleep and work together, though of course certain tasks would be apportioned to individuals or groups. In fact, it was highly unusual for individuals to work alone, the norm was to have groups of at least three.

The daily practicalities of how the Rule should be interpreted in each monastery were written down in 'customaries', in Latin *consuetudines.* These are very detailed instructions covering just about every imaginable aspect of life in the monastery. The Rule was of upmost importance to each monk. Along with passages from scripture, it was to be read and studied every day. The main place where this took place was in a building which came to be named after it, the chapter house. For it was here that a chapter of the Rule was read out each day, and, very often, a study, or homily, concerning that chapter would have been delivered to the assembled brothers, most frequently by the 'father', or 'abbot', of the community.

Chapter houses were therefore built to accommodate the whole community. Almost invariably, they were alongside the chancel of the church, and access was through the cloister. As such, their orientation followed that of the church, being on an east-west axis, with the entrance at the west, and the abbot's, or prior's seat, at the east end.

Architecturally, there are several types of chapter house. The earliest, as at Reading, are rectangular, some with an apsidal east end, others with a square end. Later examples, as at Wells and York, are round or polygonal. These date from the 13th century onwards.

Many abbots, priors and other notable persons, such as benefactors, were buried in the chapter houses.[1]

Reading Abbey - A pilgrim church

This chapter is an architectural study based upon historical records, my own research, and that undertaken in preparation of the conservation work before the re-opening of the ruins at Reading in 2019.

The following is a list of some major chapter houses in England. Reading had one of the largest, if not the largest, in the country. The following dimensions are taken from several sources, some of which differ one from another by a metre or so. I have used an average figure.

	LENGTH		WIDTH		AREA	
	ft	m	ft	m	sq ft	sq m
WINCHESTER Norman (ruined)	88	26.8	38	11.58	3344	310.67
CANTERBURY Late 14th c	90	27.43	35	10.67	3150	292.64
DURHAM Early 14th c. rebuilt 19th c	80	24.38	34' 6"	9.14	2100	223
EXETER 1225— 1230	65	19.8	30	9.14	1950	181
GLOUCESTER Late 11th to 12th c.	65	19.8	30	9.14	1950	181
MUCH WENLOCK 12th c	49	15	29	9	1421	135

READING. Below. There have been several surveys of the abbey area with different measurements given in various accounts, as shown below. As the building is still standing, and it is essentially unchanged, we can only put this down to faulty measurement or that different reference points were used.

	LENGTH		WIDTH		AREA	
STOKESEY (1721)	84	25.6	48	14.6	4032	373.76
DORAN (1835)	85	26	40	12.2	3400	315.87
ENGLEFIELD / HURRY 1800 –1900)	78	23.8	42	12	3276	304
ORDNANCE SURVEY	80	24	42	12	3360	312.15

I will next look at the first three of these abbeys, as their chapter houses are the largest, and nearest in size to that at Reading. We shall see that there are, however, significant differences between them in style and date.

WINCHESTER CHAPTER HOUSE

State: ruined   Dates to Walkelyn's time 1079+   Style: oblong rectangular, barrel-vaulted ceiling

LENGTH		WIDTH		AREA	
ft	m	ft	m	sq ft	sq m
88	26.8	38	11.58	3344	310.67

As befitting the longest church in Europe, the chapter house was one of the largest in the country. All that remain are parts of the north wall and, to the west, the southerly window and door arches, with pillars and capitals, which would have led into the chapter house. [2]

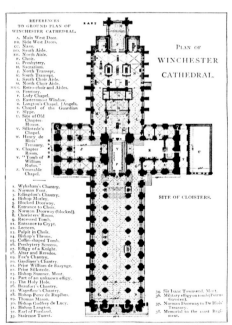

Plan of Winchester Cathedral

The chapter-house, immediately to the south, is also of Walkelin's time, and was a rectangle 88 ft. by 38 ft., covered with a barrel vault of stone, and having on the north, south and east a round arched wall arcade with shafts and cushion capitals, but only the arcade on the north wall now remains. At the west, five round-headed arches on large circular columns with cushion capitals opened to the cloister, the middle arch being wider and higher than the rest, and these still remain perfect, a most valuable example of the arrangement of an 11th-century chapter-house entrance (Victoria County Histories).

I have started with Winchester, as its dimensions are very similar to those at Reading: it was built in the same architectural style, and within fifty years of Reading. Although it did not have an apsidal east end, it did have similar vaulting, and its remaining west end is very similar to that at Reading, leading into the cloister.

View of the windows and doors, from 'inside' the chapter house looking west.

CANTERBURY

State: standing, 14th century   Style: oblong rectangular, barrel vaulted ceiling

LENGTH		WIDTH		AREA	
ft	m	ft	m	sq ft	sq m
97.3	27.43	35	10.67	3150	292.64

The chapter house at Canterbury is near to Reading's in size. It was built in the late 14th century, but it stands partly on the footprint of its Norman predecessor. It is of special interest not just on account of its size, specifically its width, but, despite being built 200 years later, it has a barrel-vaulted ceiling. It should be noted that the lower section, or storey (as it is described in the Project Gutenburg entry below), was built mid-way between the building of Reading and its own completion by Prior Chillenden. It differs from Reading in not having an apsidal east end. It is also somewhat unusual in that it lies, along with the adjoining cloister, to the north of the church.

Canterbury Cathedral, Chapter house.
*https://commons.wikimedia.org/wiki/
File:Canterbury_Cathedral_Chapter_House
_(249775103).jpeg#/media/*

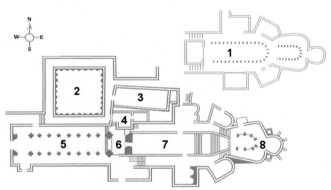

1. The Crypt
2. The Cloister
3. Chapter House
4. The Martyrdom
5. The Nave
6. The Crossing
7. The Quire
8. The Trinity Chapel

The Chapterhouse lies eastward of the wall of the cloister, on the site of the original Norman building, which was rather less extensive. The present structure is oblong in shape, measuring 90 feet by 35 feet. The roof consists of a "barrel vault" and was built by Prior Chillenden, along with the whole of the upper storey at the end of the fourteenth century. The windows, high and four-lighted, are also his work; those at the east and west ends exceed in size all those of the cathedral, having seven lights. The lower storey was built by Prior de Estria about a century before the work was completed by Chillenden.[3]

DURHAM

State: Some standing remains, 11 – 12th c. Re-built in the 19th century. Vaulted apse

LENGTH		WIDTH		AREA		
ft	m	ft	m	sq ft	sq m	
78' 6"	23.92	34' 6"	10.5	2400	223	(*BRITISH HISTORY* figures)

The Durham Cathedral Chapter house is, to a large extent, a reconstruction of the original and dates from 1895.
The original Chapter house was partially demolished in 1796 because its large scale and high ceiling made it difficult to heat, and the
18th century clergy did not like it! [4]

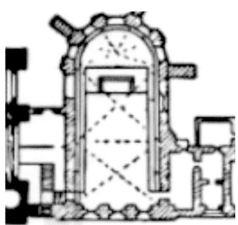

In many ways, Durham is the closest to Reading of these three chapter houses in that it has a vaulted apse. However, unlike that at Reading, the ceiling is ribbed, not barrel-vaulted.

Fig 5. Apsidal east end of the chapter house, Durham

Reading Abbey - A pilgrim church

The 'British History survey states: *Before the destruction ... it was 78 ft. 6 in. in length, with a breadth of 34 ft. 6 in. In the apse were five three-light windows with flowing tracery inserted in the 14th century and at the west end above the cloister roof a large 15th century pointed window of five lights. It consisted of two bays, each covered by a quadripartite vault, and a third bay over the apse, the vault of which was set out by keeping the four western ribs in straight lines on plan, thus making them of unequal length and throwing the keystone to the east of the centre of the apse curve.*

The transverse arches were semicircular, and the ribs of the vaults had a slightly pointed soffit roll flanked by cheverons of convex profile: in the apse the ribs sprang from large figure corbels and the soffit roll was flanked by a row of star ornaments and cheverons. A wall arcade of semicircular intersecting arches ran round the building.

The rebuilding of 1895–6, under the direction of Mr. C. Hodgson Fowler, restored the chapter house to something like its former appearance, the east end being erected on the old plan, though the original design of the apse vault was not followed, and round-headed windows of 12th-century type take the place of the 14th-century windows destroyed by Wyatt. The height to the crown of the new vault is 44 ft., above which is a low-pitched lead-covered roof. The stone bench and steps round the building have been reconstructed and the wall arcades renewed. The removal of the floor in the western part, constructed in 1796, brought to light several fragments of early sculptured crosses, probably of late 10th-century date, and also the arms of the stone chair, which have been worked into a new chair in the original position.[5]

COMMENT

I have included the above brief descriptions, as I feel they help us build a picture of Reading's place in the architectural story of when, why and how these chapter houses were built.

In the next section I will look at the post-Reformation evidence concerning Reading's chapter house.

READING CHAPTER HOUSE: KEY POST-REFORMATION RECORDS

In 1539 Reading Abbey ceased to exist. The Dissolution, with the expulsion of the monks, meant that the building no longer had a major role to play in the life of the town. Some of the monastery's buildings were converted to other uses, including a royal residence. There are sound historical records concerning its destruction and the disposal of its material assets. This has been written about elsewhere.

The following is an account of later evidence, written and pictorial, which helps us piece together a picture of what the chapter house would have looked like before its destruction. I do not claim this is a complete survey, but I hope that it gives a representative overview of the records.

1.   1650 PARLIAMENTARY SURVEY

Towards the end of the 17th century Civil War, Parliament carried out a nationwide survey of Crown lands which now passed into the ownership of the Commonwealth. In Reading this included the old abbey. The survey is reproduced in *The History and Antiquities of Reading* by Charles Coates.[6]

There is on the East side of the said mansion-house a great old hall with a very large cellar under the said hall, arched, with some other decayed roomes between the said hall and the mansion-house, with the ruins of an old chappell, a kitchen and several other rooms, fit to be demolished. (Spelling as in the original, as quoted by Coates)

Comment:

The existence of a significant cellar under the 'great old hall', raises the question as to which building is being identified. The 'great hall' (*aula* or *aula magna)* often refers to the chapter house. Use of this term dates back to the 13th century, at least. There is reference to the *aula* in the commemoration services for Henry I.[7] This is where thirteen poor people were fed. There is no means of knowing if this referred to the refectory, chapter house or some other building. On one hand, it may seem strange that the chapter house should be used as a refectory; on the other hand, we know that it was used as a meeting place, as when parliament convened there, and when Edward IV announced his marriage to Elizabeth Woodville. It may be considered equally unlikely that the refectory should be handed over for the feeding of the poor of the town. This was an event that took place on the first of each month in commemoration of the death of Henry I.

As the two buildings are so close, it is interesting, in either case, that there was a large cellar in the area.

2. 1721 STUKELEY

Stukeley describes the chapter house *as one large room 16 yards broad, 28 long, semi-circular towards the East end, with five narrow windows, three doors to the West with three windows above them. It is arched over and seems to have supported a chapel in which we fancy King Henry I was buried with his queen.*

Fig 6. William Stukeleys' drawings of c.1721 are among the first, if not the first, of the Abbey. View from the west of the Chapter House from the Cloisters.   (Courtesy Reading Library)

Comment:

The measurements here are slightly greater than later and contemporary ones. Also note the error about Henry's burial place and that of Queen Adeliza.

If Stukeley's drawing is accurate, note that the ashlar stone blocks were still in place at this time. The windows are rounded. This latter feature needs to be borne in mind when comparing it with Englefield's account, which we shall see later. We should also note how the curvature of the vault shafts start at ground level. The standing remains and other drawings show that this was not the case.

3. 1773 ILLUSTRATION

This view, drawn only six years before Englefield's detailed report (below), shows the chapter house behind part of the refectory wall, as viewed from the south.

We can see the three western openings, with two complete windows above.

To the east (far right), can be seen two of the great windows in the apse of the chapter house.

The western windows appear rounded, whilst those in the apse may be pointed. This needs to be read with Englefield's statement in mind, that all the windows appear pointed.

I am perplexed by the refectory wall which should, at this time, have reached further west. Perhaps the artist was allowing himself some liberties, in order to give a view of the openings into the chapter house.

Fig 7. 1773 Godfrey (Grose) (Reading Library)

4. SIR HENRY ENGLEFIELD 1779.

Englefield's survey was described by Dr Slade, in the 1970s, as the first *factual survey and the starting point for modern studies.*[8] It is worth reproducing the survey in full.

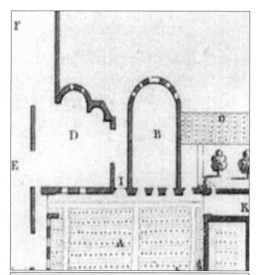

Fig 8. Englefield's 1802 version of the plan of Reading Abbey, *The History and Antiquities of Reading* by Charles Coates

South of that (the south transept), *and separated from it by a passage arched two stories high, is the great hall, once most probably the chapter house, open to the cloisters by three semicircular arches, with a window over each, and terminated to the east by a semicircle with five large windows in it. It is now difficult to say, whether or not the windows were round headed; they have much the appearance of an obtuse point, as have all the other windows remaining in the abbey, though the doors are every one round. The hall, though forty-two feet by seventy-nine, was vaulted with one semicircular arch from wall to wall, apparently with stone ribs, and the intervals filled up with a very curious substance, of which a specimen accompanies this. All those vaults which were to bear nothing were turned with this, which is evidently a tophus formed by some petrifying spring, and enclosing the impressions of twigs &c. One leaf is very fair. This substance is very soft and extremely light, bearing only the proportion off 66 to 161 of Portland stone...* [9]

Going southwards round the outside of the building, we came to a small door, and near it the remains of a stair-case. The door opens into a dark passage, once vaulted, and communicating with the cloisters by a great door.

He then describes other parts of the ruins such as the refectory, cloister and north transept. In conclusion he makes some general observations. When discussing the Gateway, that is the Inner Abbey Gateway, he talks of *the semi-saxon style which seems to prevail over most parts of the building* ...(I have retained Englefield's spelling).

Above is part of Englefield's plan, showing the chapter house (B), the south transept (D) , the cloister area (A), the refectory (K), the slype (I), which Englefield calls *a dak passage,* and the south aisle of the church (E).

5. 1791 ILLUSTRATIONS

Dating to 1791, looking from the east of the chapter house, it is possible to see where a great hole had been made in its apse. Nevertheless, the outer frame of the two windows can be made out (fig 9). Figure 10 is another view, this time from the inside, looking east.

If the representations are accurate, the windows had deteriorated since the 1773 illustration (no 3 above).

Fig 9. 1791   Reading Abbey. The ruins, from the east. The pinnacles of St. Laurence's Church appear in the background, and the east end of the Abbey Church is to the right. 18th century : print, entitled "East View of the Great Hall" [i.e. Chapter House], drawn, engraved and published by Charles Tomkins, 1791. No. 5 of his *Eight Views of Reading Abbey* (Reading Library)

Fig 10. 1791 Ruins of the Chapter House, looking west. There is a thatched, wooden lean-to building against the south wall, and two ladies pose by the north wall. Print, drawn, engraved and published by Charles Tomkins in 1791, entitled "Inside of the Great Hall".   (Reading Library)

6. 1802 *HISTORY AND ANTIQUITIES OF READING*, COATES

As we have seen (page 55), Coates collaborated with Englefield in writing the section about the Abbey. Englefield redrew his original plan, adding greater detail, whilst Coates' description of the abbey and chapter house is taken from Englefield's report.

7. 1835 THE HISTORY AND ANTIQUITIES OF THE TOWN AND BOROUGH OF READING IN BERKSHIRE (1835), JOHN DORAN

The remains of the great hall or chapter house can be viewed from the exterior; the inside being occupied by the erection of the National School. This beautiful room was eighty five feet long, and forty feet wide, with three large entrance doors from the cloister each surmounted by a window; and five large windows decorated the East end, the roof was an arched ceiling springing from eight pilasters in the side walks, each twenty feet high, the height of the room from the flooring to the centre of the ceiling was about forty feet; the walls were six feet thick above the foundations; below they were 12 feet thick, to the depth of 7 feet. [10]

The National School which had been built within the walls of the chapter house, had closed by 1835 and its house had been demolished by 1837. Prior to this, around 1833, Reading Corporation had created a trust to buy and manage parts of the ruins. The trustees were evidently conscious of the need to protect the area against vandalism and further deterioration of the site. The Borough (Corporation) as trustees, who were responsible for this section of the ruins, had run out of money, and decided they could do no more for the moment. Nevertheless, they asked the county of Berkshire, which owned the prison land, and James Wheble, who owned adjacent land, to fence in the area. Their comments also noted that this would prevent *the encroachment* of workmen employed by speculative builders on neighbouring sites.[11]

The measurements differ slightly from those given elsewhere. Once again, this may be due to differing points of reference. However, note that Doran considered that the west end openings were all doorways, and that the term 'great hall' referred to the chapter house.

8. 1847 ILLUSTRATION

The next drawing, by W. Brown, is dated 1847. It shows the upper windows as having what may be pointed arches. Whether the stonework of these arches is original, is open to debate. If not, the question needs to be asked: who replaced it and why.

The rest of the building was being allowed to fall into ruin. Why rebuild these windows?

There is also one obvious mistake, namely placing Reading in Yorkshire.

Fig 11. 1847. The east walk of the Cloister, showing the arched entrance and upper windows of the Chapter House, 1847. 1840-1849 : scan of a drawing by W. Brown, with the hand-written caption, "Reading Abbey, Yorkshire".

9. EARLY PHOTOGRAPHS - THE 1870S TO THE EARLY 1900s

Figure 12. This is one of the earliest photographs of the chapter house. It shows what may be pointed windows. As ever, though, one must remember that this does not mean they are the original openings.

Contrast this photograph with the next (fig 13), taken in the early 1900s. There is considerably more vegetation, especially around the upper windows. This would be the cause of more deterioration and structural damage.

Fig 12. 1870 –1880   Ruins of the Chapter House, looking west towards the cloister. A man, probably a park-keeper, sits at the base of the wall to the right. Glass negative by H. W. Taunt, Box 22 No. 1542 (Courtesy Reading Library)

Fig 13. 1900 –1909 Ruins of the Chapter House, looking west towards the Cloister. A man wearing a hat stands on the south side. Postcard by Francis Frith and   Company,   (Courtesy Reading Library)

10. MID TO LATE 20TH CENTURY

By the 1960s, the fabric of the ruins was in such a state that they posed a threat to public safety. In 1982 they were closed to the public. Works were undertaken and partly completed by 1991. As money ran out, a section of the dormitory wall was not included in the conservation project.

As Dr Slade noted, *medieval type lime mortar had been used and flints generally replaced as they had been.* A photographic record had been made prior to the works.

In the 1970s, Slade excavated part of the apse of the abbey church. This lay under the car park of the then prison. He noted there that the Abbey mortar was readily identifiable by its yellowish colour.[12]

Fig 14. 1955. To the right, a gentleman in a suit appears to be staring at the wall: photograph by Francis Frith and Company, (Courtesy Reading Library)

11. The 21st CENTURY

The restoration works of the 21st century were preceded by an architectural survey by Stuart Harrison, who completed a unique analysis of the site, together with a photographic record of the ruins, before work commenced.

A slaked, hot, limestone mix was used for the work.

AN ARCHITECTURAL OVERVIEW

Having seen how Reading's chapter house compares with others, I shall now make a more detailed study of its architecture. The chapter house is the most complete of the remaining buildings, and there is a great deal we can learn from it.

Despite the variations in different measurements, there is no doubting the imposing size of Reading's chapter house, and that it was among the largest, if not the largest, in England.

	LENGTH		WIDTH		AREA	
ENGLEFIELD and HURRY	78	23.8	42	12	**3276 sq ft**	**304 sq m**
Ordnance Survey	80	24	42	12	**3360 sq ft**	**312 sq m**

Although certain aspects of its architecture have been interpreted in different ways, such as whether the windows were pointed, there is little doubt but that the chapter house was built in the so-called Romanesque style. The ceiling was most probably barrel-vaulted, and the decoration, such as the blind intersecting wall arcade, is typical of that period (fig 14).

However, we should also recall that the mid-12th century was a transitional period, and places such as Durham had proto-gothic features, such as pointed arches and vaulting.

The east-end apse at Reading would have had vaulting similar to that at Durham. Although what we see at Durham is a 19th century reconstruction, it gives us a fairly accurate idea of what Reading would have looked like (fig 15).

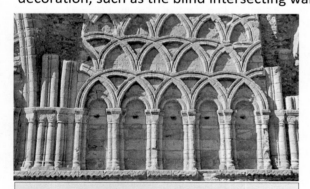

Fig 14. Wenlock. Interlaced blind arcading.

Fig 15. Durham chapter house

To create a picture of what the chapter house would have looked like, I shall examine evidence from the standing ruins, together with their analysis by Harrison, and from the historical record of previous commentaries and illustrations.

The west entrance from the cloister.

This consists of three ground floor arches and three windows above, of which the outer two are complete, the central opening having lost its top courses. We have seen that illustrations show that this was already probably the case by the 1720s.

The doorway: There is evidence of three stepped orders. It is likely that there would have been a *hood mould above.* The windows on either side indicate the existence of at least two orders. (Harrison).

The lower windows: The window to the south of the doorway, according to Harrison's 2015 survey, shows signs of a *flanking order at each side and a projecting core along its centreline, This must be related to the plate tracery subdivision of the main opening into two sub arches supported by a central shaft.* [13]

The illustration, fig 16, is an example of what this may have looked like. It is possible that the flanking orders extended the full length of the window. The possibility of plate tracery raises the question as to whether this would have been glazed and, if so, whether with stained-glass.

Harrison goes on to point out that the sides of the windows have socket holes showing where the capitals have been removed. The sills, that is the arches over the openings, are of more modern date. The upper windows and the walls above them, he says, are *almost entirely modern fabrications.*

This analysis presents us both with challenges and information on which to base any projected visual re-construction of the west end of the chapter house. It is necessary to distinguish original from later work. There is also the contrast between the 1720s illustrations and what the 2015 survey indicates.

I am inclined to the view that these illustrations are not reliable, but I would not wish to discount them out of hand, nor from convenience. Probably the best way forward is to take note of them, but both look at the survey, and make comparisons with contemporary chapter houses.

Fig 16. A cloister window at Silvacane Abbey, France. C EmDee https://commons.wikimedia.org/wiki/File:Abbaye_de_Silvacane_-_galerie_nord_06.JPG

Reading Abbey - A pilgrim church

Almost invariably, there was a set plan for the positioning of the cloister, the church, chapter house, refectory and dormitory. The cloister was the space which led to all the other main monastic buildings. The entrance to the chapter house would, therefore, have been from the covered cloister walkway, similar to those in figs. 17 & 18.

Fig 17. Cloister with door to left.
Photo by DAVID ILIFF. License: CC BY-SA 3.0"

Fig. 18. Vézelay cloister and chapter house.

Fig 19. Monreale 12th c

This held true in Reading. There is also the question as to the extent to which the surfaces would have been painted. It was normal practice to paint capitals and walls.

The upper windows: These would have looked out above the cloister roof (fig 19). They appear to have had two arch orders. However, most of the flint-work visible today is modern. Once again, it is useful to refer to the illustrations that I showed earlier, dating from the 18th century.

VIEW OF THE WEST WALL FROM INSIDE THE CHAPTER HOUSE

Once inside the chapter house, and looking back at the interior west wall, we note the following,

1. The upper flint work is a later construction, not the original,

2. The curvature of the barrel vault would appear only just to clear the upper window heads. Harrison suggests that, to compensate for this, the ceiling web may have been angled slightly upwards. If we recall that these are not the original window sills, and that in the 18th century Englefield was convinced that he saw slightly pointed windows, then I am not sure we can be certain as to exact nature of the vaulting. This is especially true in relation to the windows. Figure 20 shows Harrison's survey with suggested outlines (red lines) for the original openings and roof vaulting.

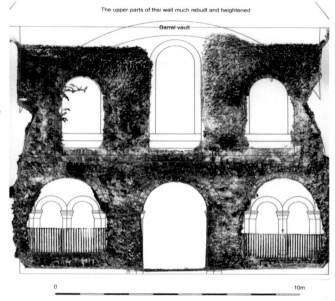

Chapter House West Wall Interior

Fig 20. West wall of the chapter house, from the 2015 Archaeological Survey, (Harrison)

When we come to consider how the windows and walls would been decorated, we can be certain that the upper windows would have been glazed and, almost certainly, this would have been with lavish stained glass.

Light from the setting sun would have bathed the interior of the space in spectacular colours. Light, or more precisely, 'Divine light', held special significance in the medieval mind, with different colours not just having metaphorical meaning, but actually imparting various aspects of the Divine.

Fig 21. Westminster Abbey chapter house. Covering the walls are murals depicting the Apocalypse. They date from the 14th century.
http://www.wilsonmj.com/2013/03/dust-jacket-bye-and-bye.html

As for the wall surfaces, it is very likely that they were painted in much the same way as we see in the chapter house at Westminster Abbey (fig 21).

THE VAULTING

The vaulting is completely lost, and even the earliest illustrations, dating to the early 18th century, show this to have been the case by that time.

It is possible that the 1650 Parliamentary survey, when mentioning the *great old hall,* was describing the chapter house. The ceiling is described as *arched.* I would suggest that the survey was indeed referencing the chapter house. It is less likely that the only alternative building, the refectory, would have had a barrel-vaulted ceiling, and its standing remains show no indication of supporting shafts. We cannot tell whether the observations in the 1650 survey are from of an existing arched vault or, more probably, based on the pilasters.

The breadth of Reading's chapter house is indeed great. Englefield describes the vault as *one semicircular arch,* supported by stone ribs. The weight of the infill, had it been Taynton limestone, would have been very heavy. Englefield says that the vaulting between the ribs was composed of tufa, which he compares with Portland stone, noting that the tufa he found on site was *very soft and extremely light, bearing only the proportion of 66 to 161 of Portland stone...*

We now know that most, by a great extent, of the stone used at Reading, came from the Taynton quarry, west of Oxford. This is a robust rock, and may be placed towards an upper density of between 1900-2050 kg/m3, whereas tufa, of the type described by Englefield, would be between 1400-1800 kg/m3 (Hayward).

It is worth while making the distinction between tufa found in the British Isles, and that used in Rome. The former fits in with Englefield's description: namely a calcareous nodular spring-water deposit. He comments upon *a tophus formed by some petrifying spring, and enclosing the impressions of twigs &c. One leaf is very fair.* This contrasts with Roman tufa, which describes a geologically recent low density volcanic rock. The word 'Travertine' is now generally used to replace the term 'tufa' in this context.

THE NORTH WALL FROM INSIDE THE CHAPTER HOUSE

The following photograph shows the north wall, with red lines indicating the position of the pilaster responds, or shafts, which supported the vault springing level sockets for the capitals and abaci. These were of separate stone and supported the transverse rib arches, which would have been the backbone of the vault across the building's 12 plus metre width.

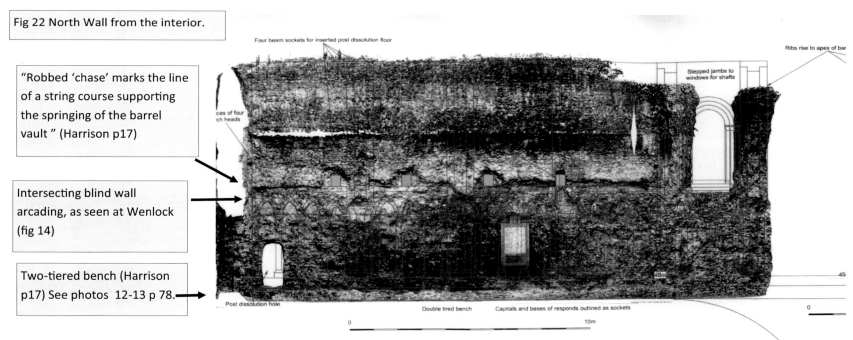

Fig 22 North Wall from the interior.

"Robbed 'chase' marks the line of a string course supporting the springing of the barrel vault " (Harrison p17)

Intersecting blind wall arcading, as seen at Wenlock (fig 14)

Two-tiered bench (Harrison p17) See photos 12-13 p 78.

Four beam sockets for inserted post dissolution floor

Ribs rise to apex of bar

Stepped jambs to windows for shafts

ces of four ch heads

Post dissolution hole

Double tired bench

Capitals and bases of responds outlined as sockets

0   10m

It is also possible to make out the two-tiered bench, which can be seen in the late 19th and early 20th century photographs shown in figures 12 and 13.

The whole building was articulated: that is there were five bays, separated by the six pilasters and ceiling transverse ribs.

Close examination shows evidence of intersecting wall arcading. I wrote about the likelihood of this some years back, making reference to the more elaborate example at Wenlock Priory. Harrison's improved photographic technique appears to confirm this hypothesis.

THE APSE

The barrel-vault, as at Durham, extended to where it joined the apse vaulting. The apse was divided into bays, divided by supporting pilasters (shafts).

Ribs rise to apex of barrel vaults

Stepped jambs to windows for shafts

le tired bench   Capitals and bases of responds outlined as sockets

10m

Fig 23. The joint of the apse and north wall

These supported ribs which joined at the apex of the barrel vault, in a manner similar to that seen in the photograph of Durham.

As at Durham, there were three windows to the east, with two more on the north and south sides, all within the arc of the apse.

Fig 23. Durham apse

THE INTERIOR

From the surviving remains, there is little we can tell about the interior appearance of the chapter house. However, by comparing it with other similar buildings, it is arguably possible to build up a representation of its likely appearance. To begin with, it is necessary to remember its purpose. All the customaries of similar monasteries mention the central role the chapter house played in the life of a monastery. The whole community gathered there daily, each morning, to hear a chapter of the Rule of St Benedict, hence its name; the Latin word for chapter being *capitulum*.[14]

The very first lines of Cluny's customary, concerning the election of the abbot, state that the whole community is to gather *in capitolo*. The new abbot's reign began in this place. It was from the chapter house that the monks would make their many ritualistic processions and to which they would return. It was a centre both of prayer and business. The orders of the day would be issued here and the offices sung. Remembering the dead was central to Cluniac life and the day started with recalling the first martyrs of the church, as commemorated in the martyrology, from which the life and death of the saints of the day were sung. The abbot, or other senior monk, would deliver a sermon. We know that the works of St Augustine were used for this purpose.

But the chapter house was also a meeting hall: the great hall, the *aula.* It was probably in the chapter house that Edward IV publicly announced his previously secret marriage to Elizabeth Woodville. Parliament met here on several occasions when it fled London to avoid the plague. It is not certain if it is the chapter house that is being referred to, but it was either here, in the refectory, or elsewhere, that on the first of each December, in commemoration of Henry I's death, thirteen poor people of the town were fed a special meal.[15] Doubtless, elaborate hangings and cushions would have been added to the furnishing on these occasions.

We have seen that the chapter house would have been richly decorated with biblical or other religious themes. The church was dedicated to the Virgin Mary and to St John, and of course, by the third quarter of the 12th century, the abbey had become a centre of pilgrimage to St James, with the hand of that saint as the main relic. The ceiling itself would most probably also have been painted, though it is unlikely that it would have seen rich mosaics, such as at Monreale in Sicily. The two-tiered seating area may have been of stone or wood, possibly with wooden backs fitting into the intersecting blind arcade.

In the centre there would have been a magnificent lectern. Here would have been placed the great book containing the martyrology, as would other books as they were read, or sung.

The abbot's throne would have been at the centre of the great apse.

One mystery is whether there was a crypt or cellar. We have seen that the 1650 Parliamentary survey mentions *a great old hall with a very large cellar under the said hall.* Could this be the chapter house, the refectory or some other building?

Whatever lay beneath it, the floor itself would have been laid with encaustic tiles. These may well have been produced locally. There are known to be tileries dating to the 12th and 13th centuries in Reading, some having been excavated in south Reading on Silver Street. [16]

We can be almost certain that abbots and other dignitaries would have been buried under the floor of the chapter house, maybe even in the 'cellar', or crypt, should one exist.

Fig 24. The chapter house looking east, Reading gaol in the background.
Photo; John Mullaney

CONCLUSION

By comparing Reading's chapter house with others built in a similar style, and at a approximately the same time, we can create a picture of what it may have looked like.

The trail of illustrations and commentaries, though by no means exhaustive, along with the most recent survey of 2016, all add to our knowledge. Fundamental is the principle that the design of the chapter house was based on its intended use as a general meeting place, as well as a space of spiritual significance.

We do well to remember that the twin pillars of the rule of St Benedict are prayer (the *opus Dei*), and care, both physical and spiritual, for the traveller, the stranger, the pilgrim. The chapter house most certainly featured significantly in the former, and it may be that it played a role in the latter.

What is more, Reading Abbey was built by Henry I as his royal foundation. He intended it not just as his own mausoleum, but as the resting place of his successors, his dynasty.

There is no doubt that, at the time it was built, and for many years after, it was an imposing building, and one befitting one of the most important monasteries in the country.

Notes

1.   https://www.dhi.ac.uk/cistercians/fountains/buildings/chapterhouse/index.php

2.   https://www.british-history.ac.uk/vch/hants/vol5/pp50-59#highlight-first

3.   http://www.gutenberg.org/files/22832/22832-h/22832-h.htm#chapter

4.   https://www.durhamworldheritagesite.com/learn/architecture/cathedral/intro/chapter-house

5.   Extracts from https://www.british-history.ac.uk/vch/durham/vol3/pp123-136

6.   *The History and Antiquities of Reading,* Charles Coates (1802)

7.   *Reading Abbey Records a new miscellany* edited B Kemp

8.   *The Town of Reading and its Abbey,* Cecil Slade p.51

9.   *Observations on Reading Abbey,* Sir Henry Englefield 1779. A copy of this may be found in Reading Central Library. A later version, with an updated plan, is in Coates' 1802 work.

10.   *The History and Antiquities of the Town and Borough of Reading in Berkshire* (1835), John Doran (p 96-97)

11.   *Reading's Abbey Quarter, an Illustrated History*, John Mullaney (p64)

12.   *Excavation at Reading Abbey, Berkshire Archaeological Journal Vol 68,* C Slade

13.   *Archaeological Survey Report in the Ruins of Reading Abbey for Reading Council,* Stuart Harrison, 2015

14.   The following three sources are relevant:

       A. *Vetus Disciplina Monastica, Ordo Clunaciensis per Bernardum*

       B. *A Medieval Latin Death Ritual, The Monastic Customaries of Bernard and Ulrich of Cluny,* Frederick S. Paxton

       C. *Reading Abbey Records a new miscellany,* edited by B Kemp

15.   *Reading Abbey Records a new miscellany,* edited by B Kemp

16.   *CFA archaeology* Report No. MK130/18 - *http://biag.org.uk/silver-street-excavation/*

Sources

Archaeological Survey Report in the Ruins of Reading Abbey for Reading Council, Stuart Harrison

(The) History and Antiquities of the Town and Borough of Reading in Berkshire (1835), John Doran

(The) History and Antiquities of Reading, Charles Coates (1802)

(A) Medieval Latin Death Ritual, The Monastic Customaries of Bernad and Ulrich of Cluny, Frederick S. Paxton

Observations on Reading Abbey, Sir Henry Englefield 1779

Reading's Abbey Quarter, an illustrated history, John Mullaney

Reading Abbey Records a new miscellany, edited by B Kemp

Reading Abbey Revealed*: https://www.readingabbeyquarter.org.uk/about/reading-abbey-revealed- History and Antiquities of Reading,* C Coates (1802)

Reading Central Library Local studies - Illustrations

(The) Town of Reading and its Abbey, Cecil Slade

Vetus Disciplina Monastica, Ordo Clunaciensis

CHAPTER 5

THE TOWERS

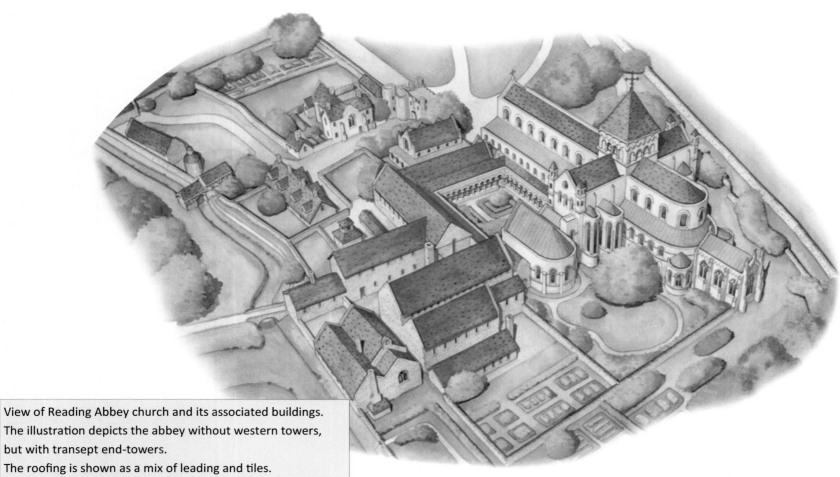

View of Reading Abbey church and its associated buildings.
The illustration depicts the abbey without western towers,
but with transept end-towers.
The roofing is shown as a mix of leading and tiles.
There is no way we can know any of these details for certain.
The design is based on advice from Professor Brian Kemp.

Illustration by John R Mullaney, FSAI
www.thetopdraw.com ©JRMullaney

CONTENTS

THE FOUNDING AND DESIGN OF READING ABBEY   94

TOWERS IN THE ROMANESQUE AND EARLY GOTHIC PERIOD   97

READING ABBEY CHURCH AND ITS TOWERS   100

SOME ROMANESQUE BUILDINGS AND TABLE A   101

 OTHER TALL STRUCTURES DATING TO THE MEDIEVAL ERA   103

 ESTIMATING TOWER HEIGHTS FROM CROSSING MEASUREMENTS AND TABLE B   103

COMMENTS   106

THE WEST END TOWERS   107

TRANSEPT TOWERS   108

CONCLUSION   108

ILLUSTRATIONS

(There are several illustrations embedded and explained in the text—others are listed here)

The Abbey   92

The Blade, Reading, and Tewkesbury compared   109

Comparative chart of the heights of some medieval towers, the Blade, and Verto housing Reading   111

THE FOUNDING AND DESIGN OF READING ABBEY

In order to understand what the tower, or towers, at Reading Abbey may have been like, it is necessary to look at when and how the monastery was founded. I have already shown how the chapter house belonged to an architectural family and how this helps us place the abbey in its wider historical context. However, there are no records about the number or style of the towers at Reading. Unlike the chapter house, whatever is written has to be based solely upon comparative research. But this is not quite the whole story. There is one medieval reference to a chancel tower, and as we have seen, Speed in 1610 depicted the abbey church with a spire, and there is an image of a church on the Second Common Seal (see page 230)

It is, therefore, worth examining in greater detail the historical and architectural background of the abbey.

The monastery was founded by Henry I in 1121 as a priory. The first head of the newly formed Reading community was Peter, a prior of Cluny Abbey in Burgundy. He brought with him some fellow monks, and others from the Cluniac Priory of Lewes joined them. They were engaged by Henry to build his royal monastery.

Following the death of King Alfonso VI of Spain in 1109, Henry had been the main sponsor and benefactor of Cluny III, arguably the most prestigious abbey in 12th century Europe, with the largest church of its time. Henry had visited Cluny and admired its life and architecture. It is therefore most likely that Reading was built in the image of Cluny, its builders initially being guided by Cluniac architects and masons, in the tradition of Gunzo and Hézelon of Liège. Whether its sculpture emulated that of the great masters such as Gislebertus, the Avenas Master, or the Perrecy Master, is a matter of conjecture, but surely there would have been some influence.

So, when we think about the overall architectural design of Reading, and specifically its great central tower, we should bear in mind its connections with Cluny. However, there was also developing in England a new architectural style. Fifty years had passed since the Norman invasion, and an Anglo-Norman genre was emerging. We may reasonably assume, therefore, that Reading would have resembled Cluny, but on a smaller scale, with its sculpture and architecture also reflecting this developing English style. For instance, most of the stone used at Reading came from the Taynton quarry, west of Oxford, not Caen in Normandy, as is often wrongly claimed. Moreover, many of its sculptures share much in common with other English Romanesque designs, such as those found in Bromsgrove and Bockleton. Yet the existence of some Caen stone capitals, attributed to Reading, does indicate a continued Norman connection for specialist work, and the carvings show both Norman and English influences.

Nor should we think of Reading Abbey as a static architectural entity, firmly fixed in the Romanesque period. The 12th century was a major transitional time in architectural techniques which, simply put, saw the emergence of the new Pointed, or Gothic, design, as exemplified in Paris by Abbot Suger's St Denis. It would be difficult to imagine that Reading was isolated from these, and later, influences. Certainly, we know that in 1314 a Lady Chapel, in the Decorated style, was added to its east end.[1]

The Cluniac monks designed their monasteries as places to fulfil the onerous requirements of their elaborate liturgy, the *Opus Dei* or *Work of God*. The monks spent many hours each day both attending and saying Masses but most of all singing the Divine Office.

This consisted of psalms, and readings from the Bible and other religious texts. When not so engaged, the choir monks, and this may well have been the majority, would have spent many hours, according to one Cluniac horarium up to a further eight hours a day, studying and practising the music to be sung. We have seen that the most important part of the abbey church, second only to the high altar, was the choir which lay to its west, under the great crossing of the church and the main tower.

To either side of the choir, to its north and south, lay the transepts, and an ambulatory ran behind the high altar. This would have facilitated movement beyond the choir as well as around the sanctuary, and the presbytery, or priests' area. Visitors could thereby circulate around the church without interfering with the monks and the *Opus Dei*. The choir area would have been partitioned off from the body of the church so that, although visitors would have been able to hear the singing and experience some aspects of the liturgy, including the rising incense and the ringing of bells, they would not have been able to participate in these services.

The second feature, and main purpose of the nave and aisles, was to provide a place of worship for its visitors and pilgrims, as well as for the monks. Cluniac houses tended to be town-centred. The church was a symbol of the Heavenly Jerusalem, the New Jerusalem, that was to come at the end of time. It was a place where it was expected that people would come to visit and to pray. Consequently, the body of the church: the nave and aisles, was designed to engage with the visitors, and comprised by far the greater area of the whole building. As mentioned, the aisles and the ambulatory facilitated circulation of the visiting laity. Side chapels dedicated to various saints, maybe containing their relics or pictures, possibly with a stained glass window above, depicting an appropriate scene, would be there for groups and individuals to see and wonder at, as they moved round the church, probably singing, chanting or making their private devotions.

Reading Abbey - A pilgrim church

Most probably, visitors would enter by the north aisle. At the east end they would be ushered to the larger chapels in the north transept, round the ambulatory behind the monks' choir, and so to the south transept and thence out down the south aisle, to exit at the west end. They may have moved into the main nave for a major service, a procession or for Mass, which would have been said at the people's altar. This latter became more formalised in time, with the erection of a rood screen.

The rood, or image of the crucifixion, would have been mounted above the screen, with an altar below and two openings, or doors, giving access to a space in front of the choir. It is possible that between the rood screen and the choir there would have been yet another screen known as a pulpitum. In the 12th century *Miracles of the Hand of St James (no. 18)* we read that the abbey's most sacred relic, the Hand of St James, was placed in a reliquary on the pulpitum. This would have had a single central opening through which the monks would process into the choir. The exact location of these screens varied and often depended on the space required in the choir. At times, when there were large numbers of monks, the screens were erected further to the west in the nave, to allow more room for the monks in the choir. At other times, such as after the Black Death in the 14th century, when numbers dwindled, the extra space was not needed and the pulpitum was positioned at the westerly entrance to the choir area.

The following ground plan of Cluny III shows these features (Fig 1). The two photographs, on either side, show extant examples of a rood screen and a pulpitum.

Rood screen - St Albans

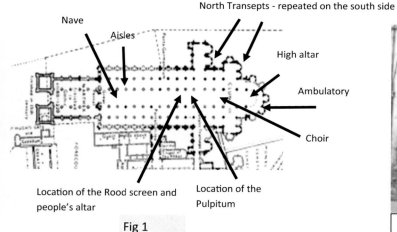

Nave

Aisles

North Transepts - repeated on the south side

High altar

Ambulatory

Choir

Location of the Rood screen and people's altar

Location of the Pulpitum

Fig 1

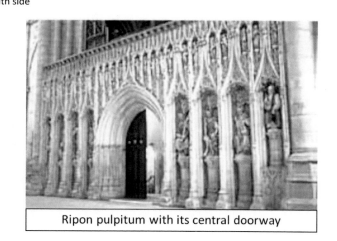

Ripon pulpitum with its central doorway

Just as the interior of the church was carefully designed to fulfil its liturgical needs, its exterior was of equal importance. In an age when most people would never have seen a building more than two storeys high, great churches such as that at Reading were imposing 'skyscrapers'. They represented divine power as mediated by the Church, and this symbolism was not lost on the population. The outsides would have been highly decorated, and parts of them, especially the main entrances, would have been brightly painted in colours symbolic of their religious significance: blue for heaven, gold and red representing Divinity and green for creation.

Their towers, reaching heavenwards, were likewise a means of bearing the same message of the Church's connection with heaven. Bells would have been hung from some towers. The sound of the bell, for monks and people alike, was the voice of God. It was a sound that many believed banished the devil.

TOWERS IN THE ROMANESQUE AND EARLY GOTHIC PERIOD

The drawing, alongside, of Cluny III, by Kenneth Conant, shows its western end before the narthex and towers were added. Originally the church was 440ft (134m) long.[2]

Its imposing presence can be seen from the drawing, also by Conant, overpage. The eastern end and the nave, as far as the western smaller extension with its towers, is contemporaneous with the start of the campaign to build Reading Abbey. At Cluny, when the west end and towers were added in the late 12th and early 13th centuries, the church was lengthened to 600ft, (183m).

Façade of Cluny III, c. 1106-20 (before construction of Narthex). K. J. C. *inv. et del.*

Reading Abbey - A pilgrim church

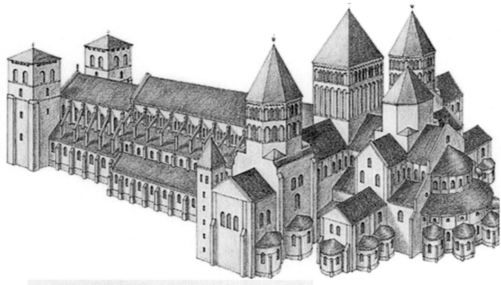

Cluny III showing the narthex and western towers.

Many 11th and 12th century churches that we see today have towers. These are most often over the choir area, and sometimes at the ends of the transepts, as well as at the west end, as shown in the illustration of Cluny.

In fact, many of these western towers were added at a later stage in the construction of the churches. This is to be expected, since the chancel was the first area to be built.

Next to be built were the transepts, reflecting the cruciform nature of the earliest churches. Expansion down the nave followed. As architectural styles, along with building techniques, evolved, it is not surprising to find these were reflected in the appearance of the nave as one moves towards the west end.

It should be said that, although we may be able to discern a style we can call 'pilgrim' or 'Cluniac', there was no rigid prescriptive pattern. Even monasteries founded directly by Cluniacs allowed for local variations in design and materials. What can be said, is that there is a Cluniac spirit which encompasses many influences, but focuses on the two main precepts of their interpretation of St Benedict's rule: namely the spiritual life of the monks and provision for the traveller, especially the pilgrim.

Consequently, there is a great variety of towers and spires. This is true not just between different countries of Europe, but even within smaller regions. Towers could be attached, detached or semi-detached. They could also be round, square or polygonal. What is common to most is the small pyramidal, round or polygonal spire, as shown in the photographs opposite. The church at Paray-le Monial in fact has both pyramidal and polygonal spires.

Paray-le-Monial, France

Poitiers, France

Trani, Italy

Today it is appreciated that the division between what we today call the Romanesque and Gothic styles is an arbitrary one, and that what occurred was an evolutionary process with no defining break. The beginning of the Gothic style is usually dated to the second half of the 12th century, as epitomised in Abbot Suger's work at Saint-Denis, Paris. However, the pointed arch and ribbed vault, which are often considered to define the 'Gothic', may be found in late 11th and early 12th century buildings such as Durham in England, Cluny in France and Monte Cassino in Italy.

READING ABBEY CHURCH AND ITS TOWERS

The conservation of the Reading Abbey Ruins, leading to their reopening in the summer of 2018, triggered a great deal of interest in the architecture of the abbey. Alongside the conservation project, another was launched to assess its size and architectural style. The Hidden Abbey Project (HAP), set out to determine these aspects of the monastery. This was a joint venture of the main landowners of the abbey area: Reading Borough Council, the Catholic Diocese of Portsmouth and the Ministry of Justice. The latter had closed Reading Gaol with a view to disposing of the site and, as such, undertook archaeological investigations conducted by MOLA (Museum of London Archaeology).

The HAP group commissioned a geophysics investigation (Ground Penetrating Radar survey or GPR) of the church area.

Several aspects of the abbey were highlighted by this renewed interest, and by these preliminary investigations. One such concerned the abbey's tower, or towers. Since the building of the Blade in Reading, near to the site of the great abbey church, comparisons had been made between the heights of the two structures

The following is an assessment of the evidence which may help determine the nature of the towers of Reading Abbey, both their style and height.

We know that by 1208 the abbey had a central tower. It existence is recorded in the annals of that year. We do not know if, at this point in time, there were any towers at the western end. As we shall see, however, it would have been usual for these to be added at some point in the abbey's history.

Having seen the connection between Reading and Cluny, it would be useful to look at what we know of Cluny's towers. Most of the information is taken from K J Conant's work and writings on Cluny.

CLUNY   Main crossing tower - height - 218ft (66.44m)   Internal crossing width 44ft (13.5m)
Overall length of Cluny church; 440ft (134m). A western end with towers was later added making it 600ft, (183m), in length.
Cluny did not acquire its two western towers until 1324 and 1342.

For several hundred years, Cluny III was the largest church in western Europe. Although it had been begun in what we may call the High Romanesque period, at the end of the 11th and beginning of the 12th century, its completion took several decades, mainly under the notorious Abbot Pons. Consequently, much of it was constructed during the later transitional period linking the Romanesque with the emergence of the so called Gothic, or German, style.

This latter, exemplified by Abbot Suger's church of Saint-Denis, developed the pointed arch and rib vaulting techniques already found in several churches around Europe, such as Durham and Cluny itself. These improvements in building methods allowed for taller, more stable, buildings which did not have to rely on the sheer mass of masonry to sustain their integrity. As a result of these technical advances, additions, such as raising the heights of towers, could be made to existing structures. We shall see whether it is possible to ascertain the likely height of Reading's central tower at the time when it was first built, and what it may have been like when it was rebuilt after the storm and fire of 1208. It is also possible to speculate about the nature and the size of other towers, be they at the west end or on the transepts.

Turning to the question of the comparison between Reading's central tower and the Blade, it is necessary to look at the latter's statistics. In the early 2020s the tallest residential building in Reading was the Verto on the old King's Point site.

READING BLADE Pinnacle height agl (above ground level) 282ft (86m)
VERTO Top floor height 150ft (52M) agl Overall height 193ft (59m).[3]

SOME ROMANESQUE BUILDINGS

The following is a list of some Romanesque buildings, or those begun in the late 11th and early 12th centuries, showing their tower heights. I have relied on various internet sites, usually the official sites of the places mentioned, for this data. I then cross referenced this information with other architectural sources. The data in *Table A* are not by any means comprehensive, but are intended to demonstrate the range of building statistics in England's main medieval churches. It will be readily seen that many were rebuilt, or added to, throughout this time frame. Nevertheless, it is clear that there is a certain consistency and conformity to be found across the range. It will also be noted that the highest towers belong to the end of the period.

Reading Abbey - A pilgrim church

Measurements for the crossing/transepts and lengths come from Bannister Fletcher, *A History of Architecture,* and from various online plans.

My sources for Reading Abbey are the current OS map and Baxter, *The Royal Abbey of Reading*, p184.

TABLE A Tower heights similar to that at Cluny (218ft, 66.44m) are underlined.

	Tower height	Date / Style	Crossing width	Transept length across	Length of church
ELY	216ft 66m	1189 transitional, restored GG Scott 19th c.	70ft 20m	200ft 60m	325ft 100m
WINCHESTER	150ft 45.7m	originally 1374 rebuilt 15th c.	100ft 30m	225ft 68.5m	350ft 106m
DURHAM	216ft 66m	originally 13th c. rebuilt 15th c.	110ft 33.5m	200ft 60m	350ft 106m
PETERBOROUGH	144ft 44m	Norman tower replaced 1350-80	74ft 22.8m	200ft 60m	380ft 116m
WORCESTER	203ft 62m	1374	100ft 30.5m	140ft 42.6m	400ft 121m
TEWKESBURY	148ft 45.1m	12th c. second half .	80ft 24.38m	122ft 37.2m	306ft 93.2m
ST ALBANS	144ft 44m	Only 11th century crossing tower standing	74ft 22.8m	200ft 60m	300ft 91m
READING	?		85ft 26m	205ft 62.5m	unknown

Different overall lengths for Reading Abbey church have been given by various people. The earliest, 420 ft (128m), was by Englefield in 1779, and the most recent, 417ft (127m), by Baxter in 2016. It cannot be stressed enough that the length, and so overall size, of Reading Abbey is unknown. All estimates are speculative, as Baxter points out, as no survey has ever been undertaken which definitively determines the siting of the west end of the nave, and so the length of the church. I would add that, without archaeological evidence, such as the discovery of the relevant footings, this latter cannot be known for certain.

OTHER TALL STRUCTURES DATING TO THE MEDIEVAL ERA

There are other well known buildings which stand outside these parameters. Notable among these are:

CANTERBURY   235 ft   76m   Note: this tower is not Romanesque but was built in the 1500s, and was tall for its day.

WESTMINSTER   225ft   68m

SALISBURY   403ft   123m   The tall spire is 180ft 5ins (55m) above the tower, making the original tower 223ft (68m) high, and so comparable with the tallest of other Romanesque towers. Salisbury's spire was added in the early 14th century by Elias of Dereham. Some claim that he had been working on the new Lady Chapel at Reading before being called by the Bishop of Salisbury to work on the Cathedral.

NORWICH   315ft   96m   The tower parapet is 146ft (44.5m). (Source, Phil Thomas, Norwich Cathedral Estates Manager 2001.) This puts it very much in the same range as other pre-tall spire Romanesque churches

LINCOLN   520ft   160m   The tower is 272ft (83m). It was raised to this height between 1307 - 1311. The Cathedral tower and the spire, the latter now lost, underwent so many changes following earthquakes, fire and re-building, that it cannot be used for comparison purposes. However, it is interesting that the crossing is 43ft (13m) sqr, and as such, falls within the same parameters of the internal crossing widths as listed in *Table B*.

ESTIMATING TOWER HEIGHTS FROM CROSSING MEASUREMENTS

Is it possible to estimate the tower height from the crossing measurement? As the tower depended on the supporting pillars for its stability, the key measurement is the internal crossing. The list in *Table A* comprises the existing dimensions of various buildings. This is raw data: I have not subjected it to any analysis, but merely present the basic figures for the reader. *Table B* presents further differentiating analysis.

One caveat is that the supporting crossing pillars are by necessity very robust, with extensive footprints. They are typically oblong and their dimensions vary from between 15 x 20ft (4.6 x 6.1m) to 8 x 15ft (2.4 x 4.6m).This means that when taking measurements, especially 'internal crossing width', it is possible to use different points of reference. This may be from one of the external edges, from a centre point, or any point within this framework. I have attempted to use the centre point when estimating the internal crossing width. Of the buildings listed, Tewkesbury is the nearest example which is comparable to Reading.

Reading Abbey - A pilgrim church

The following two illustrations show, on the left, the Ground Penetrating Radar survey with the measurements (approx.) for the aisles superimposed. The right shows the same area and measurements on a modern aerial photograph, along with the possible pulpitum outlined. Unfortunately, none of the internal pillar bases is extant, but we can estimate, from the other remains, that the would have been at the very least 32ft 9ins (10m), but more probably nearer to 42ft 8ins (13m) square. This is in line with the other tower and crossing widths evidenced in *Table B*, opposite.

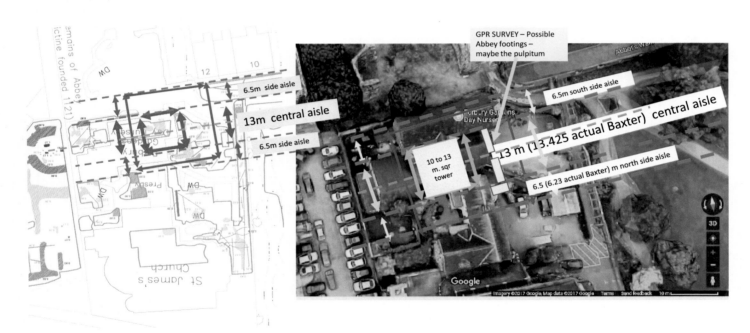

Note the direction of North

TABLE B   This table looks more closely at three sets of statistics: 1. tower heights, 2. the size of the crossing pillar bases which supported the columns for the tower, 3. the width of the crossing from a central point on these bases. I have used the official websites of the places concerned, or their guide books, and compared these with plans, making my own measurements. In all cases the figures are very close indeed, so as to make little, if any, difference. Comments particular to the building are made immediately below the statistics.

	Tower height		Crossing pillar bases		Internal crossing width	
TEWKESBURY	148ft	45.1m	18 x 8ft	5.5 x 2.4m	40ft	12.19m
ST ALBANS	144ft	44m	15 x 12ft	4.5 x 3.6m	40ft	12.19m

This is the only 11th century crossing tower still standing mainly in its original form.

	Tower height		Crossing pillar bases		Internal crossing width	
ELY West tower	216ft	66m	15 x 15ft	4.6 x 4.6m	38ft	11.6m
Central tower	170ft	51.8m	15 x 15ft	4.6 x 4.6m	70ft	21.6m

The central octagonal tower replaced the original central tower which collapsed in 1322. The nearest, in time and style, for comparison purposes with Reading, is the west tower. This was restored by George Gilbert Scott in the 19th century.

	Tower height		Crossing pillar bases		Internal crossing width	
WINCHESTER	150ft	45.7m	18 x 13ft	5.5 x 4m	40ft	12.19m
DURHAM	216ft	66m	20 x 15ft	6 x 4.6m	45ft	13.7m

The central tower was damaged by lightning and replaced in two stages in the 15th century. So, although the internal measurements are comparable with Norman churches, the tower height is not original and is now higher, facilitated by technological advances.

	Tower height		Crossing pillar bases		Internal crossing width	
PETERBOROUGH	144ft	44m	10 x 8ft	3 x 2.4m	45ft	13.7m
WORCESTER	203ft	62m	15 x 8ft	4.6 x 2.4m	45ft	13.7m

In 1175 the original central tower collapsed and the present tower was not completed until 1374. Clearly, the builders of the new tower that we see today were restricted by the original footings and pillars, but were able to build to a higher level because of advances in building technology.

Reading Abbey - A pilgrim church

Is it possible to extrapolate, from Table B, the height of Reading's central tower?

What is clear is that all the above structures share remarkably similar measurements. The exception is Ely's much later central tower which, owing to its polygonal shape and later construction, must be considered outside the scope of this examination. Nevertheless, it should be noted that its pillars share the same dimensions as seen elsewhere. From the above evidence, it would be reasonable to suggest that Reading's original central tower would have been within the following range.

	Tower height	Crossing pillar bases	Internal crossing width *
<u>READING</u>	144ft to 216ft 44m to 66m	None surviving	44ft 13.25m

* The width of Reading's internal crossing, c. 44ft (13.25m), is based on Baxter p213 and the plans as detailed above.

We should recall that Cluny's crossing tower height was 218ft (66.44m) and its internal crossing width 44ft+ (13.5m) sq at the pillar's central point.

COMMENTS

In so far as conclusions may be reached at all, it would seem that the original tower at Reading may have between 144ft (44m), as at St Alban's, and 216ft (66m) as at Ely and Cluny. It should be remembered that, in common with most Cluniac and Romanesque towers, it would most probably have had a small pyramidal spire, if square, or a similarly small polygonal spire if the tower was also polygonal.

It is also quite probable that some additions and changes were made to the central tower over Reading Abbey's long history, as is the case for most of the towers on today's cathedrals. Some, such as Salisbury, had tall spires added. It is therefore possible that a larger spire, wooden or otherwise, was added at a later date, between the 14th and 16th centuries. If this was the case, then the tower would have been significantly higher. However, there is no record of this and the only diagram we have, Speed's map of 1610, shows what looks like a pyramidal spire. His map was drawn some seventy years after the Abbey's dissolution, and there are records showing that the spire had been removed sometime previously, following the dissolution of the monastery in 1539. It is most likely that Speed's map was intended to be figurative or representational, rather than architecturally correct.

Over the course of time, some towers fell down. Many were rebuilt following some disaster or another. This may have been the case at Reading.

Reading Abbey's annals tell us that on the 12th March 1208, a whirlwind and lightning struck the abbey around the tower, setting fire first to the north and then the south transept. This probably necessitated rebuilding the tower, which by that date may have been in the Early English, rather than Romanesque, style. One could speculate, from the figures above, that the original tower was at the lower end of the heights given, about 44 metres high, whereas the second tower may have been higher at c. 65 metres high.

Before the restoration work of 2019 on the ruins, undertaken by the Diocese of Portsmouth in conjunction with Historic England, within the grounds of St James' church, there were scorch marks on the standing flints of the north transept and on the two fallen blocks near the entrance to the church. It is tempting to speculate that these date to the 13th century fire, but one should not read too much into this, as there are several other possible reasons for them, such as the depredations of the 17th c. Civil War, or the possibility that a cottage with a chimney had been built against the north transept remains.

The above figures and analysis are preliminary and partial, but could form a basis for further discussion. I am not drawing any definite conclusion as to the tower's height in relation to the Blade, except to say that it would have been unusual, even unique, had the tower (without a tall spire) been the same height as the pinnacle of the Blade. It would, however, be reasonable to speculate that Reading Abbey's central tower may have reached, or slightly exceeded, a level equivalent to the top floor of the Blade.

THE WEST END TOWERS

Many Romanesque churches had towers, often twin towers, at the west end. It was usual for these to be added, as at Cluny III and Ely, some time after the main body of the church was completed. There is no way of knowing when, or even if, Reading had such towers. The GPR survey was inconclusive in this respect. Excavations, or a more detailed GPR, to see if there are foundations, may substantiate their presence.

As the area has been extensively dug over, and changed, over the intervening centuries since the Dissolution, it is quite possible that even if such archaeology did take place, no further evidence would come to light. One may reasonable speculate that such a prestigious abbey would have had an elaborate west end, maybe with a narthex or galilee chapel, and with towers added at some point, but this is by no means certain.

TRANSEPT TOWERS

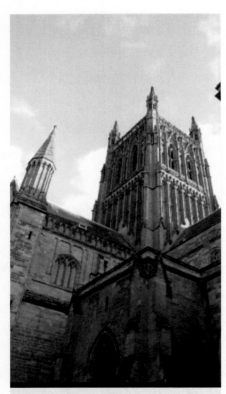

Worcester Cathedral, north transept

It is most likely that the gables of the transepts would have had towers with pinnacles, as seen in the photograph of Worcester Cathedral. These would have been smaller than the central or western towers, and would have acted as end-buttresses.

As AWN Pugin noted, pinnacles had a functional role in medieval architecture. Their downward thrust aided the stabilisation of the building. It is therefore most likely that Reading Abbey would have had such towers and/or pinnacles, but there is little chance that their size and design can be determined from existing remains.

CONCLUSION

The above is based on work looking at Romanesque, and especially Cluniac, churches, not just in England but across Europe. As part of this research, I have been examining the theory proposed by some (especially Kenneth Conant), that there is a proportional relationship between the various parts of Romanesque buildings. This appears to hold true with regard to some ground plans and some elevations. However, as can be seen in the sample *Table A*, there is a deal of disparity when it comes to comparing tower heights and other dimensions. It is possible that there are several reasons for this.

There may be some benefit in examining the thickness of retaining walls. Lindy Grant comments on this aspect in her book *Architecture and Society in Normandy 1120-1270*. As we do not have this information for Reading, I have been unable to make any analysis, or do any calculations in this regard.

Whenever we look at existing 12th century buildings, we should remember that their towers, and overall church dimensions, are not always as originally planned. Subsequent building work, demolitions, and the accretions of history, have significantly changed the proportional relations. This is demonstrated in several of the above examples - see *Tables B* and *C*.

It is also possible, as frequently occurred, that plans and their execution were changed over various building campaigns, so that the original designs and the subsequent elevations do not correspond.

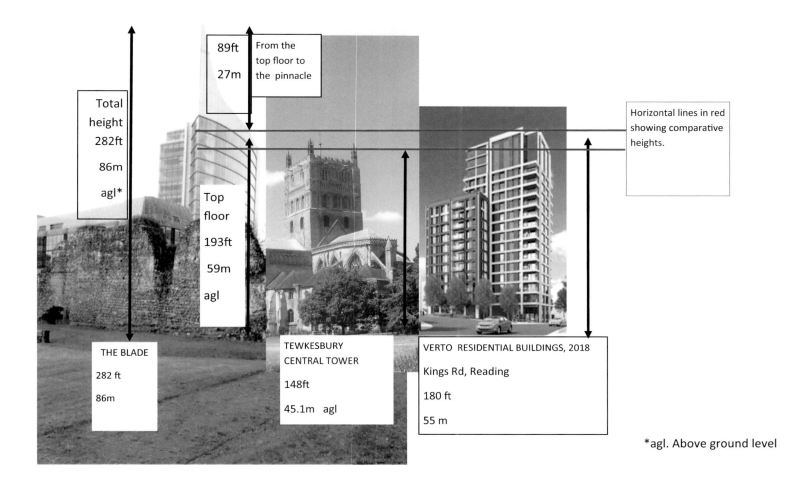

89ft

27m

From the top floor to the pinnacle

Total height 282ft 86m agl*

Top floor 193ft 59m agl

Horizontal lines in red showing comparative heights.

THE BLADE

282 ft

86m

TEWKESBURY CENTRAL TOWER

148ft

45.1m agl

VERTO RESIDENTIAL BUILDINGS, 2018

Kings Rd, Reading

180 ft

55 m

*agl. Above ground level

The above is a rough impression of the comparative heights of the buildings mentioned. It should be noted that, because of the angle of the photographs, this comparative illustration is intended merely to give a guide to how towers of various heights would appear from ground level.

Reading Abbey - A pilgrim church

Reading Abbey tower — Comparative heights chart and concluding comment

The chart opposite gives the comparative heights of the buildings that I have examined, and the likely height of the central tower at Reading.

Reading Abbey's main central tower would have fitted into the overall pattern of mid to late 12th century towers. It is most likely that a small pyramidal spire would have capped the tower. This would have added several metres to its height, but it is most unlikely to have exceeded 70 m. There is also the possibility, some may argue probability, that a tall spire was added at some time, in which case its height would have been raised considerably.

As we have seen, there is no way of knowing whether there were any towers at the west end. However, it is very likely that there were smaller towers at the corners of the north and south transepts.

Most probably, the tower or towers would have been square, but again, it is possible that one or more may have been polygonal or round.

NOTES

1. The Decorated or Second Pointed Style, from late 13th to the 14th centuries, describes the artistic movement, principally associated with architecture, which saw the development of pointed arches, ribbed vaulted ceilings, buttresses and extensive stained glass windows within the context of the more delicate stone-work. It is most probable that Reading's Lady Chapel was in this style.

2. Conant K,J, *Carolingian and Romanesque Architecture* 800 – 1200.

3. Sources – the Blade site *http://www.skyscrapernews.com/buildings.php?id=1910* - and *https://www.emporis.com/buildings/182026/the-blade-reading-united-kingdom* .
   The Verto building *https://www.emporis.com/buildings/1470968/verto-reading-united-kingdom*
   The 'Emporis' website was functioning at the time of researching this book, but not at the time of publication.

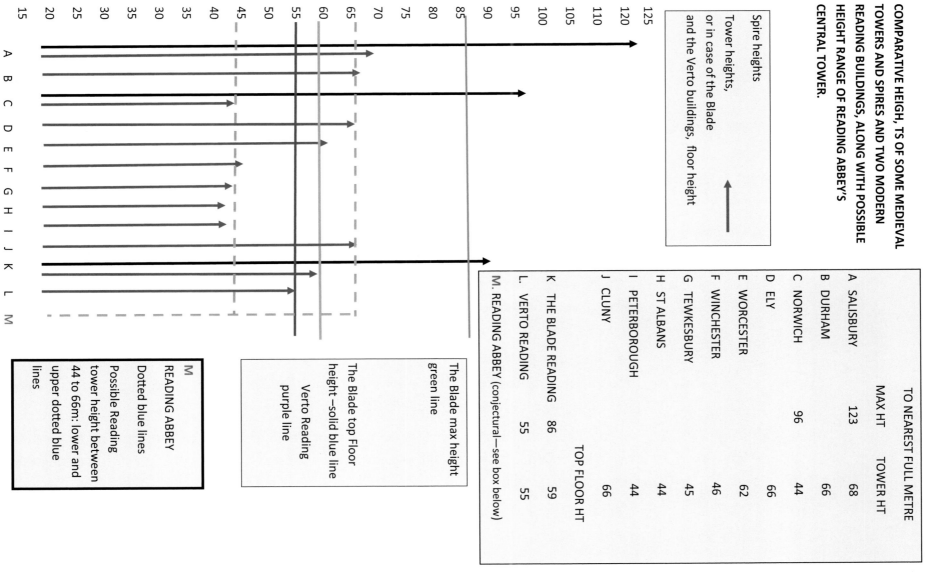

COMPARATIVE HEIGH, TS OF SOME MEDIEVAL TOWERS AND SPIRES AND TWO MODERN READING BUILDINGS, ALONG WITH POSSIBLE HEIGHT RANGE OF READING ABBEY'S CENTRAL TOWER.

Spire heights
Tower heights,
or in case of the Blade
and the Verto buildings, floor height

	TO NEAREST FULL METRE	MAX HT	TOWER HT
A	SALISBURY	123	68
B	DURHAM		66
C	NORWICH	96	44
D	ELY		66
E	WORCESTER		62
F	WINCHESTER		46
G	TEWKESBURY		45
H	ST ALBANS		44
I	PETERBOROUGH		44
J	CLUNY		66
			TOP FLOOR HT
K	THE BLADE READING	86	59
L	VERTO READING	55	55
M.	READING ABBEY (conjectural—see box below)		

The Blade max height
green line

The Blade top Floor
height—solid blue line

Verto Reading
purple line

M
READING ABBEY

Dotted blue lines

Possible Reading
tower height between
44 to 66m: lower and
upper dotted blue
lines

111

CHAPTER 6

NORTH TRANSEPT– MORTAR ANALYSIS

Dr Kevin Hayward and John Mullaney

PURPOSE AND SCOPE OF THE WORK

Following the completion of the conservation project of the ruins of Reading Abbey, known as *Reading Abbey Revealed,* Historic England agreed to subsidise similar work on the standing remains of the north transept. These are in the grounds of the Catholic Church of St. James, which are owned by the Catholic Diocese of Portsmouth.

Questions had been asked as to what extent these standing ruins represent the original structure, and whether they had been altered in some way.

5 m approx.

Flint core of the apsidal chapel in 2018.

The formation of the flint core appears to differ at a higher level, roughly from between 3 to 5 metres, as can be seen on the photograph. The lower level flints are mixed in with mortar, showing no regular pattern, whereas the upper levels are laid in courses.

It was suggested by both Historic England and by Reading Museum that this may be the result of some conservation work in the 19th or 20th centuries. One way of checking if there had been later conservation work, was to examine the mortar.

I contacted Dr. Hayward, who has acted as consultant petrologist in all my researches, and we decided to take mortar samples from the stack. It is normally possible to identify and distinguish medieval mortar from that used in the 19th and 20th centuries.

But before writing about the results of these investigation, I will put the north transept into its historical context.

In Chapter 1 we saw how the nave, side aisles and transepts of Cluniac monasteries were designed both for the monks and for visitors and pilgrims.

Processions were an integral part of the *opus Dei*. They were viewed as mini-pilgrimages, and as such they were both solemn and elaborate. Various parts of the abbey church were planned with this mind.

We need to imagine a typical saint's day procession, where a dedicated altar, with the image of the saint, would be decorated, and surrounded by many candles and incense burners. The monks would have started the liturgy in the chapter house, chanting the appropriate psalms of the Office for that saint. Following a cross bearer and thurifers, the abbot would then have led the monks, maybe up to one hundred, possibly carrying an image or relic of the saint, out through the cloister. From the cloister they would have entered the south aisle of the church. Here visitors and pilgrims would have joined the procession, swelling the numbers to several hundreds.

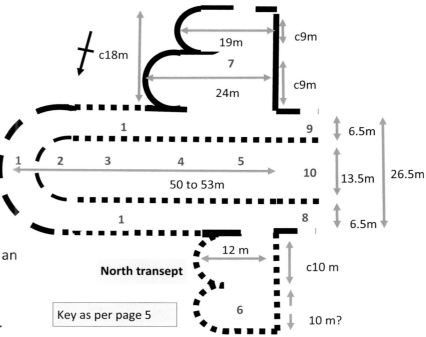

North transept

Key as per page 5

If it was a special feast day, newly-cut reeds would have been scattered on the tiled floor, and rich drapery would have been hung over the choir stalls and around the side altars. In daylight hours, the rays of the sun would have filtered through the stained glass, mingling with the smoke of the incense and the many candles placed by pilgrims in front of shrines and altars. When dark, or in the cold of winter, the church would have been warmed by the candles and heavily laden with the scents of bees-wax and incense, rising high into the vaulting.

We can now see why the church had to have such generous dimensions. Likewise, the transepts were spacious and designed to accommodate large numbers.

At Reading both transepts had two apsidal chapels, as shown on the plan. Each chapel would have had an altar, most probably dedicated to a particular saint. I have speculated, for instance, that the larger of the two chapels in the south transept, may have been dedicated to St James, and that the relic of the hand of St James would have been brought there on his feast day, the 25th July.

Returning to the examination of the north transept, the only part remaining is the southerly wall of the south chapel. Its overall height is about 8.15m.(Harrison *The North Transept.* p3).

Tomkins 1791.   Courtesy Reading Library

However, one anomaly is that an 18th century illustration (left), does not appear to show the same profile as in a late 19th, or early 20th century, photograph (right).

Had the window opening, or indeed any other part of the structure been 'rebuilt'?

Window opening c.1900

I also looked at other clues, such as Englefield's 1779 survey, (see page 53).

A small house built by the late Lord Fane

His plan shows a small house and its garden, which, in his notes, Englefield says was *built by the late Lord Fane.*

This is shown standing against the ruins in the illustration mentioned above. The plan has the house in the correct position, against the ruins of the south chapel of the north transept or, more accurately, of the north ambulatory wall immediately to its east. It should be noted that the chimney, and so flue, do not appear to be attached to the ruins. This is important for our later observations. It is possible that there were two different houses at different times.

The abbey window would have been in the ambulatory wall, east of the north transept. This window arch has now completely disappeared. It should be noted that Englefield, when discussing the chapter house and other parts of the ruins, wrote, *it is now difficult to say, whether or not the windows were round headed; they have the appearance of an obtuse point, as have all the other windows remaining in the abbey, though the doors are every one round.*

This is an important observation, from one who saw the ruins before the changes, restorations and conservation projects of the 19th and 20th centuries. Certainly, some of the early illustrations and even photographs, such as the one shown here, could be interpreted as substantiating Englefield's observation. Note, however, that he says the evidence is inconclusive, and the angle of the point is not obtuse.

****

I shall now return to how we approached the problem concerning the apparently different building techniques noted above. There were two issues that needed to be resolved.

Firstly, was it conceivable that the differing layering was consistent with the whole stack dating back to the medieval period, and secondly, could a mortar analysis help in the dating process?

One explanation for the first problem is that, up to a certain level, the builders may have built up the ashlar blocks or wooden shuttering and poured in the infill mix of flint, cement and other material. Above a certain level, three to five metres, it was easier to layer the core in much the same way as a modern bricklayer would build a wall. This would account for the difference in the appearance of the composition between the two levels. In the lower sections there is much more mortar and other infill material, whereas the upper levels are in courses, with the flints bound more tightly together. Layering courses of flint was more common after the mid-13th century, though not unknown beforehand.

There is evidence that this was done on the other parts of the abbey site and that the technique of herring-bone layers was used to strengthen the courses. This latter technique was used by builders of Cluniac monasteries in France, and it should be remembered that the first monks called to found Reading were Cluniacs brought over to England by Henry I in 1121. It was, however, a comparatively widespread method, with examples in England stretching from the Roman era, through Saxon times and throughout the middle ages. See 'Comment 2' below'.

NORTH TRANSEPT MORTAR SAMPLES (Dr Kevin Hayward)

The numbers refer to where the mortar samples were taken. The Figure numbers refer to the figures 1 and 2 .

1 and 2. Type A, Light cream-grey lime gravel mortar 2.5 YR 8/1 with ovoid chalk
inclusions — primary medieval mortar (Fig 1)

Fig 1.

Fig 2.

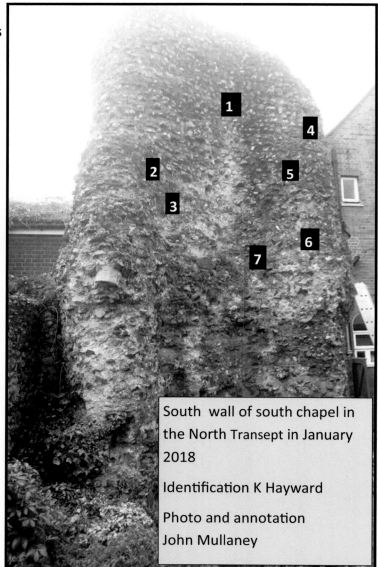

South wall of south chapel in the North Transept in January 2018

Identification K Hayward

Photo and annotation
John Mullaney

3.	Mid to late 19th or 20th century mortar. ("Roman cement"). Darker colour. (See comment 1, below). (Fig 2)

4.	Type A . White grey 2.5 YR 8/1 Light cream lime gravel mortar with 25mm brown flint pebbles rare charcoal. Ovoid chalk inclusions c 10mm. Rare shell. Hummocky tufa like appearance. Possibly primary medieval mortar

5.	White gravel mortar with 25mm brown gravel flint pebbles and large ovoid chalk humps, but very similar to Type A with one small piece of White-grey 2.5YR light cream gravel mortar with 25 brown flint pebbles, rare charcoal. Ovoid chalk inclusions c10mm. Rare shell similar. Possible primary medieval mortar.

6. Type A White grey 2.5YR 8/1 light cream concretionary lime gravel mortar with 25mm brown flint pebbles. Rare charcoal. Ovoid chalk inclusions c 10mm. Rare shell. Hummocky tufa like appearance. Finer than no 4 above. Possible primary medieval mortar

7. Type A White grey 2.5YR 8/1 light cream lime gravel mortar with 25 mm brown flint pebbles, rare charcoal. Ovoid chalk inclusions c 100mm. Rare shell. Hummocky tufa like appearance . This is slightly harder than items 4 and 5 above but the same sample recipe. Possible primary medieval mortar

Samples 1 - 3 taken July 2019; samples 4 - 7 taken January 2018.

COMMENTS

1. These, along with other samples, were taken from every face of the ruins. There is little difference in the spread of the types of mortar. Most of it, by a long way, is primary medieval mortar. However, at various points, modern, so called "Roman mortar", dating from the second half of the 19th into the 20th century, appears haphazardly both on the front face and on the reverse side of the standing remains at St James' church. These consist of patches of cement which appear to have been placed over the flint and existing mortar in recent times, presumable to stabilise areas that were crumbling. They form only a small fraction of the whole.

The conclusion must be that the structure dates to the medieval period and that the area with the layered appearance, therefore, likewise dates to the same time frame. In short the layered flints are not a modern rebuilding.

2. The building method at Reading was commented upon by Englefield. He wrote: *The vast strength of the walks and the perfection of their cement is a circumstance very worthy of notice. They were evidently built by laying course upon course of the coating stone* (ashlar blocks), *and running the interior parts full of fluid mortar, mixed with small flints. Where the walls were not coated with stone, I fancy boards were used to confine the liquid wall, and their traces are in some places visible.*

The use of shuttering, as we would refer to it today, was not uncommon and was used from Roman times.

Although Englefield mentions two possible ways in which the abbey was constructed, the fact that there are layers of flints and more careful work such as herring-bone, indicates that a third method was also employed, namely 'flintlaying', similar to bricklaying.

4. The dark staining on the face of the apse wall raised some questions. A representative from Historic England, among others, speculated that it may the consequence of a fire, or a chimney flue from a house.

This is a possibility but, for the reasons pointed out earlier, it is unlikely to be the small house erected by Lord Fane, or at least the one shown in the illustration. On closer examination several of the burn marks, it is unlikely that it could be the consequence of a fire during the time of the abbey. A devasting fire was recorded in the abbey's annals for St Gregory's day, 1209, but it is highly improbable that the fire would have penetrated the ashlar to such an extent as to cause the discolouration .* Fire was a common problem during the middle ages, and the evidence from other buildings does not support the theory that a fire at Reading could have caused the scorching.

Stones at the foot of the chapel wall

5. It is worth mentioning the stones at the base of the chapel wall. These had been hidden for many years, covered with a pile of flints and other debris. They are tied into the wall. The more easterly end has the base of a single shaft. The most westerly three stones have mason's marks, the most spectacular being a saltire inside a square.

They are laid tightly together, but with room for some infill. The infill is unlike the hard mortar reported above; rather it resembles a modern dry mix. Of course it is possible that this is just dust and debris from other sources. However, there are gaps at points between the stones and so it might be expected that these would have been filled in.

All are made of Taynton stone.

Mason's mark

* Following the restoration work covering the stack with slaked-lime, this discolouration is no longer visible.

6. Finally, the great column base, in Taynton stone, on the south of the transept wall merits a mention. Englefield's plan indicates its existence and it is in the correct position to match the base for the supporting east column of the south transept. When I uncovered this, I was struck both by its completeness and by the high quality of the craftmanship. It is the most complete base on the whole abbey site.

This, and the fineness of the mason's art, was noted by Historic England as worthy of special attention. It was also commented upon by several people, such as Stuart Harrison in his report to the Diocese of Portsmouth, and by Professor Anne Curry of the University of Southampton.

What is noticeable is the lack of mortared joins. The carving is so exact that each block sits tightly and firmly with its neighbour. The mortar in the core is of the same light cream lime gravel mortar as seen elsewhere. There are some patches of late 'Roman mortar' as described above.

7. The use of herringbone layering to strengthen the bond is an interesting feature which is to be found in several places throughout the abbey ruins. Further reference to the use of flint in building may be found in *The Grove Encyclopedia of Medieval Art and Architecture*, Volume 1 p234

CONCLUSION

The mortar samples from the north transept show that its remains mostly belong to the same building period and that the change in appearance is not due to later additions in post-medieval times.

After these samples were taken, most of the stack was treated with slaked-lime, using the same method as for the main body of the ruins. The result is that the evidence discussed above is no longer visible, nor probably accessible.

It would be of interest to know whether, following the 2018 conservation work, it is possible to take similar mortar samples from other parts of the ruins. They may be able to help determine, for example, whether the window openings, such as those in the chapter house, are original and if not, to what extent they have been altered, and when this work was carried out.

CHAPTER 7

THE STONES OF READING ABBEY
Dr Kevin Hayward and John Mullaney

There are very few ashlar blocks still on the abbey site. The stones that can be seen are mainly the pillar bases and those scattered at random in the flint and mortar core, which is what we mostly see today. During the 19th century, some stones were collected and incorporated into structures such as the archway tunnel between the Forbury Gardens and the ruins. Many more appear all over Reading and beyond. We shall be taking a look at some of these in this chapter. By way of an introduction, the following is some information about the stones in general.

When the abbey was built, much of it was faced in dressed stone slabs, known as ashlar. These were mostly made from Taynton limestone. I shall be saying more about this later. There may have been other types of ashlar blocks, but if so, these were few and far between. Also, much of the carved stone, such as that set into the archway, was also from the Taynton quarry near Oxford.

There are some carved stones from Caen in Reading Museum. These are probably from the abbey, although they were found at Sonning, not on the abbey site. Caen stone, sometimes called Cane stone, is a prestigious, high quality limestone which would have been especially brought over from Normandy.

What would the abbey church have looked like? Taynton stone turns a golden-brown colour with age. The church was an impressive building, and we must imagine this golden edifice towering over the town, visible for many miles. It is likely that the exterior, especially the west front, would have been lavishly painted. It would have had niches for statues of saints and biblical figures. The church was dedicated to the Virgin Mary, Mother of Jesus, and St John the evangelist. It is almost certain that they would have been represented at the entrance and these, like all the other statues, would have been brightly coloured.

Moreover, the colours chosen would not have been arbitrary. To the medieval mind, different colours represented different aspect of creation and of the divine. For instance, red or gold represented the Godhead, whilst green portrayed creation and earth, and blue was associated with heaven.

Not all the flint walls were covered with ashlar. It is often possible to see which surfaces had ashlar, as the keying holes are visible. From the early medieval period, flint walls were commonly rendered with lime coating. This is commonly believed to have been the case on the dormitory wall at Reading.

Below is an interesting section of the refectory south wall after the conservation work was completed.

Note the herring-bone layering of the flints. There is also a line of ashlar stone blocks. Was this carefully constructed flint wall limewashed?

THE STONES

I shall begin by giving an analysis of the types of stone that have been found at Reading. This has been written by Dr Hayward

PETROLOGY OF ARCHITECTURAL FRAGMENTS

Dr Kevin Hayward

The underlying geology of this part of the Thames Valley and through much of south-east England is devoid of stone suitable for fine carving. The rock is often too young and soft and frequently consists of clays and unconsolidated sands and gravels. This means much of the stone used in the carving of the abbey must have come from afar. Fortunately, Reading's excellent riverine links afforded to it by the River Thames allow suitable stone to be easily barged downstream from older Jurassic limestones in the Cotswolds. Furthermore, stone can be barged upstream, via the Thames Estuary, from maritime sources as far afield as the North Downs, Lincolnshire, Dorset and even the continent.

Most of these finer rock types identified as architectural fragments, or ashlar, from Reading Abbey are termed freestones. Freestone is limestone or sandstone with a soft, open, porous texture that enables the rock to be worked or carved in any direction, and it is often hard enough to withstand external weathering.

The types of freestone identified from Reading Abbey form part of the medieval stone package typical of many large ecclesiastical, palatial and defensive buildings in London and south-east England.

In terms of frequency at Reading these are:

Taynton stone

Use: Very common stone type, both from the in-situ remains of Reading Abbey, loose blocks of architectural stone including the famous Reading Abbey stone and blocks reused into later post medieval walls and cellars throughout Reading.

Rock Type: Orange-brown banded shelly oolitic limestone. The surface consists of alternating bands of hard grey shelly (oyster) and ooids (small round calcite grains – that often weather out giving the rock a pitted surface)

Geological source: Burford/Taynton stone - Middle Jurassic (Bathonian) Taynton, Burford - West Oxfordshire.

Caen stone

Use: So far only identified petrologically in the large number of ornately carved capitals (the Keyser capitals). These, however, were recovered from Sonning.

The regal connection with Normandy resulted in large consignments of stone being supplied for use in ecclesiastical projects in London, and in southern (Canterbury Cathedral) and eastern (Norwich Cathedral) England. However, this has inevitably led to the assumption that a lot of the stone used in Reading Abbey is from this source.

Rock Type: Fine condensed cream, yellow or yellow brown limestone (packstone). In thin section, the rock is made of tiny black snail pellets (peloids). Its fine surface can be conducive to the application of pigment (paint).

Geological source: Caen stone Middle Jurassic (Bathonian) Caen, Département Calvados (Normandy France)

Barnack stone

Use: So far only identified in a reused fragment in the wall alongside St James's Church. This rock, outside of Cambridgeshire, is used in the production of sarcophagi. The example (alongside), from Westminster Abbey, probably dates from the 12th century. The quarrying and supply of this rock goes into disuse after the 13th century, as the quarry largely runs out of stone.

Rock Type: Very hard sparry shelly limestone with occasional ooids

Geological source: Barnack stone Middle Jurassic (Bajocian) Barnack Village, Cambridgeshire near Peterborough (extensive use in Peterborough Cathedral)

Reading Abbey - A pilgrim church

Purbeck marble

Use: So far only identified petrologically in a reused column shaft section in the wall alongside St James's Church (below left). The rock is polished black, forming striking column bases, shafts within an abbey or cathedral in contrast to yellow rocks e.g. in Salisbury Cathedral. (below right).

Rock Type: Fine dark grey sparry limestone packed full of small 10mm complete freshwater snails *Paludina carinifera* Shelly Wackestone

Geological source: Purbeck marble, Purbeck Group, Durlston Formation (Lower Cretaceous), Swanage-Langton Matravers, Isle of Purbeck, Dorset.

Reigate stone/malmstone

Use: So far only identified petrologically in an ashlar block in the arch. In medieval London this was the most common rock type in the use of not only ashlar (e.g. Westminster Abbey refectory Wall), but window mullion (tracery) mouldings.

Rock Type: Very low density fine-grained lime-green (glauconitic) limestone). Fine surface can be conducive to the application of pigment.

Geological source: Reigate-Mertsham stone Upper Greensand, Upper Cretaceous, Reigate-Mertsham (East Surrey). or Malmstone Upper Greensand (Farnham District).

Tufa

Use: Not identified so far in Reading Abbey (other than a fragment that may possibly have come from the chapter house). Elsewhere e.g. Westminster Abbey, associated with vaulting e.g. 11th century Pyx Chamber.

Rock Type: Tufa – Low Density Hard calcareous spring water deposit full of voids.

Geological source: Holocene river/spring water deposit - many possible sources along the Thames and Kennet Valley e.g. Woolhampton.

COMMENT (John Mullaney)

The above assessment demonstrates the overwhelming use of Taynton stone in the building of Reading Abbey. However, much of the fine stone was removed after the Dissolution. Consequently, it is possible that there was a wider use of Caen stone than indicated in the finds. As Dr Hayward points out, the Caen stone capitals in Reading Museum were not found on the abbey site, but in Sonning. I shall be looking at this in more detail later.

The lack of tufa is surprising. Unlike Caen stone, this is not prestigious material and not easily refashioned. There is little reason why it should have been removed. Yet Englefield claims that the chapter house vaulting was made of tufa, and so we would expect to find more on site, as he did.

The sole example of Purbeck marble is also surprising. This is in the wall separating St James' from the Forbury Gardens. The sample is a cross section of a pillar. This would have been part of a range of pillars, for example as used in clerestories. However, the dearth of more samples may be explained by its prestigious and so desirable nature for re-use elsewhere. Wherever that may have been is a mystery.

THE HIDDEN ABBEY STONES PROJECT

Reading Museum holds a vast collection of abbey stones. As part of the Hidden Abbey Project, a subsidiary investigation, the Hidden Abbey Stones Project (HASP), was begun to find out more about abbey stones on the site and in the wider area. The following is a sample of the results of this investigation.

Location: Caversham Court Gardens: Catalogued 2017

Type of stone: Taynton

Description: This single block of carved limestone has mouldings typical of the 12th and 13th centuries, as depicted in Villard de Honnecourt's 13th century work. It has two runnels which were most probably designed to retain window fittings.

Windows of this design appear very late in the Romanesque period during the transition between the Romanesque and Gothic periods. They are associated with the pointed windows of the first, second and third pointed periods. (In England; the Early English, Decorated and Perpendicular).

The rounded mouldings are indicative of an earlier style, still reflecting the Romanesque period. Lorenz Lechner, writing in 1516, described how the size of a mullion was based on a calculation of its proportion to the thickness of the walls into which the window was placed. There were two types of mullion, the old and the young, the former being the larger. If this is true then, following his calculations, it is possible to work out the thickness of the original walls. It may well come from the Lady Chapel, built in 1314 in the 'Decorated' style.

Function: a mullion stone from a window into which was inserted a leaded glass window, most probably stained glass.

Extract from Villard de Honnecourt's book showing various templates for masons to follow. Among these, it is possible to identify mullion patters similar to the stone which was found in Caversham Court Gardens in 2017.

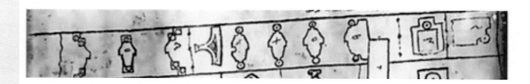

Location: Caversham Court Gardens: Catalogued 2017

Type of stone: Taynton

Description: This single block of carved limestone is of a type known as 'whistle' stones, so called because they look like whistles. Some such stones have perfectly rounded shafts, others are elliptical. The tie-in section, or tongue, is carved at a right angle to the shaft. This particular stone has red colouring which appears to be remnants of paint. If so, it is a rare example of original paint on Reading Abbey stone.

15cm

7c

12cm

Function: It is likely that this was part of a column shaft as shown in the diagram. The tongue, or projecting part of the stone, would have served to tie the shaft into the body of the wall and would not have been visible. In fact, the purpose of the design may have been to give the impression that this elegant shaft work was free standing. The column would thus appear to be in front of two walls that were joined at an internal right angle. (See diagram).

Location: Reading — Newtown: Discovered and catalogued in 2017 in the garden of a house in School Terrace

Type of stone: Taynton

Description: The design is typical of 12th century Romanesque sculpture.

Function: Probably a cornice or horizontal moulding forming a ledge. This could be over a window or door or even along a length of stonework, either at he base or top of a wall. One function would be to direct rainwater away from the wall. Although it has red colouration, Dr Hayward advised that this is not the remnants of medieval paint.

Reading Abbey - A pilgrim church

Location: Central Reading : Discovered and catalogued in 2017 in the in the grounds of St James' church, within the north transept of the Abbey.

Type of stone: Taynton

Description: The design is typical of 12th century Romanesque sculpture. The fact that it appears to be tapered, suggests that it was a voussoir.
Other examples are to be found at Bromyard (Herefordshire), Bockleton (Worcestershire) and Tickencote (Rutland).

BOCKLETON

Function: Probably a voussoir with roll mouldings. It would have served as one of the stones in an archway as shown in this photograph of the south doorway into Bockleton church, Worcestershire. The Norman style of arch was typically rounded and the joint-lines between the stones radiated from the arch's centre.

Location: Kidmore End: catalogued 2017

Type of stone: Taynton

Description: A single block of stone with a carving of a head which has a hole though its mouth. The head is worn and may represent either a real or mythical animal. It does not look as if it was ever meant to represent a human head. The large block, or corbel, behind the head, has a hole which serves to collect water before being discharged through the mouth of the of the head. See next page.

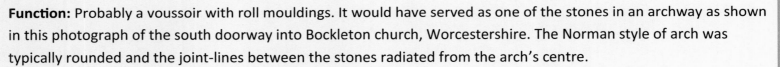

Function: As such a large block of stone was expensive, it is clear that this piece of masonry was not purely decorative, but served a structural function. Where a stone was purely decorative, it would not have been necessary to countersink it into a wall to such a depth. In common with Romanesque and Gothic grotesques and gargoyles, this larger part would have been fitted into the main masonry to give the whole piece stability.

Corbel

A corbel: a projecting piece of stone or wood to carry the weight and thrust of arches or entablatures. It was essential that the block was well secured so that the down-thrust would be borne by the wall.

Another use of a corbel was in a "corbel table". Here several corbels were employed to support the eaves of a roof. For a stone to serve as a corbel the top part would have to be flat so that a stone or wooden structure could rest on it.

Sometimes, a corbel would have a hole pierced through to flow water to flow through and away from the wall, as here.

Wokingham stone

Location: Wokingham: catalogued 2017

Type of stone: Taynton

Description: Two fragments of what look like pieces of rib vaulting came to light in a garden in Wokingham.

The question is, 'did these come from Reading Abbey, or from some other building?' The existence of the same pattern in the 19th archway leading from the Forbury Gardens into the Ruins would suggest that these did come from the abbey, as the archway is made up of stones found on the abbey site.

Forbury Gardens - archway

We must acknowledge the possibility that the same masons, working with the same materials, to the same designs, may have been employed elsewhere. This is almost certainly the case in the similarities between some of the stones at Windsor and Reading.

An example of similar, if not identical, carvings may be seen by comparing those on these two illustrations.

The upper photograph is of chip-carved stone originally found in the herbarium of Windsor Castle.

Below, the same pattern is to be found in a stone set into the exterior wall of St James' church in Reading.

There are several possible explanations for this, one being that the Windsor stone was brought from Reading at the time of Queen Mary Tudor. We have records of 'Cane' (Caen) stone being brought from Reading to Windsor to construct the Poor Knights' Lodgings. On the other hand, it may be that the same masons had been employed in both locations, or indeed different masons were working to the same patterns.

THE DOUAI STONES

Location: Douai Abbey, Woolhampton.

Type of stone: Taynton

Description: Two grotesques

Grotesque 1. It is possible that this served as a corbel. The top of the head is flattened, as the second photo shows

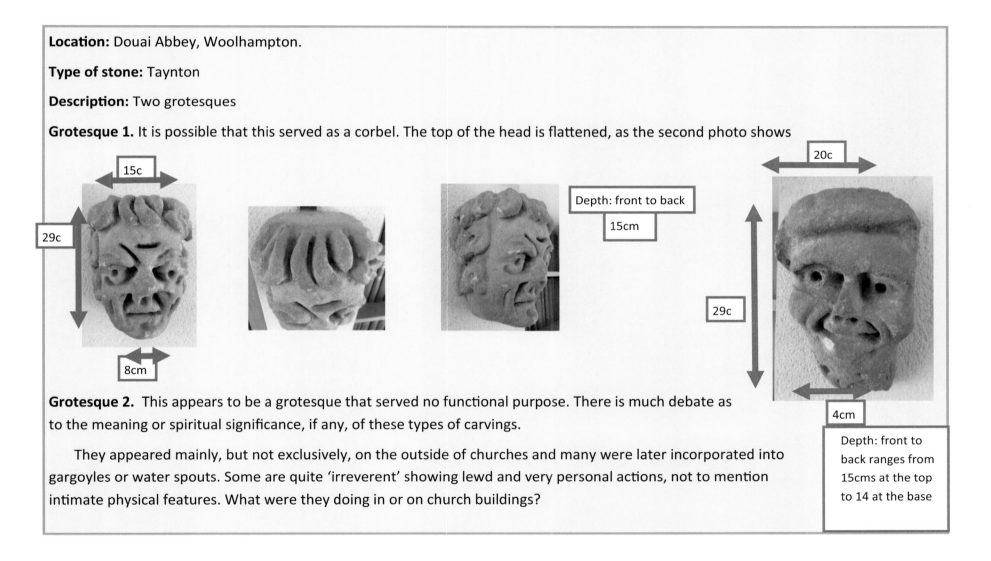

Depth: front to back

15cm

20c

15c

29c

8cm

29c

4cm

Depth: front to back ranges from 15cms at the top to 14 at the base

Grotesque 2. This appears to be a grotesque that served no functional purpose. There is much debate as to the meaning or spiritual significance, if any, of these types of carvings.

They appeared mainly, but not exclusively, on the outside of churches and many were later incorporated into gargoyles or water spouts. Some are quite 'irreverent' showing lewd and very personal actions, not to mention intimate physical features. What were they doing in or on church buildings?

Reading Abbey - A pilgrim church

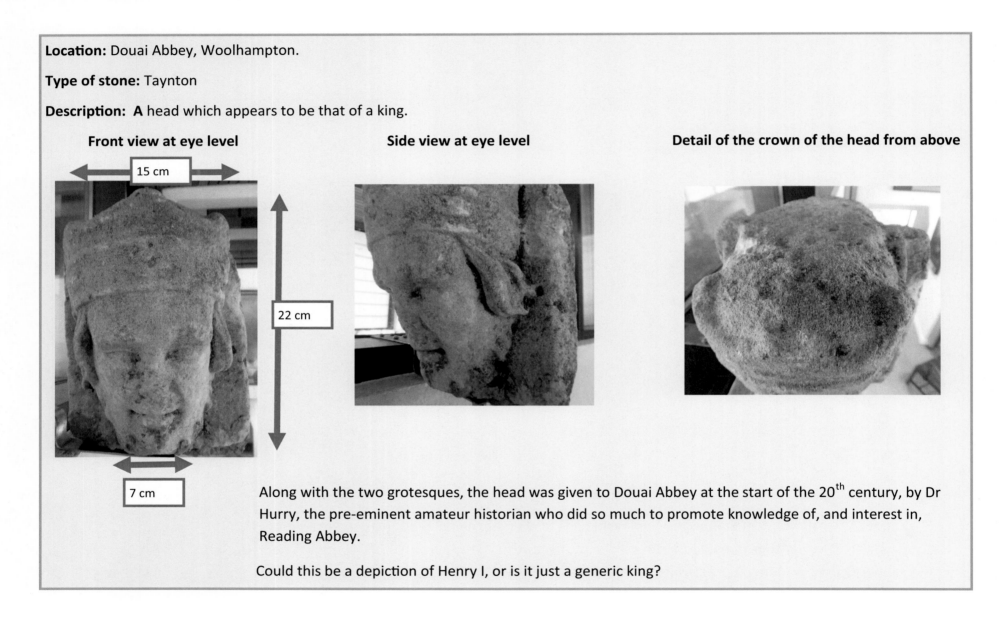

Location: Douai Abbey, Woolhampton.

Type of stone: Taynton

Description: A head which appears to be that of a king.

Front view at eye level   Side view at eye level   Detail of the crown of the head from above

15 cm

22 cm

7 cm

Along with the two grotesques, the head was given to Douai Abbey at the start of the 20th century, by Dr Hurry, the pre-eminent amateur historian who did so much to promote knowledge of, and interest in, Reading Abbey.

Could this be a depiction of Henry I, or is it just a generic king?

There are similarities between the head at Douai Abbey and those of the kings of Judah, dating to the 13th century, in the Musée de Cluny, Paris. These once adorned the façade of Notre Dame. Mistakenly, they were thought by the revolutionary mob to be those of the kings of France. So, having decapitated the living king, the mob turned its attention to these statues, dressed as they were in the clothes of Capetian Kings. They were lost for nearly 200 years, but fortunately were rediscovered in 1977 and are now on display at the French National Museum of the Middle Ages. Notice the similarities in carving, and especially the crown, of the Douai head and those in Paris.

Reading Abbey - A pilgrim church

The Reading Museum capitals

On the 22nd June 1916, Charles Keyser read a paper to the Society of Antiquaries entitled: *Some Norman capitals from Sonning, Berkshire and some sculptured Stones at Shiplake and Windsor Castle, probably brought from Reading Abbey*[1]

Keyser recounted how he had been engaged, since 1912, in excavating the Holme Park Estate, Sonning. The next ten pages of his paper are an analysis of these stones, in which he concluded that they most probably originated from Reading Abbey. The meeting concurred with the secretary's opinion that these stones were made from *a fine-grained oolitic* material that was *probably Caen stone.*

The second half of the work consists of detailed photographs of the stones which, at the time of writing, 2022, reside in Reading Museum. Although these were not found on the Reading Abbey site, it is generally accepted that this was their place of origin.

NOTE

1. *Some Norman Capitals from Sonning , Berkshire and some sculptured stones at Shiplake and Windsor castle, probably brought from Reading Abbey.* Keyser C . Proceedings of the Society of Antiquaries, London 28, 1915 –1916.

CHAPTER 8

READING ABBEY'S STONES AND WINDSOR CASTLE
Dr Kevin Hayward and John Mullaney

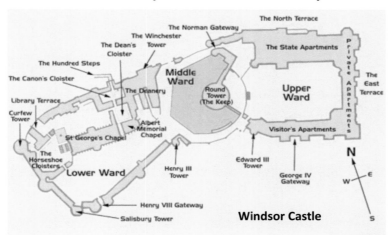

Windsor Castle

Windsor Castle

POOR KNIGHTS' LODGINGS   THE HERBARIUM

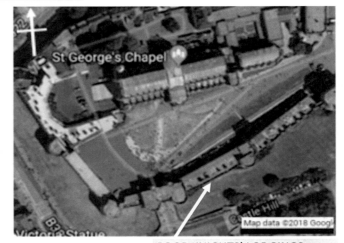

POOR KNIGHTS' LODGINGS

Reading Abbey - A pilgrim church

In 1557, Queen Mary Tudor began the construction of the Poor Knights' Lodgings at Windsor Castle, south of St George's Chapel. The masons' accounts describe how various materials were removed from Reading Abbey.

> Reading – The stones for the building were fetched from Redding Abbey by water,
> Reading – Carpenters viewing the Roofes at Reading and Wallingford by the day   12d
> Reading – Masons taking downe the great stones of the dores and windowes in the Chappell of our Lady there by the day &c.   12d
> Reading – Labourers digging stones out of the walls there per diem   7d
> Reading – Masons Chusing of stones there per diem   10d
> Reading – Labourers digging of Cane Stone out of the windows for ye Batlements in the New Lodgings per diem   7d

The existence of these records has been well documented and various attempts at identifying the origins of the stones have been made over the last 150 years or so. (Baxter, *The Royal Abbey of Reading*, p217-220)

It should be noted that there are two separate groups of stones. Those mentioned in the 16th century document refer to the battlements of the Poor Knights' Lodgings. However, in the early 20th century, Charles Keyser who discovered the stones at Holme Park, now in Reading Museum, claimed that a further group of stones in the Herbarium of Windsor castle had come from Reading in the 16th century.

In 2016 Baxter challenged some of these assumptions. He pointed out that, whereas the stones mentioned in 1557 had been taken from the Lady Chapel at Reading, which had been built in the Decorated style of the early 14th century, the stones in the Herbarium are in the Romanesque style. It is just as likely that the stones previously identified by Keyser as originating in Reading came from other earlier buildings in Windsor itself. Baxter refers to works by Tighe and Davis (1858), but most importantly of all, he repeats Sir John Hope's conclusion (1913), that 'it is therefore difficult to assign such fragments their proper birthplace'. Baxter also points out that the undeniable similarity of the carvings of the Reading and Windsor stones does not prove that one came from the other. He states, 'we can say with confidence that the same sculptural workshop was involved'. In this case, we can add that the same masons were very likely using the same types of stone, following the same decorative patterns, and employing the same stone working techniques. I shall examine the evidence for these assertions.

HISTORICAL BACKGROUND - WINDSOR

By the 1120s Henry I had enlarged the castle at Windsor started by his father, William the Conqueror. In cementing his power base, William had selected one of the first outcrops of raised terrain west of London, with its commanding views of the Thames Valley. Henry's own building campaign in Windsor was carried out between 1107 and c.1110. In opposition to his eldest brother Robert, known as Robert Curthose, he had seized the throne in 1100 on the death of their brother, William II (William Rufus). The castle was one way of underpinning Henry's authority. The significance of the scale of his building at Windsor was recorded by the contemporary chronicler Henry of Huntingdon, who wrote in his 'Historia Anglorum', *Eodem anno cum rex curiam suam tenuisset ad Pentecosten apud novum Windelsores quam ispe aedificaverat*. "In the same year (1110), the king (Henry) held his court at Pentecost (Whitsuntide), at New Windsor, which he himself had built".

ARCHITECTURAL BACKGROUND - READING

The building of Reading Abbey began in 1121, in the Romanesque style, with rounded arches and massive pillars. The building was begun under the direction of Peter, a prior of Cluny Abbey in Burgundy. Fellow Cluniacs from the foremost Cluniac priory in England, St. Pancras at Lewes, joined him. Within a couple of years, Hugh of Amiens, sometimes known as Hugh de Boves, prior of St Pancras, was appointed as the first abbot of Reading, which became an autonomous Cluniac abbey. There can be little doubt, therefore, that the design of the early abbey at Reading was in the Romanesque style, possibly with Burgundian Cluniac influences.

Though its early design was Romanesque, an event in 1208 may have had an impact on its later appearance. A devastating whirlwind, with lightning and subsequent fire, engulfed the central tower and burnt first the north then the south side of the church. (*Annals* – Kemp p20—21). The text leaves a degree of uncertainty as to whether the whole church was burnt, or whether this refers only to the tower area and the north and south transepts.

Whatever the case, reconstruction would have been urgently needed. By the early 13th century, the time of the disaster, it is likely that the First Pointed or Early English style would have been employed in rebuilding the damaged areas. If this was the case, it would have entailed the use of pointed arches supporting ribbed, rather than groin vaulting, and probably not barrel or tunnel vaulting, though this is not impossible. Any new sculpted carvings would most likely have been in accord with this new style. These would have included arches, windows, tracery and patterns consistent with this 'Gothic' aesthetic.

Reading Abbey - A pilgrim church

PETROLOGICAL BACKGROUND (This section is by Dr Hayward.)

Geological Setting

The Castle at Windsor lies on an outlier of Upper Chalk (BGS Windsor Sheet 269), the closest outcrop of Chalk to the west of the City of London. Elements of chalk ashlar and moulding stone are associated with some of the earliest 12th century structures (Hayward pers. obs.) as are the associated much harder flint nodules contained with this part of the Upper Chalk of East Berkshire. Other local sources of stone include sarsen, or greywether (Dewey & Bromehead 1915, 93) a hard grey cryptocrystalline sandstone, again shaped as ashlar and rubble stone from the earliest structural phases. The principle outcrops lie at Chobham Common and "the Camp"[1], from the geologically young Eocene Barton Beds, 10km to the south as some 7km west of the River Thames.

However, stone suitable for finer ashlar and more intricate architectural ornamentation and construction, known as "freestone" (Sutherland 2003)[2], needs to come from much further afield from older Middle Jurassic outcrops. Fortunately Windsor's excellent riverine access to outcrops of the orange, or golden, brown banded shelly oolitic limestone Taynton stone (Middle Jurassic – Bathonian) West Oxfordshire via the River Evenlode and thence the Thames, means that it has become the principal freestone type used in the castle. The more prestigious light yellow Caen stone (Middle Jurassic - Bathonian) Normandy, France is also widely used, either being shipped across the English Channel and thence upstream via London and the River Thames, or reused via a ready "quarry" of stone from Reading Abbey after its dissolution in the 1540s.

Site Visit November 16th Stone Types

Hand specimen identifications of the stone types used in the ashlar and mouldings of the internal and external facing wall of the 16th century quarters at Windsor Castle, indicate that they are of two varieties.

Type 1 (90%) Taynton stone Brown-orange banded shelly oolitic limestone (Middle Jurassic – Bathonian West Oxfordshire) crisply executed and cut suggest primary quarrying and supply of this stone during the 16th century.

Type 2 (10%) Caen stone – light yellow packstone (Middle Jurassic – Bathonian Normandy) again a majority are crisply executed ashlar elements and door jambs suggesting primary quarrying and supply of this stone during the 16th century. Combined these two rocks create a chequer-board effect of orange and yellow ashlar facing

However, it was not possible to determine, what the petrology was of the c 2-3 reused mouldings incorporated into the external ashlar face. This was because they were at a height of 5 metres - The matching art-historical style with examples from Reading Abbey, would clearly indicate that these elements were recycled following the dissolution of the Abbey in the mid-16th century. Given their colour – slight orange tinge it seems more probable that these are examples of Taynton stone.

Bibliography

British Geological Survey (1981) 1:50,000 Geological Map 269 (Windsor).

Dewey, H, & Bromehead, C.E.N. (1915). The geology of the country around Windsor and Chertsey. *Memoir of the Geological Survey England and Wales. Explanation of Sheet 269*. HMSO, London.

Sutherland, D. (2003). *Northamptonshire stone*. Dovecote Press.

THE POOR KNIGHTS' LODGINGS

South face of the *Poor Knights' Lodgings*

We have seen that there are written records of stones being taken from Reading for use in the Poor, or Military, Knights' Lodgings. The following is an account of from the Victoria County History - Berkshire, Vol 3

From the great gate-house there extends eastward along the castle wall a long range of lodgings for the Military Knights. It consists of a series of seven two-storied ashlar-faced houses towards the west, a square tower in the middle built of coursed heathstone, which is the residence of the governor of the knights, and a further series of six houses towards the east. The latter date from 1359–60, and are also built of heathstone, but were altered to their present form in 1557–8, when the western range of houses was also built. The tower is the old belfry of 1359–60 and contained the chapel bells until their removal to the Clewer tower in or about 1478. The single house west of the tower (the others are arranged in pairs) has attached to it the remains of the 13th-century bastion that here projects from the castle wall, and formerly contained a common hall, kitchen and pantry for the use of the Poor Knights.

It was almost completely rebuilt by Sir Jeffrey Wyatville, and now forms a residence for one of the castle officials. Each house has on the ground floor a four-centred doorway and a two-light window, and on the first floor another two-light window and one of a pair of lights conjoined over the coupled doorways. The tower is three stories high and flanked at the corners by buttresses. The whole range underwent a very complete restoration in 1840–50.

Externally the nether lodgings have also a Marian facing of sandstone, now pierced, where none was before, with a number of 19th-century windows. In the cellar story these are square-headed loops, in the main floor trefoiled lights, and in the upper story pointed or trefoiled lights.

The battled parapet and the chimney stacks are likewise new. The 13th-century round tower has for a long time been reduced to its present height and has a modern casing of heathstone pierced with three tiers of Wyatville's windows. The old belfry has fortunately preserved its original exterior, except that three tiers of modern windows have been inserted in it. The lofty heathstone wall east of the belfry, against which the upper lodgings stand, is possibly temp. Henry II, but now exhibits four rows of modern windows similar to those of the nether lodgings.

From this account, it can be seen that the lodgings were 'almost completely rebuilt by Wyatville'. He carried out his work between c.1827 and c.1840. The VCH specifically mentions the 'battled parapet', stating that the 'battled parapet and chimney stacks are likewise new'. It is reasonable to assume, therefore, that the stones brought from Reading in 1557 for the battlements were either reused or replaced. We shall look at this later.

THE HERBARIUM

The Herbarium, November 2018

Until recently, there was a collection of carved stones in the area in the moat known as the Herbarium. Keyser counted over one hundred, and suggested that they had been brought to Windsor at the same time as those from the Lady Chapel. We have seen that these are in the Romanesque style, and that Baxter therefore challenges this assumption. It is of course possible that they were brought at the same time as those from the Lady Chapel but were not recorded. However, considering the detail of the 16th century records for the disposal of abbey property, it would be expected to see them mentioned, although the records may have been lost.

It is worth considering that at least some of the stones in the Herbarium may originally have been in the battlements, but were discarded when these were rebuilt by Wyatville. The stones have now been removed from the Herbarium .

What is of interest is the similarity of the patterns and stone type to those found at Reading. There are also similar stones incorporated into the walls of the Poor Knights' Lodgings.

COMPARISON OF SOME OF THE STONES AT WINDSOR AND READING

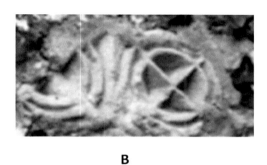

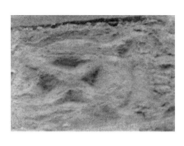

A	B	C

Photographs A and B courtesy of Ron Baxter   *Photograph John Mullaney*

Stone   A - in the 'Herbarium' at Windsor.   Stone B - in the north wall of the nave of St James' church Reading

Stone   C – Windsor – South wall of the Knights' Lodgings

D	E

D and E, original photographs of two stones discovered by Keyser in 1914 at Holme Park.

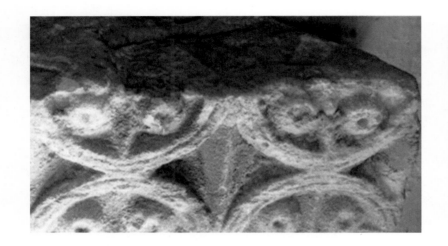

F   *Photograph courtesy Ron Baxter*

Stone F - in the Herbarium Windsor.

G   *Photograph: Kevin Hayward*

Stone G - in the south wall of the Poor Knights' lodgings

THE POOR KNIGHTS' LODGINGS

As we have seen the 'Poor' or 'Military Knights' Lodgings', including the battlements, were almost completely rebuilt by Wyatville,.

PETROLOGICAL ANALYSIS

Dr Hayward identified several types of stone in the walls. This included Caen (A - page 145) and Taynton (B - page 145) stone as well as sarsen, as identified by Dr Hayward (D - page 146).

A. Caen stone, distinguishable by its whitish colour, in the north and south walls of the Poor Knights' Lodgings.

B. South wall. Golden Taynton stone mixed in with other stones.

C . Sculpted Taynton stone inserted into the south wall

D. North wall. Example of a sarsen, as described in Dr Hayward's report above. (page 138 ff)

E. Example of 'packing'

The structure also included packing stone in the mortar, where smaller pieces of stone are inserted to maintain a consistent appearance of the wall (E).

As is to be expected, the south wall showed more signs of weathering, however this is less severe than might be expected after 500 years. There are certain stones that do appear more weathered, and therefore indicate that they came from an earlier building. Some of these are Romanesque in style and so probably date to the 12th century. Some are also similar in design to stones found at, or associated with, Reading Abbey. We have seen however that this does not prove they came from Reading, as they could just as likely have come from Henry I's building of New Windsor, as recorded by Henry of Huntingdon.

ARCHITECTURAL ANALYSIS

The first impression on seeing the south wall of the Lodgings was that this was not a Tudor structure. This accords with the record of substantial renovation, and 'of a completely new building', dating to the first half of the 19th century.

The are plenty of specimens of Caen and Taynton stone in the wall. However, very few, if any, have the appearance of dating back 500, let alone 900, years. This opinion is based upon the lack of weathering, the style of the stonework, and the fact that the stones themselves would appear to have been cut specifically to fit the existing structure, and are not spolia from an earlier building. The VCH mentions that there was building work in 1359 -1360. It is of course possible that some of the stones were taken from this previous build, recut to size and refitted in the 19th century.

The next task was to determine whether any of the stones could be those which the records show were brought from Reading. The only written record states that Cane (Caen) stone was taken from the Lady Chapel windows for the battlements, along with other unspecified 'great stones from the doors and windows'. The record does not indicate where these latter were to be used. It is possible that they were later placed elsewhere in the Lodgings or indeed in the castle's reconstruction. It was not possible to take a close look at the existing battlements but photographs were taken. These show a uniform row of dressed stones.

The north wall shows very little weathering and its overall presentation is in keeping with being mainly the result of 19th century interventions.

Photograph; John Mullaney

The next two photographs show one of the doorways and its jambs.
These are of Caen stone, but again appear to be purpose-prepared for this location.

The south wall shows a distinct lack of weathering, except for a few stones which clearly come from an earlier Romanesque building.

One would expect much more evidence of weathering on a south wall.

The overall presentation, such as the shape of the windows, once again dates this to the 19th century restoration.

Photographs Kevin Hayward

South wall of the Poor Knights' Lodgings from the west. (Photograph John Mullaney)

COMMENT

None of the above raises any doubts concerning the original location of the Poor Knights' Lodging nor that its basic structure dates to the Tudor period. Nor does it disprove the historical evidence that stone was brought from Reading to Windsor in the middle of the 16th century.

Reading Abbey - A pilgrim church

However there is little, if any, evidence that the stones visible today are those mentioned in the 16th century account, or that they had their origins in the Lady Chapel of Reading Abbey. Once more, it should be noted that some of these stones may have come from Reading and were incorporated in the 19th century restoration. There is just no way of telling if this was the case.

One final consideration concerns the date of Reading's Lady Chapel. We know that it was built c. 1314. It may be useful to place its construction in a wider historical context. This was in the middle of the troubled reign of Edward II. His wife, Isabella of France, was about twelve in 1308 when Edward married her. Isabella was the daughter of Philip the Fair, King of France. The future Edward III, their son, was born in 1312. By this date the Duchy of Normandy, including Caen, was ruled by France, and was not part of the English crown's lands. Consequently, Caen stone was likely to be even more expensive and more difficult to obtain than at the time of either Henry I or Henry II, in whose Norman territories Caen had stood. One must ask whether the Caen stone of Reading's Lady Chapel had been taken from some existing source in England, or indeed from some other part of Reading Abbey itself.

THE LADY CHAPEL

The Lady Chapel at Reading would have looked very much like that at Chichester. It was built in the Decorated style. This is distinguishable by its pointed arches and fine geometric and curvilinear window tracery, with narrow mullions which facilitated the use of leaded stained glass windows. The pointed arches, with their corresponding vaulting, also reduced the need for wide and deep retaining walls. This design in turn permitted much wider windows, with more light entering the building. Unlike the rounded apses of the Romanesque period, the chapel would have had a square east end, allowing for a magnificent 'wall of glass'. The photograph opposite shows just how little space is taken up with masonry, so creating a light and spacious interior.

The ceiling would have had quadripartite ribbed vaulting. This directed the weight and downward thrust of the roofing onto the supporting pillars. The greater the weight, and so downward thrust onto the pillars in larger buildings, the more the need for exterior buttresses (and finally flying buttresses), to act as a counter to the downward and outward force on the retaining pillars and walls. In the cases of Chichester and Reading, only simple angle buttresses on the corners and wall buttresses along the sides, as shown in the photograph, would have been required.

We saw above that the 16th century document about Reading Abbey says that Cane (Caen) stone from its windows was taken for the battlements, and that other 'great stones' were brought to Windsor. The photographs of Chichester today show the likely appearance of Reading's Lady Chapel before its destruction.

Chapel ©Richard

Chichester Gillan

cathedral Lady

Chichester cathedral Lady Chapel ©Richard Gillan

CONCLUSION

In many ways, Windsor serves to corroborate previously noted evidence and theories regarding the style and design of Reading Abbey. However, the combination of a petrological analysis of the stones, and of placing them in their architectural and historical setting, has helped clarify certain aspects of the links between Reading and Windsor.

Though a matter of judgement and opinion, it is doubtful that the Romanesque stones in the Poor Knights' Lodgings came from Reading, as Keyser believed. If they were, they have been reworked to such an extent as to make their identification virtually impossible.

Nevertheless, there is clearly a strong artistic link between the stones at Reading and Windsor. As Baxter points out, this shows the close connection between the two buildings and the masons working on them.

This is a significant point, as it demonstrates the importance of Reading Abbey to Henry I. If Windsor was a symbol of his military and secular power, Reading Abbey was a statement of Henry's esteem for, and connection with, the Church.

It would not be too much to claim that Windsor and Reading represent the twin foundations of Henry's kingship: his right to rule through both secular and divine authority.

CHAPTER 9

The 'Reading Abbey Stone'[1]

In February 1835, a letter from Mr James Wheble of Woodley Lodge, was printed in the *Reading Mercury*. Wheble, a rich Catholic landowner and antiquarian, announced the discovery of the most complete and largest piece of sculpture found on the Abbey site. [2]

Perhaps even more significant, is that the stone was discovered in the centre of the chancel, near to Henry I's burial place. The photograph above shows it with four short columns and a central plinth. These were added in 1840, when the carved stone was converted into a baptismal font for the newly built St James' church.

Wheble, a staunch Catholic, had bought much of the abbey site when it appeared the area might be sold for development. He wished to retain this 'holy space' and carry out excavations on it.

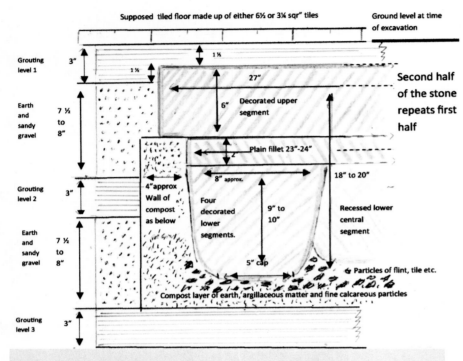

Supposed tiled floor made up of either 6½ or 3¼ sqr" tiles

Ground level at time of excavation

Grouting level 1   3"

1 ¾

1 ¾

27"

6"   Decorated upper segment

Second half of the stone repeats first half

Earth and sandy gravel   7 ½ to 8"

Plain fillet 23"-24"

2

Grouting level 2   3"

4" approx Wall of compost as below

8" approx.

18" to 20"

Four decorated lower segments.

9" to 10"

Recessed lower central segment

Earth and sandy gravel   7 ½ to 8"

5" cap

Particles of flint, tile etc.

Compost layer of earth, argillaceous matter and fine calcareous particles

Grouting level 3   3"

Cross section diagram, of 'The Reading Abbey Stone',
based on the description by James Wheble. The 'Stone' is shaded green.
The *5" cap* refers to one of the four 'capping neckings' mentioned by Wheble
as having been *levelled by pieces by tile, flint &c.*
These *caps* are now supported by the four 19th c. pillars.
Drawing ©J. Mullaney

In late 1834, immediately on acquiring the site, Wheble began his excavations, and his workmen soon uncovered the stone.

Wheble was of the opinion that the Stone had been carefully buried at its point of discovery: that it had not fallen there by accident. His reasons were based on the way the stone had been buried.

He tells us that *it was found to be in an erect position, levelled and squared in a line, taken East and West, down the centre of the choir,* and that *it rested upon the third or undermost layer of grouting, having pieces of tile, flint &c. (to obtain the level) placed beneath the four capping neckings.*

Wheble was at pains to report that the Stone had been carefully laid on a 2 inch layer of what he terms a *compost* consisting of *earth, argillaceous matter and fine calcareous particles.* which had been laid over the lowest layer of the *grouting*. The care with which it had been treated was underscored by the fact that *pieces of tile, flint etc.* had been *placed beneath each of the four capping neckings* to obtain *the level*. In short, its burial had all the hallmarks of a ceremonial interment.

In describing the top of the *abacus*, as it appeared from above, Wheble wrote: *In the centre of the flat surface of the abacus a mortice hole of 6 inches square penetrates downwards to the bottom, but two angles of the hole, to the depth of 2½ inches, have been rudely rounded off, thus affording some 11 by 9 inches of space there.*

Much of this is still visible. However, when the Stone was converted into a font, at the time of the opening of St James' in 1840, the centre was gouged out and this feature has vanished. Wheble described the hole as a mortice. He does not suggest what its companion piece, which presumably had a tenon, might have been. Nor does he say how deep this hole was. He merely states that it *penetrated downwards to the bottom.* This latter was 6 inches square, with two of the top edges being bevelled, *rudely rounded off* to *a depth of 2½ inches.* He then says that this gave an opening at the top of the hole of 11 by 9 inches. This would indicate that all four sides had been bevelled to the approximate depth he mentions, creating an oblong opening narrowing down to the square aperture.

Cut away section of the centre of the Stone at the time of its discovery.

2½ " deep bevelled section

6" sqr hole to an unspecified depth

Overhead image of the Stone at the time of its discovery

9"

11"

6" sqr

27"

27"

Drawings © John Mullaney

Wheble's letter tells us that when the Stone was first discovered it was richly painted, for he writes: *it was delightful to behold the freshness of the ancient colours,- black, white and red, in many of the intricacies of the tracery.* He concludes the article by saying that it is a treasure, *though no longer bearing its primitive magnificence of decoration.*

In April 1835, just two months after Wheble's article appeared in the *Reading Mercury,* the same paper printed a report on the Stone, speculating as to its provenance and use.

Wheble had already initiated the debate as to its origins and purpose. Clearly, news of its discovery had excited interest, not just in Reading but further afield. Mr Britton of London was quoted as saying it was unique. This is probably John Britton, the renowned antiquary, author of many books concerning the history of architecture. One of these, the *Architectural Antiquities of Normandy,* was illustrated by Pugin. An earlier book by Britton, about the architecture of Britain, had acknowledged Sir Henry Englefield who first surveyed the abbey in the late 18th century.

Other authorities, writing from as far afield as France, had offered various opinions as to the Stone's origins and purpose. Whereas Britton believed that the Stone was *the capital from a cluster of columns,* a certain Baron T. said it was in the *Romane* style, *called 'Saxon' in England,* and that such *clusters of columns are rare* and to be *found in Dol, Brittany.* He dated the Stone to the 10th, or very early 11th century.

Reading Abbey - A pilgrim church

The baron commented on the fact that the central block is square. Generally, he noted, these are circular. He went on to say: *were it a specimen of the architecture of the middle ages in the south of Europe, there would be nothing extraordinary in the middle block being square.* The writer of the *Mercury* article claims that this leads us to proposing that the Stone takes us *back to the times of St. Ethelwold, Bishop of Winchester, and famed for his talents in sacred architecture, of Queen Elfrida, and the ravages of the Danes under Sweyn.*

Without naming the source, the newspaper says that another gentleman from London had suggested that the Stone *was originally used as the top of a pedestal on which the shrine of some relic, or an image, was placed; and the round holes in the abacus were intended to hold branches for lamps.*

The Stone's Material Composition

When starting this research, I was unable to find evidence that any scientific study had been made regarding the petrology of the Reading Abbey Stone. Some comments came from Keyser and Baxter.[3] It would appear that Keyser and other members of *Reading Society of Antiquaries* believed that it was made from Caen stone, and all describe it as oolitic limestone.

In late 2014 Dr Kevin Hayward made an examination of the Stone. This revealed that the Reading Abbey Stone was indeed made from a single block of oolitic limestone and that the quarry could be identified as Taynton.

Dr Hayward also noted that the style of carving bears remarkable similarities to that found at Lewes Priory, although the stone type there is Marquise Oolite from the Boulogne region of France. It should be noted that when Henry I founded Reading Abbey, the first monks came from the Cluniac Benedictine monastery at Lewes.

The carved stonework in the Museum's collection from Reading Abbey was examined by Bernard Worssam in 1995 and 1996, and his identifications are recorded in the relevant entries of Reading Museum's database. He noted that some of these are made of Caen stone. These include voussoirs, a few springers and most of the capitals. Others, including a few capitals, most of the springers and some voussoirs, were identified as Taynton stone.

Although the Reading Abbey Stone is made from a single block, it consists of three sections. Moreover, there have been changes, both to its top and to its base, made by the addition of the wooden cover and the pillars, or shafts, on which it stands. These are consequent upon its 19th century conversion into a font.

The topmost section consists of the 27" square (approx.) slab with decorated sides. Next comes the plain fillet, followed by the ornate lower part with its four rounded caps, and the central piece or block. Baxter describes these as *four corner capitals, on the four recesses between the capitals, and the deep, square impost block.* The four corner capitals, or caps, are rounded at their bases.

Before we examine the Stone as a whole we shall consider its three main sections and what commentators have said about them.

The Upper Part of the Stone

Wheble wrote that *the upper member, or abacus, forms a square of 27 inches, the surface of which is flat and unwrought. Each side of the abacus is 5½ in. and a deeply-cut, ornamented, chain-like pattern runs continuously along the four sides.*

The four holes, commented on by Wheble, and in the 1835 *Reading Mercury* article, have received no further attention that I have been able to find, apart from the comment by the anonymous gentleman from London. And yet they offer another level of uncertainly as to the origins and purpose of the Stone. It may be that they even present an explanation of its original placement and function

The Fillet

The fillet is the undecorated section just below the abacus and above the decorated 'capitals'. Wheble was the first to apply the term to this part of the Stone when he described this section as a *species of fillet.* Apart from Wheble's original description, this feature has been ignored by the commentators. It is undecorated and comparatively smooth.

.

The Lower Section

This is by far the most ornate part of the Stone.
Intricate carvings cover two sides of this sub-section, and all four sides of the central block.

Wheble's measurements differ slightly from those by Baxter in the 'Corpus of Romanesque Architecture'. However, because of the unevenness resulting from the carvings, when I made the same measurements, I found that both sets were within what may be considered a reasonable margin of error.

The central section is described by Baxter as follows: *The impost block is of simple square design but carved on all four faces with an overall design of interlacing foliage scrolls enclosing oval fields filled with furled leaves..*

In his original report, Wheble noted that *two sides have unfortunately suffered from a rather cautious and workmanlike mutilation.* This indicates that there was no decoration on these two sides when the Stone was uncovered. It was on these two empty spaces that Wheble felt free to fix two brasses commemorating the stone's discovery and the founding of the abbey. These are still in place at the time of writing.

The part of the stone covered by the brasses has never been subjected to any critical analysis. Wheble states that the presumed carvings had already been removed or mutilated before his discovery. Closer examination of the areas where the brasses are fixed might indicate that there may have been carvings present.

Theories about the Origins and Purpose of the Stone

Wheble considered the top section of the Stone to be an abacus: the top section of a pillar capital.

However, in spite of using the term *abacus,* he was clearly unsure about the Stone's origins and purpose. He appears to question the possibility of it being the top of a capital but muses on what other purpose it could have served. In his original letter, he writes: I *am not aware, Mr. Editor, that any similar block, whether of stone or of wood, ornamented or unadorned, could have been serviceable to the forms of catholic worship in the situation where this stone was discovered.* However he goes on to speculate: *was it adapted to support a sarcophagus, or rather a slab on which reposed some recumbent figure? Could it have been the basement for a Holy Rood or Cross? Or for a font? Or a chaunter's desk? Was it, in its primordial state of splendour, a portion of, and an ornament to, the monastery said to have preceded that erected by Henry?*

So, what have been the theories as to its original purpose?

1. A Pillar Capital

Today this is the most commonly accepted theory as to its origins and purpose.

This photograph is from the cloister in the monastery founded by the Benedictines in Santillana del Mar, in Cantabria, northern Spain. This was one of a series of monasteries on the pilgrimage *camino*, or 'way', to Santiago de Compostela, and is contemporaneous with the early days of Reading Abbey. The picture shows how the Reading Abbey Stone capital may have looked if it was the capital of a cluster of pillars in a cloister. However, there is no central column within the quadripartite structure of the Santillana pillars. Another difference is that the abacus is undecorated, and moreover far less pronounced than we see in the Reading Stone.

2. An Altar or Shrine Base

We saw that, from the moment of its discovery, there was speculation that the Stone may have served a different function from the common opinion that it was a capital. Could it indeed have been an altar or a base on which to place a feretory or some other sacred object? Was the six by six inch hole part of a tenon and mortice joint? Is it reasonable to speculate that the Reading Abbey Stone may have been such an 'altar', and that the central hole was a slot for the feretory containing the hand of St James which was placed there on special occasions, such as his feast-day on July 25th? A similar explanation would allow for some other object, such as a holy rood, as suggested by one of the early commentators, to be placed in the hole. Perhaps various objects of veneration were positioned there at different times, according to whichever feast was being celebrated on a particular day.

Such a theory would fit in with the explanation given by one of the 1835 correspondents regarding the purpose of the holes. *One gentleman in London, is of opinion that "it was originally used as the top of a pedestal on which the shrine of some relic, or an image, was placed; and the round holes in the abacus were intended to hold branches for lamps".* This latter conjecture would bring into play all the four holes.

3. A Lectern or Chanter's Desk

As late as 1923, the possibility that the Stone was not a capital appeared in the *Victoria County History*. This makes a comparison with the famous stone lectern in Crowle. The footnote in the VCH referring to the church of St John the Baptist, Crowle, mentions *a remarkable marble lectern of the late 12th century, locally said to have come from Pershore Abbey at the time of the Dissolution.*

The Victoria and Albert Museum has another example of a lectern resting on a stone plinth. Their website says:

This 12th-century 'Wenlock Marble' lectern is from Much Wenlock Priory in Shropshire, being found in the ruins of that establishment. It would have stood on top of a column or pillar, at the top of which was a square capital, neither of which have survived. Much Wenlock Priory was a Cluniac establishment (founded 1079 and 1082), built on the site of an earlier church founded in 680 by Merewalh, King of the Magonsaete, whose daughter was canonized. St. Milburga was buried here. Northern European lecterns were usually made of wood or metal. This is one of only three 12th century surviving lecterns in England made from stone that came from Shadwell Quarry near Wenlock. All are decorated with foliage and animal heads. Though without specific iconography to indicate its location, it probably sat near the High Altar to support liturgical books rather than in the Refectory where monks were read to during meals.

There are several points in this account which have particular relevance to the Stone. Firstly, the Wenlock stone lectern would have stood on a stone pillar on top of which there was a square capital. Secondly, it came from a *Cluniac establishment*. Thirdly, stone lecterns were less common in northern Europe. Fourthly, the lectern would most probably have been placed in front of the high altar. There are, however, also differences such as the nature of the carvings, which are more ornate than those on the Reading Stone.

Of special interest is that, in all these cases, it is clear that the 'lectern' section fitted onto, or into, a 'capital'. It would appear that in some cases the capital had a mortice which accommodated a tenon joint. This would certainly account for the hole at the top of the Stone. The size of the Crowle lectern is comparable with that of the Reading Stone. The Reading Stone is 26 x 26", approximately, and that at Crowle is just over 25 x 25". The recess (top opening) at Reading is 11 x 9", that at Crowle is 11 x 11".

Analysis of the theories regarding the carvings on the Stone

The carvings on the Reading Stone are in low-relief. Although one might expect a certain consensus among expert opinion, the transition periods between Saxon, Saxon-Norman and Norman-Romanesque are difficult to differentiate. Consequently, an element of subjectivity divides opinion about the stylistic character of the carvings.

We are left with the apparent distinction between the design on the upper part (abacus), and lower segments. The following drawings trace the outline of the design of the abacus.

  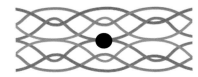

Close examination of the pattern shows that it consists of two parts; an upper and a lower. and that the lower reflects the upper. The first drawing, on the left, is of the upper half only. The black dot shows the hole in the side of the abacus. It will be seen that the lines are not plaited and can only be said partly to interlace: they do not strictly speaking interweave one with the other.[4]

The second illustration, on the right, demonstrates how the lower section is merely a mirror image of the upper part. Although the lines touch, they are in fact distinct, though not separated, at these points.

Reading Abbey - A pilgrim church

The simplicity of the Stone's 'interlacing' contrasts with the more complicated interwoven Saxon and Viking patterns. It has been suggested that as the abacus carvings represent a continuous unbroken pattern all round the Stone, they are distinct in style, as well as methodology, from those of the lower section.

The patterns on each of the parts of the lower section are totally distinct one from the other. True, there is a cohesive balance of character, but there is no evidence of a 'story', or the development of a theme. Because there is much more wear and tear on the abacus than on the lower section, it is also impossible to work out if any of the infill carvings are representative of anything or if they are merely patterns.

To a great extent, it is for the informed viewer to decide whether the top and bottom carvings are of a similar style. It is sufficient to point out that the lower carvings are more intricate, with complicated differentiated patterns and fine beading, or pearling, similar to, though not the same as, those on the Keyser and Zarnecki capitals in Reading Museum. The abacus carvings, though intricate, are much simpler and repetitive, appearing as they do on all four sides.

It should be noted that the chasings in the top carvings are also simpler than those in the lower section. This may have been a matter of style, chosen by the mason. Moreover, there is no pearling on the upper segment of the Stone.

In the lower section we find what Dr Baxter identifies as the Byzantine blossom. Much has been made of this motif. Several authorities have traced it to an earlier period than post-Conquest, 12th century, England. It is this that I shall examine next.

One of the most celebrated pieces of Saxon carving is on the shaft of the East Stour Cross, which several authorities such as Cramp, Kendrick and Drinkwater, among others, all date to the late Saxon period. Cramp talks of the exotic ribbed *acanthus type* flowers *or Byzantine blossoms* which may even have their origins in Islamic designs, such as seen in the cedar of Lebanon panels in the el-Aqsa mosque in Jerusalem. Drinkwater says that *the date of the East Stour shaft cannot be ascertained with complete accuracy, but it would seem reasonable to attribute the work to the period of the latest ornament found on the stone,* namely, *the palmette or Byzantine blossom.*

Whatever its origins, various versions of the Blossom, or palmette, motif were in use well before the Romanesque period. As Drinkwater says, the importance of the East Stour cross shaft *lies in the variety of its ornament.*

As with the case of the East Stour shaft, each side of the Reading Abbey Stone contains a distinct pattern. There is, however, a unifying theme of variations of the palmette motif. This occurs, for instance, on the impost block, as well as on the outermost sides along with interlacing work.

CONCLUSION

Several alternative theories have been given for the Stone's carvings. It could be that the upper and lower carvings date to different periods and so were carved by different masons.

Alternatively, they may have been executed at the same time but in different styles, possibly because different masons with different skills were at work. Thirdly, it is possible that the Stone, or part of it, was carved around the time the 1121 abbey was founded, but using motifs recalling an earlier era.

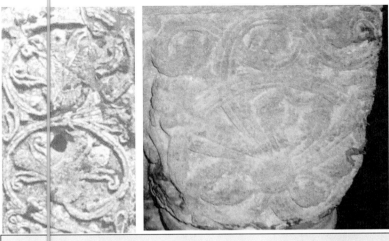

Left: East Stour shaft showing the palmettes or Byzantine Blossom motif. Right: Reading Abbey Stone and the Byzantine Blossom

Perhaps a companion stone, or even parts of one, carved from the same material and with similar designs, may be found either in the Abbey or indisputably connected with it. Some questions, such as why the Stone came to be interred in such a singular way, may remain unanswered, but such a discovery may help unravel one the Abbey's abiding puzzles.

At the time of writing, set into the wall separating the school playground from the passage between Abbots Walk and the Forbury Road, there is a single block of Taynton stone with what appears to be the same pattern as on the abacus. This is so weathered that the pattern is indistinct, but its existence does add to the mystery of the Reading Abbey Stone.

NOTES

1.   For a fuller account of the contents of this chapter see *The Reading Abbey Stone,* Mullaney, J.

2.   *Reading Mercury* 20th April, 1835

3.   *The Royal Abbey of Reading,* Baxter, R.

4.   *Grammar of Anglo-Saxon Ornament* (in *Corpus of Anglo-Saxon Sculpture*) page xxviii ff, Cramp R.

CHAPTER 10

THE STONE OF THE 'CORONATION OF THE VIRGIN'

Photo © Chris Widdows

ONE OF THE MOST IMPORTANT PIECES OF MEDIEVAL SCULPTURE IN ENGLAND

It is no exaggeration to say that this is one of the most important pieces of medieval sculpture in England. Along with some of the other stones now in the Museum, it was discovered in 1949 by the eminent art historian, George Zarnecki, at Barn Acre Cottage, near Borough Marsh Farm, on the opposite bank of the Thames to Shiplake. In the 1990s Bernard Worssam, confirmed that it is carved from Caen stone.

Most of the Museum's stones that were not unearthed by Zarnecki in 1949 came from Holme Park, Sonning, and from Borough Marsh, Shiplake. They were discovered by Charles Keyser just before the 1914 -18 war. Keyser was told at the time that his original finds at Holme Park had been brought from Borough Marsh. Consequently, he made further excavations in that area and uncovered more stones. This was not quite the same location as Zarnecki's later finds; nevertheless it is generally assumed that there is a connection between the two groupings. Although some have high quality carvings, they do not feature explicit representations of important religious dogma, such as that portrayed on the stone of the Coronation of the Virgin.

I began by giving a name to the sculpture. It is commonly known as such. However, I am making an assumption: that it is indeed a representation of the Coronation of the Virgin Mary. It is a claim disputed by some.

Before examining the evidence for this attribution, I should say that the fact that the stone has figures, whoever, or whatever, they represent, itself makes it one of the most significant of the Reading Abbey stones. This leads to the next and most important part of my researches: namely to show how the art and architecture of the abbey were intrinsically related to its purpose.

I said, at the start, that the abbey, including its church, was built with specific purposes in mind. Primarily, these were to fulfil the Cluniac interpretation of St Benedict's rule: firstly that the monks' duty was to observe a life of prayer, the *Opus Dei,* and secondly to care for the traveller, the pilgrim, and the needy. The design of the building was determined by these two injunctions. What I have described so far has been a very mundane account of the architecture and individual stones. The rest of the book will look at the more spiritual aspects of the abbey.

There is no better place to start than an examination of this stone. I hope to convince the reader that it is indeed a representation of the doctrine of the crowning of Mary, the mother of Jesus, as 'Queen of Heaven'.

As mentioned, the abbey, in the Foundation Charter, was dedicated to Mary and the apostle John the Evangelist. Later, having acquired the Hand of St James, it also became famous as the pilgrim church of St James.

Fig 1, The Quenington carving over
the south door

THE STONE'S ICONOGRAPHY

I am beginning with another sculpture: at St Swithin's church, Quenington, Gloucestershire (fig 1). The carving, a tympanum over the south door of the church, depicts 'Mary, Mother of God', enthroned with her son, Jesus Christ, who is placing the crown on her head. The apparent simplicity of the image belies a much more complicated theological and artistic provenance.

The tympanum most probably dates from the early to mid 12th century, making it the oldest known sculpture of this religious theme in Europe.

If the Reading stone (fig 2), does indeed show the same image, this would make it one of international significance. It too would be one of the first carvings, if not the very first in all Europe should it pre-date Quenington, to illustrate this doctrine.

But does it indeed show the same figures? The Quenington carving is complete, whereas that at Reading is a part of a pillar capital, which has lost most of its detail.

What we see in Reading is a seated female figure. We can make out an outstretched arm, an elbow with the upper arm raised so as to reach over the head of the female figure. In the Quenington carving, the arm belongs to a seated male figure who is holding a crown over the head of the female figure.

The supposition is that the same story is being told in both carvings. This viewpoint is reinforced by the fact that both female figures are holding something to their breasts. One theory is that this is a dove, the symbol of the Holy Spirit, by which the Virgin Mary conceived Jesus and which is shown in scenes of the Annunciation.

Fig 2

HISTORICAL BACKGROUND TO THE ICONOGRAPHY

Though rare in sculpture, the iconography depicts a recurring and developing theme in the Christian church from at least the 6th century. The place of Mary in the Christian story of 'salvation history' has been debated down the centuries, and art has always been used to convey current thinking and teaching.

The belief in the role of the Virgin as the Mother of God, (*the one who gives birth to God* - the Θεοτόκος 'theotokos' or 'deipara'), appears in some of the earliest Christian writings and associated art works. One very early depiction, dating to the 6th century, is in the church of Santa Maria Antiqua, Rome.

The tradition that when Mary died, her soul, with her body, was taken to heaven, can also be found in early 6th to 8th century texts, such as in the account of St John the Theologian. By the 10th to 11th centuries, this dogma was deeply embedded in Catholic teaching in the west. In the eastern Orthodox church, there existed the tradition of the 'Dormition', (*Koimisis* - Κοίμησης) or falling asleep. This stated that Mary's soul was raised to heaven, and after three days her body was also taken up. The debate centred on two issues: firstly, whether Mary died, and secondly, if so, whether her body was also taken to heaven. An alternative, but minority, narrative was that she did not die but was taken straight to heaven.

Returning to the Stone: although discovered elsewhere, it is generally believed that it came from Reading Abbey. Its likely date, its subject matter, and the fact that it is made of such prestigious material, all point to it coming from a very high status building. Reading Abbey is therefore an obvious choice.

Santa Maria Antiqua, Rome.
6th century

THE STONE'S PLACE IN 12TH CENTURY RELIGIOUS PRACTICE AND BELIEF

As we have seen, the stone of the 'Coronation' was most probably carved in the early to mid 12th century, at the time when Henry I founded the monastery in Reading Abbey. We know that Henry had close connections with the Benedictine monks at Cluny, in Burgundy. Indeed, he was one of their major benefactors, and Cluniac Benedictine monks were the founders of Reading Abbey. The stylistic evidence from its architectural remains would indicate that he engaged Norman craftsmen, though it is possible that local Saxon masons were also employed.

Santa Maria in Trastevere, Rome.

mid 12th c. mosaic

of the crowned Virgin

It was expensive to ferry Caen stone across the channel. This contrasted with the cheaper and more easily transportable stone from the Taynton quarry, near Oxford. Much of this was used in building Reading Abbey. However, the use of Caen stone for the 'Coronation Stone', shows the prestige of the carving. Moreover, the fact it was used for this image in particular, reinforces its importance in the minds of those who made it, and looked upon it.

At the time the abbey was being built, a teaching closely associated with that of the Coronation of the Virgin, that of the 'Immaculate Conception', was being hotly debated across Christendom - not least in England. The dogma of the 'Immaculate Conception' is often misunderstood outside the Catholic world. This states that Mary was conceived naturally, with a human mother and father, in a normal biological way, but without the inherited guilt associated with the first (original) sin of Adam and Eve. It was believed that Mary, as the future mother of 'the Saviour', was not subject to the penalties of this sin, one of which was considered by some to be death and the decomposition of the body. Hence, the belief grew that either Mary did not die or, if she did, then her incorrupt body was taken to heaven, where she was crowned by her son. It is notable that Hugh, the first Abbot of Reading and a Cluniac Benedictine, observed the feast of the Immaculate Conception on December 8th every year, at Henry's request. In contrast, Roger, bishop of Salisbury, Henry's friend and chancellor, did not observe this feast at Sarum.

'ECCLESIA' or 'THE CORONATION OF THE VIRGIN'

'MATER ECCLESIA' or 'MATER ECCLESIAE' ('Mother Church' or 'Mother of the Church')

There has been some debate as to whether the Reading stone and that at Quenington represent 'The Church' (*Ecclesia*), rather than the Coronation of the Virgin. As far as I can find, those images representing 'Ecclesia' show the Christ figure embracing the seated female figure, rather than holding out a hand and placing a crown on her head. It is, of course, more than likely that the two concepts were interlinked. Mary was considered 'Mother of God' and 'Queen of Heaven', and was also identified with being the 'Mother of the Church', *(Mater Ecclesiae)*.

One early representation of *Ecclesia,* the Church herself, is from the time of Desiderius (c 1026 –1087), the great reforming abbot of Montecassino, later Pope Victor III. Figure 1 is from one of the *Exultet Rolls.* The text is lavishly illustrated, and was designed for the Easter Vigil service and the liturgy centred around the Paschal Candle. The famous hymn, the *Exultet* ('Let the hosts of heaven rejoice'), which initiates the Easter ceremonies, contains the words *gaudeat et tellus* ('let also earth rejoice'). Tellus was the Roman goddess of the earth, the counterpart of the Greek 'Gaia', and is used here to symbolise Earth as opposed to Heaven. She is shown at the top of the picture (fig 1) suckling a cow and a serpent.

Fig. 1

Fig. 2

In figure 2, the 'Church', *Ecclesia,* is personified as a woman, as in figure 1, holding up the pillars of the church, flanked on one side by clerics and on the other by the laity. Over her head are the words *mater eccťa (mater ecclesia –* 'mother church') .

By the 13th century the symbolism of *Mater Ecclesia* was well established and was appearing in carvings and stained glass. The imagery in the stained glass window (fig 3), shows a female figure holding a cup into which flows the blood of the dying Jesus, demonstrating the spiritual and physical unity of Christ with His Church.

The female figure is not Mary, Christ's mother, the female figure usually depcited at the foot of the cross, but it is that of *Ecclesia*. On the other side is another female figure. This is *Synagoga*, representing the Jewish nation. She is blindfolded, and often portrayed with the broken tablets of Moses or, as here, a broken staff. The blindfold demonstrates her rejection of Christ. The broken tablets could also be a reference to the 'Old Law' of the Old Testament, which had been replaced by the 'New Law' of Christ's kingdom.

As ever, there are levels and layers of symbolism which were familiar to the people of the Middle Ages, who would have heard sermons on these themes throughout their lives.

Fig 3

Fig 1

Ecclesia and Synagoga are not always shown at the foot of the cross. A frequent depiction, as at Marburg, (early 13th century), merely depicts the characterisation of the two figures. The viewer was clearly expected to understand the story and message behind the images (fig 1).

ANOMALOUS DEPICTIONS.

When considering such representations, there is sometimes disagreement about whether the female figure seated beside Christ in Glory is his mother Mary, and so *Mater Ecclesiae* (Mother of the Church) or *Mater Ecclesia* (Mother Church), that is the figure of Ecclesia.

As I have pointed out, it would appear that, where depictions of the female figure show Christ placing a crown on her head, this is referencing Mary, His mother, being crowned Queen of Heaven by Christ. The words of several contemporary hymns such as *Regina Coeli* and *Salve Regina* bear out this theory.

However there are apparently some ambiguous illustrations, such as that shown earlier in the church of Santa Maria in Trastevere (page 168). Here Christ is seated alongside a crowned female figure. It has been suggested that this is *Ecclesia* and not Mary.

One of the inscriptions in the mosaic, from the *Song of Songs,* reads "his left arm will be under my head and his right arm will embrace me" (*Leva eius sub capite meo et dextera illius amplesabitur me,* Song of Songs 2:6, 8:3). The other two texts refer to Mary. The Old Testament prophets Isaiah and Ezekiel foretold the coming of the Christ, and one of these prophecies appears on a scroll: "Behold a virgin shall conceive and a bear a son" (*Ecce virgo concipiet et pariet filium,* Isaiah 7:14).

I leave it to the reader to decide if the mosaic in Rome refers to Mary or Ecclesia.

THE CORONATION STONE AS A TREASURE FOR THE 21ST CENTURY

Reading is fortunate to have such a rare sculpted depiction of this important religious theme, possibly one of only two in England dating to the mid 11th century.

If we recall that, in the Foundation Charter, Reading Abbey was dedicated to the Mother of God and ever Virgin Mary, *(monasterium in honore et nomine dei gentricis semperque virginis Mariae et beati Iohannis evangeliste),* it is easy to see why such an image should be associated with the monastery.

Indeed it has been suggested, by several art historians, that it is very likely that the tympanum over the great west door would have been a representation of Mary, and there would have been no better carving than that showing her being crowned Queen of Heaven. It has also been suggested that this pillar capital could have come from the cloister, and that a similar carving to that found at Quenington may have stood over the entrance to the chapter house.

It should be said that figurative carvings were intended to recall to mind some spiritual aspect of the monks' life as they moved around the monastery. Seeing a particular representation, a monk would have silently said an appropriate prayer, contemplating the meaning of the image in front of him. This would have become second nature throughout his monastic life.

Whether originally from the abbey or not, and even if we leave aside the religious element, when we look upon this stone we are viewing a most beautiful work of sculpture, which holds a special place in the history of art in England.

NOTE

1. In pictures of the *Annunciation,* the dove, representing the Holy Spirit, is often shown hovering over Mary's head, with its beak directed towards her ear. This almost universal representation has been linked with the belief that, as St Augustine says, "God spoke through his angel and the Virgin conceived through her ear". *Deus per angelum loquebatur et Virgo per aurem impregnabatur*, St. Augustine *(Sermo de Tempore, xxii.)*. The turtle-dove is a frequently used symbol of Christian constancy and devotion.

The turtle-dove is often referred to in poetry as a symbol of fidelity; thus Gottfried von Strasburg (died c.1210) calls the Virgin Mary a turtle-dove in faithfulness. (One excellent analysis is the MA thesis about the 'Physiologus', by Mary Allyson Armistead.

CHAPTER 11

THE COMMEMORATION SERVICE FOR HENRY I

A document, concerning the ceremonial surrounding the annual commemoration of Henry's death on the 1st December 1135, is to be found at the end of a 13th century manuscript of the *Summa de Dictamine* or *Summa Dictaminis* by Guido Fava. I shall be referring to this as the *Reading manuscript (Reading ms.)*.

Originally from Westminster Abbey, and now in the British Library, (Additional Ms 8167, fo. 200r-v), the account gives instructions on procedure during the two days of commemoration, that is on the eve, or vigil, and the day itself, namely the 31st November and the 1st December.

That it was a solemn commemoration, liturgically speaking, is demonstrated by the fact that the *Office of the Dead* was sung with full ritual. But it was also a time of celebration, with special feasting for both the monks and for 'thirteen poor people' who were to be fed in the *aula* (hall) of the Abbey.

The manuscript is not a detailed liturgical account of every part of the Masses, and of the Divine Office, to be said to commemorate Henry's death. It is rather a list of instructions written, most probably, to clarify the rituals, where there was room for alternatives and doubt. The Latin, and its English translation, are from Professor Brian Kemp's book *Reading Abbey Records, a new miscellany*. In this chapter the English translation appears first, followed by the Latin as transcribed from the manuscript by Kemp. This allows us to see the actual words used by the medieval writer, who must surely have been a monk of the community. Kemp gives us a verbatim translation with some explanatory footnotes. As ever in any translation, especially one which reaches back over several hundred years, there are difficulties in discerning the original intention of the writer.

Throughout this chapter I show carvings from the church of St Lazarus, Autun, in Burgundy, near Cluny. Building started almost exactly at the same time as at Reading. The stone carvings are attributed to Its most famous sculptor, Gislebertus, and his school.

The main building material is local sandstone. As this is not suitable for carving, the great west door tympanum and the pillar capitals of the main apse are made of hard whitish limestone as found near Tournus, Chalon and Beaune. The other capitals are all made from a different thick-grained oolitic limestone, like that found at Charolais.

The illustrations are from *Gislebertus Sculptor of Autun* by Denis Grivot and George Zarnecki.

I offer some explanations, but I would encourage readers to look deeper for themselves, maybe listen to some of the chants online and discover the sounds of the liturgies. I hope that listening to the beauty of medieval Latin, expressed through the chant, will give some idea of what it would have been like to have been in Reading Abbey in the 13th century.

I have divided the text into sections. These correspond to where it would appear that the medieval author moves from one ceremony, or part thereof, to another. I have then written a commentary about each section. These comments analyse the text where I consider it needs clarification. I also place the original work into a wider context, to explain some of the references which may not be immediately apparent to someone unfamiliar with medieval liturgical practices, especially those associated with the monastery of Cluny. I have made particular reference to this aspect of Benedictine liturgy, because Reading Abbey had been founded by Cluniacs and continued to follow many of its customs.

By the time the *Reading manuscript* was written, in the mid 13th century, Reading Abbey was most certainly an independent monastery. However, many contemporary documents refer to it as having Cluniac influences. From what we read in the manuscript, this was true of the liturgy. It would suggest that Reading still followed much of the Cluniac concept of monastic spirituality, with firstly its concentration on the paramount importance of the *Opus Dei,* the daily prayer life of the monastery with its special devotion to the *Officium mortuorum,* and secondly the duty of care for the poor and the traveller.

Cluniac monk of the 12th century

Wikimedia commons https://
commons.wikimedia.org/wiki/
File:Cluniac_monk.jpg

It has been argued, by such as Werckmeister, that the iconography of the north portal is based on the Office of the Dead, and was part of a penitential ritual. The Office of the Dead incorporates the themes of penance and forgiveness shown on the west portal at Autun, and also makes allusions to Lazarus and the Last Judgment. As this chapter shows, the Office of the Dead was to Henry's commemoration services

Several early monastic treatises show that penitential rituals existed in the tenth century. For instance, one describes how: "On Ash Wednesday, those sinners ready to undergo public penance, were to present themselves in front of the church, clad in sackcloth and barefoot, prostrate themselves before the bishop, and proclaim their guilt." After their penance, the bishop conducted them into the church and they were then told that, as Adam was expelled from Paradise, so they, too, were ejected from the church because of their sins. Only after completing their penance would they be re-admitted.

ANALYSIS

SECTION 1

"What particularly is done in the Abbey of Reading for the soul of king Henry the founder of that place.

Concerning the anniversary of King Henry, our founder, the things that are to be performed on the two days at his commemoration and absolution. All ought to be present who in any way can be, and at 'Verba mea' after chapter in the choir"

[Q]uod specialitatis fit in abbatia Radingie pro anima regis Henrici fundatoris illius loci.

[D]e anniversario Regis Henrici fundatoris nostri ad cuius recitationem et absolucionem que utroque die facienda est. Omnes adesse debent qui aliquo modo possunt et ad 'Verba mea' post capitulum in choro.

COMMENT

Absolucionem: Accusative singular of *absolutio*. The normal spelling in later times is with a 't' rather then a 'c', which was used at the time of this work.

The term 'absolution' refers to the belief that prayers for the dead are able to cleanse the soul of any remaining sin and so guarantee salvation from eternal damnation. This is a corollary to the doctrine of purgatory, which had become well defined by the 13th century, but which had its roots in early Christianity, as the works of such as Ambrose, Augustine and Peter Chrysogonus demonstrate.

The prominent role of the Office of the Dead (*Officium mortuorum*) in Cluniac monasteries underpinned this core aspect of the spiritual life of the monastery, its Hours, (Matins, Lauds and Vespers), being said after the Office of the Day. It would appear that Reading continued this Cluniac tradition.

The Last Judgement. The tympanum of the west doorway. The Archangel Michael, on the left, weighs a soul, as a devil attempts to tilt the balance in his favour, and the Archangel Raphael, bottom right, sounds the trumpet of doom.

Recitationem: Accusative singular of *recitatio*.

This refers to the recitation of the psalms. It does not mean that there was some sort of sermon, eulogy or 'celebration' of Henry's life. Such a concept would have been unthinkable to the monks as part of the *Opus Dei.* Another part of speech, a verb, of the same word, *recitatio,* is used in the next section.

Verba mea

Kemp explains in a footnote that this is an 'Introit' to a Mass. There were many different 'entrance prayers', or 'introits', particular to differing Masses, depending on the time of year or special feast day. These were part of the 'proper' of the Mass: those prayers specific, or *proper,* to certain feasts, as opposed to the *Ordinary of the Mass,* which contained those sections that did not change, such as the *Kyrie* and *Agnus Dei. The Reading manuscript* only mentions the *Verba mea* and not the Mass said on that day. However, several extant 10th and 11th century manuscripts show that Ps 5, *Verba mea,* was used as the introit on the Saturday immediately preceding mid-Lent, or *Laetare,* Sunday. Although the service for Henry was not mid-Lent, but at the end of November and beginning of December, it would have been an appropriate Mass to say for the 'salvation of the King's soul', as instructed in the Foundation Charter

Originally the introit was considered to be an antiphon, (a verse before the main psalm - *Antiphona ad introitum* or 'Entrance antiphon'), rather than the opening prayer of the Mass. Manuscripts, dating to the 10th and 11th centuries, such as at St Gall, mark it with an 'A', for 'antiphon'. In the case of this *Verba mea,* we may be looking at an introit commonly used for a 'Mass of the Dead' since the liturgy concerns the 'absolution of King Henry'.

This particular introit was also considered appropriate for a funeral Mass as it is one of the 'dirge' psalms. These are so called because of the use of the Latin word *dirigere* meaning 'to lead': a word which appears, in one form or another, in these psalms. The word refers to God's grace and action in 'leading' the dying person through the attacks of evil spirits whilst the person lies dying. The 'dirge', or the act of leading and protection from the wiles of the devil, may be attributed to the intervention of a saint, or an angel or even of the Virgin Mary.

The soul, at the moment of death, is brought into the 'bosom of Abraham'. The image of Abraham's bosom is used in the writings and sculptures that would have familiar to the monks at Reading. In some cases, as in the works of Peter Chrysogonus, the 'Bosom of Abraham, is not necessarily 'Heaven', but a place that the 'just' go to until the Last Judgement, when they are finally admitted to Paradise.

Reading Abbey - A pilgrim church

Dives and Lazarus.
Capital from the doorway of the
north transept.
Abraham is holding Lazarus in his bosom.

In the Gospel of Luke (16:19–31), we encounter this concept in the parable of Dives, the rich man, and Lazarus, the beggar. Lazarus is taken into the bosom (*kolpos - κόλπος*) of Abraham, whilst Dives is condemned to Hades. The sculpture by Gislebertus. on the left capital of the north doorway at Autun, depicts Lazarus in the lap, or bosom, of Abraham. The terms *kolpos* in Greek, and *bosom* in English, are both highly charged words with ambivalent connotations. Jerome's vulgate uses the words, *sinus* ('bosom', 'lap'). Whatever the theological niceties of these words, there can be no doubt that the monks of Reading would have been very familiar with this story and its implications when considering the life of Henry I.

The *dirige* psalms all share this theme. Another example is v.9 of Psalm 5 which reads *Domine deduc me in iustitia tua propter insidiatores meos, dirige ante faciem meam viam tuam* ("Conduct me, O Lord, in your justice: because of my enemies, direct my way in your sight"). The Cluniac death rituals mention the dangers of death-bed temptations, especially despair, and the need for God's directing grace through this difficult time, this final journey, the ultimate pilgrimage. Psalm 5 was considered relevant for use at Henry's Mass as it was also associated with a life of prayer, both public and private.

An alternative explanation is that the *verba mea,* at this point, refers to the opening psalm of the first nocturn of Matins in the Office of the Dead. As the service described in the *Reading ms.* is immediately after morning chapter, this is less likely than the above explanation. The morning chapter was not followed by Matins.

...post capitulum in choro. This is ambiguous. It could be read that the 'chapter' was in the choir. This is unlikely, and it probably means that after chapter, in the Chapter House, the monks would then go to the choir, in the church, for the morning Mass. At this point the psalm *Verba mea* was sung as the Introit to the Mass and all the monks were expected to attend.

An alternative free translation would be;

"After Chapter, all are required to be present for the 'Introit', *Verba mea,* at Mass in the Choir"

SECTION 2

"After the things have been read out in chapter that are customarily read in the daily order, the table of the office composed for the dead is recited, as on double feasts."

Lectis in capitulo que ordine cotidiano legi solent, recitatur tabula officii pro defuncto scripta sicut in dupplicibus festis.

COMMENT

The meaning of Double Feasts

To understand the reference to double feasts, it is necessary to look at the categorisation of feast-days and how this was reflected in the Divine Office. From the thirteenth century, there were three kinds of feasts: *simplex, semiduplex,* and *duplex.* All three were governed by the rules of the Divine Office and *Opus Dei.*

The simple feast commenced with the chapter (*capitulum*) of First Vespers, and ended with None. It had three lessons, and took the psalms of Matins from the week-day office; the rest of the office was like the semi-double.

The semidouble feast had two Vespers, the nine lessons of Matins and ended with Compline. The antiphons before the psalms were only intoned. In the Mass, the semi-double always had at least three *orationes* or prayers.

On a double feast the antiphons were sung in their entirety, before and after the psalms. At Lauds and Vespers there were no prayers of intercession (*suffragia*) of the saints, and the Mass had only one prayer (*oratio*) and only then if there was no commemoration prescribed.

The ordinary double feasts are called *duplicia minora*: occurring with feasts of a higher rank.

For the more important feasts, an office of nine lessons was established and this came to be known as a semi-double office, and later such feasts were called doubles. Hence, before the thirteenth century, we find celebrations of simple feasts, of semi-doubles and of doubles. Durandus, writing in the thirteenth century, tells us of the existence of doubles major and doubles minor:

Reading Abbey - A pilgrim church

The word "double" ('duplex') is derived, some authors hold, from the ancient custom of reciting two offices or saying two Masses on the same day - one for the current feria and one for the feast (festa). Other authors say that the word is derived from the ancient practice of chanting twice or in repetition the complete responses and versicles. And, above all, the recitation of the full antiphons before and after each psalm, at Matins, Lauds and Vespers, was called "duplication," and this name, it is said, was given to the office (double, duplex) in which the practice of duplication took place.

We read in the *Reading manuscript* that Henry's commemoration ranks along with the most solemn and most important of church feasts, such as Christmas.

The Flight into Egypt.
Pillar capital in the choir.
It has been proposed that some of the sculptures take their inspiration from local mystery plays.
This might explain the 'wheels' depicted under the donkey, as either a wooden model was drawn through the town, or a real donkey was placed on a cart.

As a side note, it is worth mentioning that in the Latin, on this occasion, the Office is referred to as the 'Office for the Dead', *pro defuncto.* This is in the singular, so could be translated here as 'Office for the Dead Person' and not in the plural, *pro defunctis.* Nor is the term 'of the Dead', *defunctorum,* used at this point. Later in the manuscript, however, there is reference to "offices of the dead", *officia defunctorum,* (see section 14), so it would appear both terms, 'for the dead' and 'of the dead', were used. In fact, in the *Vetus disciplina* of Cluny, the distinction is made between Masses and Offices 'of the Dead', *mortuorum,* and those for a particular individual, *pro defuncto.* This is also explicitly stated in the *Consuetudines* of Farfa (Ch 56 *Extra Locum Fratri defuncti cernitur usus*).

The distinction, on one hand between a specific prayer for a particular dead person and, on the other hand, general prayers for the dead, was addressed in the 14th century *fasciculus morum* ('handbook of practice'). The redemptive power of the death of Christ and of each individual Mass created a problem with regards to the efficacy of Christ's death. If His death was sufficient to 'save the souls of all mankind', what was the value of the Mass, or indeed of prayers for the dead? If a single Mass was the Act of Salvation, what was the value of having many Masses? These were contradictions that the philosophers and theologians of the 14th century struggled to reconcile.

The solution proposed in the *fasciculus* is that Masses, and prayers, such as the Office, where the whole liturgy was dedicated to the 'salvation of the soul' of a particular person, benefitted that individual directly, whereas general prayers for the dead, even if names were mentioned in the process of the liturgy, was just that: a general prayer of petition and thanksgiving. Hence it was possible to find a Mass or Office 'for' a person, *pro defuncto,* and a Mass or Office 'of the dead', *defunctorum.* Clearly, by the standards of scholastic logic, this was an unsatisfactory explanation. However, for our purposes in analysing the *Reading manuscript,* we can see that both terms were acceptable and most likely had distinct significance.

The problem did not lessen over the following centuries, and, in part, it was this paradox that led the Protestant reformers to condemn 'prayers', let alone *Masses,* for the dead and to concentrate on the redemptive power of Christ's death and the doctrine of predestination.

SECTION 3.

"At the invitatory, which is 'Circumdederunt', four brethren in (copes)* are designated   At the third responsory four brethren (are designated), at the sixth five, at the ninth six".

Ad Invitatorium, quod est 'Circumdederunt', quatuor fratres in (cappi)s notantur. Ad tercium responsorium quatuor, a sextum quinque, ad nonum sex.

<u>*Note. Words in brackets added to clarify the meaning.</u>

COMMENT

This passage refers to the Hour of Matins or Nocturns. It was only at Matins, (*Nocturnes*), that three sets of psalms and antiphons were sung.

A very early commentator of the Divine Office, Amalarius, writing in the 9th century, noted that Matins consisted of three nocturns (*De ecclesiasticis officiis* – "Concerning the Ecclesiastical Offices"). However, he stated that at a funeral vigil there should be no invitatory psalm, as this was no place for *Venite exultemus,* "Come let us rejoice". He was referring to Psalm 94 which is the Invitatory psalm which proceeds the singing of any of the nocturns. This account does not tally with what we read in the *Reading ms.* which explicitly mentions an 'invitatory'. However, almost three centuries separate Amalarius' description and the founding of Reading Abbey. Moreover, the Office had developed significantly by the 13th century.

Reading Abbey - A pilgrim church

The rubrics for saying the Office of the Dead are complicated. They read:

Dicitur Invitatorium (Ps 94) in die Commemorationis omnium defunctorum, et quoties dicuntur tres Nocturni, aliis vero temporibus omittitur, et inchoatur ab Antiphona Psalmorum Nocturni, et dicitur tantum unum Nocturnum cum suis Laudibus, hoc ordine: Secunda et quinta feria, primum Nocturnum. Tertia et sexta, secundum Nocturnum. Quarta feria et Sabbatho, tertium Nocturnum.

"The Invitatory (Ps 94) is to be said on All Souls' Day and as often as all three nocturns are sung. At other times it is to be omitted and is to be begun with the Antiphon of the Psalms to the Nocturns. Only one Nocturn, with its corresponding Lauds, is to be sung in the following order: The First Nocturn is to be sung on Mondays and Thursdays, the Second Nocturn on Tuesdays and Fridays, and the Third Nocturn on Wednesdays and Saturdays."

Each nocturn includes three psalms with antiphons, and three lessons from the book of Job, each lesson being followed by a 'response', taken from the same book. The ninth 'response' is *Ne recorderis peccata mea,* 'Do not remember my sins'.

Professor John Harper of the University of Bangor commented: *The inclusion of an invitatory is unusual (except on All Souls' Day) - at least in the English secular forms.* Moreover, the normal Invitatory for Matins of the Office of the Dead is ***Regem, cui omnia vivunt, Venite adoremus.*** This, in part or in full, is repeated after each verse of Psalm 94. As a help to understanding the structure of the Office, I am including the full text, with rubrics, here:

Invitatorium:
Regem, cui omnia vivunt, Venite adoremus.

Psalmus 94:
Venite exultemus Domino, iubilemus Deo salutari nostro:
praeoccupemus faciem eius in confessione: et in psalmis iubilemus ei.
Regem, cui omnia vivunt, Venite adoremus.
Quoniam Deus magnus Dominus, et rex magnus super omnes deos:
quoniam non repellet Dominus plebem suam:
quia in manu eius sunt omnes fines terrae:
et altitudines montium ipse conspicit.

Venite adoremus.

Quoniam ipsius est mare, et ipse fecit illud:

et aridam fundaverunt manus eius: venite adoremus, et procidamus ante Deum:

ploremus coram Domino, qui fecit nos:

quia ipse est Dominus Deus noster: nos autem populus eius, et oves pascuae eius.

Regem, cui omnia vivunt, Venite adoremus.

Hodie si vocem eius audieritis, nolite obdurare corda vestra, sicut in exacerbatione secundum

diem tentationis in deserto:

ubi tentaverunt me patres vestri: probaverunt, et viderunt opera mea.

Venite adoremus

Quadraginta annis proximus fui generationi huic:

et dixi, semper hi errant corde:

ipsi vero non cognoverunt vias meas:

quibus iuravi in ira mea, si introibunt in requiem meam.

Regem, cui omnia vivunt, Venite Adoremus

To listen to a version of the Gregorian chant
https://www.youtube.com/watch?v=B_a_rGrUAbs

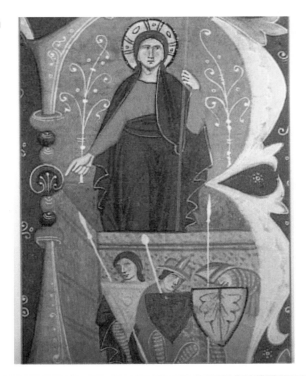

Picture attribution, Aurora Surgit https://www.youtube.com/watch?v=B_a_rGrUAbs

SECTION 4.

"The entire church is to be adorned with the finest hangings, and before the prayer of Vespers the seats are to be provided with covers."

Tota ecclesia melioribus pallis ornanda est, et ante orationem Vesperorum forme operientur bankalibus.

Dream of the Magi.
Pillar capital in the choir.
Pointing to the star, the angel speaks to the magi, touching the hand of one whilst his companions sleep.
This is the only sculpture at Autun with traces of the original colours: red, blue, green and gold.

COMMENT

The whole church, not just the chancel, was to be richly adorned. This is consistent with the event being considered equivalent to the most sacred of days: double feasts. The 'pallium' is a cover, usually associated with an altar covering, or the shawl like vestment bestowed as a special honour to church dignitaries. The second part of the sentence is rather more difficult. Kemp's translation is given above. The word 'bankalibus' is the ablative plural of 'bankale' usually spelt 'bancale', which many medieval dictionaries translate as 'cushions'.

Whichever way this sentence is translated, the church and seats were richly adorned for the two days of Henry's commemorative services.

It should be noted that the description in the *Reading ms.* does not follow the liturgical order of the Office Hours. The Vespers referred to here must be those of the first day, that is the Vigil. There would have been little point in adorning the church at Vespers towards the end of the second and final day.

I suggest the following sequence of events on the Vigil.

1.   30th November - (Eve of the day commemorating Henry's death)
Morning chapter - probably followed by the Matitudinal Mass. (Items 1 and 2 in my analysis)

2.   Sext followed by the Main or High Conventual Mass and None said at 3pm

3.   Church is decorated

4.   Vespers of the day (item 3), followed by Vespers of the Office of the Dead, and Compline

SECTION 5.

"After Vespers, with all bells ringing inside and outside, and the lord abbot with cope having entered the choir, the hebdomadary shall begin the antiphon 'Placebo'. The lord abbot, after the antiphon at 'Magnificat' has begun, will cense the High Altar and the king's tomb with two copes assigned for this, who at the end of the third psalm will enter the choir with censers, and after the censing of the altar and tomb shall proceed to cense the lord abbot."

Post Vesperas sonantibus omnibus signis deintus et deforis, et domino abate cum cappa chorum ingresso, incipiet ebdomadarius Antiphonam 'Placebo'. Dompnus abbas, incepta Antiphona ad 'Magnificat', incensabit maius altare tantum et tumbam Regis cum duobus in cappis ad hoc assignatis, qui circa finem tercii psalmi intrabunt chorum cum turrabilis, qui post incensacionem altaris et tumbe pergunt incensaturi dominum abbatem.

COMMENT

The word for bell is not present in the Latin, however the use of the verb *sonare, (sonantibus)* indicates a loud sound and this is reinforced with the words instructing that the sound is a signal, *signis* (literally *'with signs'*) to be made both inside *(deintus)* and outside *(deforis)* the church. *Signis* is frequently interpreted as meaning 'with bells'. It is used in the *Vetus Disciplina, De Die Natali Domini,* "iterum pulsatis signis, Missa illa Lux fulgebit, incipitur". *(Concerning Christmas Day,* Ch 5. p289 Hergott). The same term is used by customaries of many monasteries, including Farfa. In those of Cluny, the phrase *pulsatis signis* is used on numerous occasions.

'After Vespers', the hebdomadary is instructed to sing the *Placebo*. This is the clearest indication that Vespers of the 'Office of the Dead' was to be sung immediately after the Vespers of the day. The *Placebo* refers to the line *Placebo Dómino in regione vivorum,* ("I will please the Lord in the land of the living"). These are the last lines from the first verse of Psalm 114. They are used as the antiphon for the first psalm of Vespers in the 'Office of the Dead': Psalm 114 *Diléxi, quóniam exáudiet dóminus vocem oratiónis meæ,* ("I have loved, therefore let the Lord hear the sound of my prayer"); it is usually referred to as *Placebo Domino* or just *Placebo.*

The practice of reciting the hours of the Office of the Dead immediately after the Office of the Day is a particularly Cluniac custom. The tradition was that, during the abbacy of Odilo at Cluny (994 –1049), he instituted the feast of All Souls, dedicated to prayers for the dead. This was soon adopted by the Catholic church in general.

Reading Abbey - A pilgrim church

Part of the Cluniac observance was this concentration on prayers for the dead, which included the daily recitation of the Office of the Dead. We know from both Bernard (*Vetus disciplina*), and Ulrich (*Consuetudines),* that by the 11th century it was a Cluniac practice for the Office of the Dead to follow the Office of the Day.

The above translation of the opening verse of Psalm 114 is not straightforward. There are several versions of the Latin, let alone possible translations. For example, one such exegesis points out that the verb *Dilexi* means to 'please' or 'give pleasure' and that *quoniam* should be translated as "therefore", rather than "because". In other words, in this interpretation the meaning to the monks would be that Henry had done good in his life, and so the Lord would hear his prayers, rather than he did good in life because the Lord had heard his prayers. The use of the subjunctive "let the Lord hear", *exaudiet,* would support this view. This is just one possibility, but it does reflect the fascination the medieval mind would have had in 'playing' with words and syntax together with their possible meanings and their potential implications.

We read that the church was to be richly decorated and the festivities began just before the Liturgical Hour of Vespers. As we have seen, this must refer to the Vespers of the Day, as the next instruction is that after Vespers the hebdomadary begins the antiphon *Placebo* which starts the Office of the Dead.

Flight into Egypt. Pillar capital in the choir.

This view is of the same carving shown on page 178, but from a different angle.

It demonstrates the depth of the stonework and the outstanding technique Gislebertus brought to his art.

SECTION 6.

"The abbot says the two collects at Compline, standing and intoning, that is, *Presta domine quesumus* and *Fidelium"*

Duas ad complend' collectas dicit abbas stando et cum tono, videlicet 'Presta domine quesumus' (Kemp in his footnotes says 'suggested reading' for *presta*) ***et 'Fidelium'.***

COMMENT

***Duas … collectas* ("two … collects").**

The Collects were originally prayers before Mass used to 'gather' or 'collect' the people together, often said in the procession to the church. They became formalised as the prayers at the start of Mass. Here they are transferred to use in the Office.

Compline.

The last 'Hour' of the Office is Compline. This was said immediately before bed. Kemp states that the Collects he mentioned are the most probable suggestions. As only the Hours of Matins, Lauds and Vespers form the Office of the Dead, this refers to Compline for the Office of the Day.

The Collect was the same for Prime and Compline. The Collect, or in this case two Collects, come in the concluding section of each of the Hours. The Collect *Fidelium* was later omitted at Compline and replaced with a blessing. It would appear that they were both said at Henry's commemoration. The words are: *Fidelium animae, per misericordiam Dei, requiescant in pace. Amen* ("May the souls of the faithful (departed), through the mercy of God, rest in peace. Amen").

It is interesting to note how the chant is described in this case. The verb used is *dicere (dicit)* which literally means 'to say' ('he says'). But the instructions then clarify this by instructing that it should be said *in tono,* 'intoned'. I shall be examining, in section 10, the more complicated and contentious use of another word, *indirectum,* to describe how the chant is to be 'said'.

SECTION 7.

"From the beginning of the *Placebo* until after Compline the next day four candles shall burn brightly at the tomb, two at the head and two at the feet, apart from the others which are lit at every office, as on the principal feasts".

Ab incepcione 'Placebo' usque in crastinum post completorium ardebunt iugitur quatuor cerei ad tumbam, due ad capud et duo ad pedes, preter alios qui ad omne officium accendentur, sicut in festis principalibus

COMMENT

The time-span covered is from the first psalm of Vespers on the vigil, that is the first day of the ceremonies, to the end of Compline on the day itself. One puzzling word is *iugitur*. Kemp translates this as 'brightly'. It appears to be an adverb based on *iugo (-are)*, 'bind together', hence 'brightly', in the sense of 'all together'.

It is clear that these four candles are "in addition to", *preter,* the usual number of candles that would have been lit during such a significant feast day.

The 'just' being led by an angel into paradise.

The west doorway tympanum

Pilgrims are represented by two figures carrying staffs and scrips (pouches) and badges: a cross for Jerusalem and a scallop shell for Compostela.

The full inscription above reads:
Quisque resurget ita quem non trahit impia vita et lucebit ei
sine fine lucerne diei. Gislebertus hoc fecit.

"Thus, whoever does not lead an impious (wicked) life shall rise again, and the eternal light of day will shine upon him.
Gislebertus made this".

Only the underlined words are shown in the section of the carving shown here.

SECTION 8.

"Once the royal Matins with additions has finished, and with all bells ringing inside and out, the aforesaid four persons wearing copes shall enter beginning the invitatory, which is *Circumdederunt*, where in place of the *Gloria* they shall say *Requiem eternam*. All the other things set down in the table are said. At the second, fifth and eighth lesson the altar will be censed, as will the tomb and the convent as on the principal feasts."

Finitis matutin(alibus) regalibus cum appendiciis suis, et pulsatis omnibus signis deintus et deforis, intrent predicti quatuor cappis indutis, incipientes Invitatorium 'quod est Circumdederunt', ubi loco 'Glorie' dicent 'Requiem in eternam'. Cetera omnia sicut in tabula notata dicentur. Ad secumdam, quintam et octavam lectionem incensabitur altare et tumba et conventus sicut in festis precipuis.

COMMENT

Finitis matutin (alibus)

Kemp has inserted ...*alibus* to fill in a missing part of the text. The normal words for the Canonical Hour of Matins is *Matutinum* or *Matutinae.* It should be noted that, later in the text, the word *matutinalis* is used in full to describe the Morrow Mass (cf Section 14). The *Vetus Disciplina* likewise uses this form for the Morning Mass over 150 times, for Lauds at least three times and on one occasion for the Hour of Matins.

Kemp's insertion of *alibus,* as an ablative plural, is therefore consistent with this usage.

regalibus

Still part of the ablative absolute construction, this adjective gives a precise description of which Matins were recited. The Royal Hours are more frequently associated with the eastern Catholic and Orthodox churches, but it would appear that the term 'Royal Matins' was applied also to Matins when one of the Royal Psalms opened the first nocturn. The Royal Psalms commonly found for Matins are nos. 20 and 21. These are especially found in Matins for Sundays in November and December. It is worth looking at these to see what the *Reading manuscript* is most likely referencing.

Psalm 20

Psalmus 20 *Exaudiat te Dominus in die tribulationis: protegat te nomen Dei Iacob.*

Psalm 20   May the Lord hear you in the day of tribulation. May the name of the God of Jacob protect you.

Psalm 21

Psalmus 21 *Domine, in virtute tua lætabitur rex: * et super salutare tuum exsultabit vehementer.*

Psalm 21   The king rejoices in thy strength, O Lord; * and in thy salvation he shall rejoice exceedingly.

It should be noted that the numbering of the psalms differs, depending on which version is being used. The Vulgate uses the Greek numbering, (G). Today, the Hebrew numbering (H) is often used. There are ten 'Royal psalms' (H:2,18,20,21,45,72,101,110,132,144).

The numbering used here is the Hebrew version.

It would appear that the meaning of the above is that the Royal Matins, with all its extra parts, had to be completed before the Invitatory for Matins of the 'Office of the Dead' was begun. We have looked at the question of the 'invitatory' above.

This was announced with the *pulsates … signis.* As before, Kemp gives the translation of *signis* as 'bells'. *Pulsare* may also mean to knock or beat upon. We know, from the Cluniac customaries, that clappers, and not bells, were used to announce the impending death of one of the community. Bells were, however, sounded on the death of a brother. Consequently, as the ceremony concerns the deceased Henry, I suggest that either translation, bells or clappers, may be used. The clappers may have been similar to wooden football rattles. These are still part of Catholic ritual during Holy Week, in the 21st century.

incipientes Invitatorium quod est 'Circumdederunt'

The text then says that the Invitatory *Circumdederunt …* is to be sung, the second time this is mentioned (Section 3, above). This was a standard Invitatory for the first antiphon for Matins of the Office of the Dead. However, there may be some confusion over which psalm this refers to. In the transcript Kemp put the inverted commas around *quod est.* I think they should just be round *Circumdederunt.*

As we have seen, the phrase *Cirumdederunt me dolores mortis* (The sorrows of death have surrounded me"), appears in Psalm 114. Variations of these words are to be found in Psalm 17, verses 5 –6; *circumdederunt me funes mortis et torrentes diabuli terruerunt me.*

(The bonds of death have surrounded me and the fires of the devil have made me fearful), and *funes inferi circumdederunt me praevenerunt me laquei mortis.* (The chains of hell surrounded me, and the snares of death have overcome me). Another version of Psalm 17, *Cirumdederunt gemitus mortis; Dolores inferni circumdederunt me.* (The groans of death surround me; The sorrows of hell surround me), was used as an Introit at Mass.

This is the same psalm which, as we saw earlier, is known by the word *Placebo* and which begins Vespers. (See Section 5).

As to be expected at the Office of the Dead, the *Requiem aeternam* (eternal rest), is said instead of the *Gloria*. I believe this is additional confirmation, if any is required, that the two Offices were said. In this case, the so called 'Royal Matins', or celebratory Matins of the day, preceded Matins for the Office of the Dead.

The ceremony was enhanced by the censing of the altar, tomb and, it says, *conventus,* after the readings of the second, fourth and eighth lessons. The word *conventus* could mean the whole monastery or, more usually, those gathered for the ceremony. It may even include, or just refer to, the physical area of the church where the Office was being sung: namely the choir. The Cluniac customaries instruct that the whole community should be involved in the liturgy. Those monks who were unable to sing were specifically mentioned as to be given the roles of crucifer (cross carrier), thurifers and acolytes. It can be seen here that, whilst the choir monks would be singing, or preparing to sing, these brothers, dressed in copes, would be placing candles around the chancel and tomb, and bearing the thuribles for censing. In the Cluniac tradition the copes would have been richly embroidered. So, just as the sound of the chant was central to the liturgy, so too were the colour, light and holy scents of the whole ceremony.

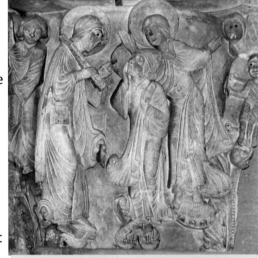

The road to Emmaus.
Pillar capital in the choir.

There has been some doubt as to what is being represented here, but Christ is shown with the pilgrim's staff and scrip, as seen on the images of the pilgrims on page 186.

sicut in tabula (*just as* set down in the table of instructions)

The word *tabula* refers to the general liturgical instructions, which would have included the rubrics for which version of the Office should be said, including the psalms, canticles and readings, as well as the ceremonial surrounding it. The whole document is redolent of the rubrics for non-liturgical dramas such as the Winchester *Visitatio Sepulchri* (Visit to the Holy Sepluchre). Liturgical dramas were plays based upon episodes in the life of Christ, such as meeting the travellers on the road to Emmaus, or the arrival of the three Marys at the empty tomb of the risen Christ, the *visitatio sepulchri*.

There are several thousand such dramas across Europe, and they share certain features with the Reading Abbey manuscript. This is not to say that we should view the commemoration of Henry's death as a drama. We are presented with a strictly liturgical account. However, both the linguistic and compositional structures are similar, in fact identical, to that of the rubrics for the dramas. These liturgical references in the rubrics belong to a specific linguistic register and vocabulary, which the two have in common.

What follows is a comparative analysis of the Winchester *Visitatio* drama and of the *Reading manuscript*.

The Winchester *Visitatio Sepulchri* and the *Reading manuscript*.

Readers will, by now, be familiar with the format and language of the *Reading manuscript*. They will have seen the relationship between the 'instructions' and the content of the liturgy that they are describing. As a comparison, what I give here is the non-liturgical introductory rubric of the Winchester *Visitatio*. The instructions place us on Easter morning, when the three holy woman go to the sepulchre where Jesus had been laid following the crucifixion. Three monks take on the roles of the holy women and a fourth, wearing an alb, or white tunic, represents Jesus. The rubric tells us how he should steal off to the sepulchre, whilst the other three search the area for the tomb.

> *Dum tertia recitatur lectio, quatuor fratres induant se, quorum unus alba indutus acsi ad aliud agendum ingrediatur, atque latenter sepulchri locum adeat, ibique manu tenens palmam, quietus sedeat.*

> *Dumque tertium percelebratur responsorium, residui tres succedant, omnes quidem cappis induti, turibula cum incensu manibus gestantes ac pedetemptim ad similitudinem quaerentium quid, veniant ante locum sepulchri.*

> *Whilst the third lesson is being recited four brothers should put on their vestments. One of them should put on an alb, as if he were going somewhere else, and should secretly go into the sepulchre, and there, holding a palm in his hand, he should sit still.*

> *Whilst the third responsory is being recited, the other three should follow, all wearing copes, swinging incense-filled thuribles and, walking carefully, as if looking for something, they should approach the place of the sepulchre.*

Just as, in the *Reading manuscript,* the rubric frequently begins by placing the action in its liturgical setting, so we are here immediately made aware that the above takes place at the "third reading". In the same manner as the *Reading ms.* then gives 'stage directions', so too the *Visitatio* gives instructions as to the number of brothers, what they should wear, how they should walk and where they are to sit or stand.

Linguistically, there is the same interesting mix of indicative and subjunctive moods. Together with the speaker's name or role, the rubrics usually provide information about what the speaker is to say or sing. The subjunctive form of the verbs with a qualifier (e.g. *quietus sedeat),* serving as the imperative is therefore logical. This applies to most of the verbs used in rubrics of Easter plays and in the *Reading ms.*

However it is not a universal rule in either texts: there are examples of such rubrics using the indicative form. Some of the rubrics avoid the subjunctive for verbs such as *dicere, cantare.* Nevertheless, the subjunctive is sometimes found for the directorial aspect, e.g. *intrent,* in both documents. Another similarity is that the participants can be replaced with a pronoun (as for instance *ille, illa*) or a numerical designation (*prima, secunda, tertia,* first, second, third), provided that the character's name or status has already been given in a previous rubric, or that it is clear from the context of the dramatic text.

I have included this brief look at the linguistic stylistics of the *Reading manuscript* to indicate its close relationship with a long standing tradition in liturgical, ceremonial and dramatic instructions with which the monks, and the laity, of the mid-13th century would have been familiar.

AMENDED TRANSLATION changes in red.

Once the royal Matins with additions has finished, and with all the bells (*or* clappers) sounding as a signal, both **inside and outside, the aforesaid four persons wearing copes shall enter at the beginning of the Invitatory** for the Office for the Dead, **which is** *Cirumdederunt* **(Psalm 114), when, in place of the** *Gloria,* **they shall** sing the *Requiem eternam.* **All the other things set down in the** rubrics **are** to be recited. **At the second, fifth and eighth lesson the altar will be censed, as will the tomb and the convent.** This will be done **as on principal feasts.**

The Fourth Tone or 'key' of medieval music.
Nave capital. Copy of a Cluny capital .

The ringing of bells is mentioned on several occasions in the 'Commemoration'. Could these be the type of bells that would have been found at Reading?

SECTION 9

"After the repetition of the ninth responsory there follow the two customary psalms and the two aforesaid collects, (cf Section 7) which at this time are said not by intoning but spoken; and then, with all the bells ringing as previously noted, the 'Exultabunt' is begun by the hebdomadary. Around the beginning of the canticle 'Ego dixi', the lord abbot and those accompanying him shall withdraw to re-vest themselves in copes. And at the 'Laudate dominum in sanctis eius' the lord abbot shall return to his stall, re-vested, and with him his fellows, who are to cense the altar and the tomb as stated previously. On return to the said chapter, and the customary absolution having been made, the absolution shall be pronounced again."

Post repeticionem noni responsorii. (sic) *sequuntur duo psalmi consueti et due collecte premise que tunc non cum tono sed indirectum dicentur. Et tunc, pulsatis omnibus signis sicut prius prenotatum est, incipitur ab ebdomadario 'Exultabunt'. Circa principium cantici 'Ego dixi' exeat dompnus abbas as revestiendum se et etiam duo qui ei sociabuntur in cappis. Et ad 'Laudate dominum in sanctis eius' redeat ad stallum suum dompnus abbas revestitus et cum eo socii eius, qui incensare debent sicut predictum est altare et tumbam. In capitulo dicto versu et facta absolucione consueta, iterum fiet absolucio.*

COMMENT

This section is still dealing with Matins, followed by Lauds. It was customary for Lauds to follow immediately after Matins. *Exultabunt* refers to the antiphon *Exultabunt Domino* which introduces Psalm 50, *Miserere mei Deus: secundum magnam misericordiam tuam,* (Have mercy on me, Lord, according to your great mercy), the first psalm of Lauds for the Office of the Dead.

There follow Psalms 64, 62, 66 and the canticle *Ego dixi* (Ezechiae - Isaia 38], *Ego dixi in dimidio dierum meorum: vadam ad portas inferi* (I have said in the middle of my life, I will go to the gates of hell), The *Ego dixi* is followed in turn by Psalms 148, 149, 150 and the canticle of Zacharia *Benedictus Dominus Deus Israel:* (Luke 1.).

There is a break between this canticle and the next psalm mentioned, number 148, *Laudate dominum in sanctis eius* when the abbot returns to his stall and the tomb is censed.

sequuntur duo psalmi consueti due collecte premise que tunc non cum tono sed indirectum dicentur

"there follow the two aforesaid collects, which at this time are said, not by intoning, but *spoken.*"

The above instruction is the most problematic in the whole document. It concerns the way in which the two collects, which are also mentioned in Section 7, are to be said or sung. *... non cum tono ...*

It is necessary to ask whether the instruction ***non cum tono sed indirectum dicentur*** also refers to the two psalms. If this were the case one would expect the relative pronoun, **que,*** to be the masculine **qui,** since it would refer both to the psalms and the collects. The word 'psalmi' is masculine and so the pronoun, though also referring to the word for collects, which is feminine, would be masculine and should read ***qui***. I conclude therefore that the instruction **non cum tono** refers only to the collects.

*The spelling "que" is consistent with the other similar endings quoted in the Reading ms. It is of course a version of 'quae', the feminine plural of the relative pronoun qui, quae, quod. What this spelling does show is that at Reading, as well as at Cluny, the pronunciation of the 'ae' dipthong is 'e' (as in the English word 'day') and not the classical 'ae', pronounced as in English 'my'.

due collecte premise ... indirectum dicentur

I have come across several explanations for the word *indirectum*.

1. Kemp choses the literal translation, namely that the words are spoken.

2. Apel, in his magisterial work on Gregorian Chant, examines this term (*Gregorian Chant Ch 4, p 179*). 'Direct' psalmody, he explains, is the simplest form of psalm singing. The psalm is sung straight: namely it is not preceded or concluded with an antiphon or any other text. He goes on to say *it is most clearly represented by the 'psalmus directaneus ('psalmus in directum', sometimes misspelled 'indirectum') which is sung for some Psalms during the Little Hours of certain days of somber* (sic. US Eng.) *character, for which an especially simple manner of singing was deemed proper.* Apel goes on to say that the music follows a very *elementary recitation formula.* This view is supported by Peter Wagner, *Introduction to the Gregorian Melodies,* p23, where he says this *consisted of a psalm being performed from beginning to end without responsorial or antiphonal additions. It does not, however, mean that it was spoken in the sense that an ordinary speaking voice was used*.

3. Peter Wilton of the Schola Gregoriana points out that the verb *dicere* ("to say" or "to speak") is used freely to describe 'intoning' rather than merely 'speaking'. *When liturgical books say "said" they tend to mean 'chant simply', rather than to complex music. The boundary between singing and saying was drawn differently. The ordinary speaking voice would most likely not have been used.*

Turning to the meaning of the word *indirectum,* he says: *"in directum" involves chanting on one note for the first half of each psalm verse, ending with the "metrum" (descending a semitone and then another tone on the two syllables preceding the final accent), and in the second half of the verse simply reciting on one note. Longer psalm verses are divided into three phrases, the first ending with the "flex" (dropping a third after the final accent), and then the remaining two phrases are as described above.*

4.   Professor John Harper wrote, *Often such memorials or commemorations would be recited privately, or very simply. And this brings me to 'indirectum'. I have wondered from the outset whether this is a term comparable with 'sine nota' found certainly in sources of the Use of Salisbury. There are differences of opinion about this. Some suggest that it means spoken – but in a resonant building that is not an effective means of articulating a text; others (including me) favour an interpretation which is without decoration – so sung on a monotone.*

In the *'Vetus disciplina'* for the abbey of Hirsau, in modern-day Germany, regarding the tonsure of a novice, we read the following:

The tonsure is administered in the same way. (This refers to the preceding instructions regarding the cutting of hair). *Those present at the Mass will be the officiating priest, the librarian with the book, and the novice master with the scissors, and the cloth to collect the hair, given to him in the sacristy by the chamberlain. The hair, cut off by the priest, is collected in this cloth and held by the novice master.*

The service starts with the words 'May the Lord be with you' and with the prayer 'Grant we beseech thee...'. Next the priest blesses those present with holy water and then makes the tonsure cut. The young man begins the antiphon, 'You are the Lord', using the 'indirectum' tone, that is without any modulation of voice. And then, when this verse is concluded, the monastic choir continues with the verse 'Preserve us..' followed by 'Glory be to the Father...', and they repeat the antiphon (introduced by the novice), *but this time they sing it.* [3]

We learn here that, once the novices have been blessed with holy water and have received the tonsure, one of them intones the antiphon *Tu es Domine.* The directions are very clear: namely that this is done *indirectum* and the explanation is that this means without any modulation of the voice *(id est, sine modulatione vocis)*. The most probable, if not only, explanation for this phrase is that the antiphon is sung in a monotone. This cannot mean 'spoken'. The choir or 'Convent' then take this up and go on to sing the rest of the same antiphon, following the verse beginning *Conserva* finishing with *Gloria.* This follows the expected pattern of *Antiphon— Psalm Verses – Gloria Patri — repeated Antiphon as conclusion.*

It is possible that the newly tonsured novice was not expected to sing the antiphon, as he would not as yet have had the necessary training. The full sung version of the antiphons would have been most demanding and required much experience.

CONCLUSION

There are, therefore, several possible interpretations of the term *indirectum,* and so the meaning of the sentence. On balance, most commentators think it unlikely that the words would have been merely 'spoken'. However, the chant would have been very simple, possibly on a monotone, and without any elaborate introductory antiphon or melisma (cf pp 205-206). As one would not expect an antiphon to precede a collect, and if the words were not merely spoken, the most likely explanation is that given by Harper.

Section 7 and section 10 use of the words *cum tono*

One explanation of the phrase *cum tono* is that it is referring to the tones associated with each of the eight modes. As Apel says (p209) *the earliest sources e.g. the 'Commemoratio brevis de tonis et psalmis modulandis of the ninth century'* (Beneventan Gradual early 11th c), *present the psalm tones as a fully developed system of eight 'toni', one for each mode.* I suggest that the *Reading ms.* is instructing the cantor not to use any tones associated with the modes, because the collects are to be 'said' *in directum: tonus directaneus.*

A solution to this problem may exist in the text of the *Reading ms*. In Section 7 we read that the collects are to read by the abbot, who says (*dicit*) the two collects standing and ***cum tono***. We should note that in this instance the verb *dicere* is used and it clearly means chanting or singing, not just speaking. Whereas the *tonus* was set by the antiphon, in this case, as there is no antiphon, no tone is set but the collects are to be said *in directum,* that is in the simplest form possible, namely in a monotone.

In the collection of the *Vetus Disciplina,* the term *tonus* is used frequently. Moreover, on several occasions it is explained as meaning *cum modulatione.* Clearly the term *tonus* is an instruction to use one of the tones, that is the words are sung to varying notes. The phrase often used is *in tono.* Whereas *non cum tono* means that the words are to be produced *sine modulatione,* this does not mean that they were produced in an ordinary speaking voice.

Suicide of Judas, Nave, south side, capital

SECTION 10

"And immediately after Sext a peal of bells is rung until the abbot and the whole convent are revested. And after the peal of bells the abbot is to proceed to his seat by the tomb upon the pavement to the south side, associated with the prior (if…) or another prelate should not be present. And then after the precentor has started the responsory, *Subvenite*, (cf. p29 Paxton) the commendation of the soul will be fully carried out with the customary antiphons, psalms and collects, with the convent revested. Nine rule the choir.
The responsory is sung by four, the tract by six."

Post Sextam vero statim pulsatur classicum donec abbas et totus conventus revestientur. Post classicum vero ingrediatur abbas ad sedile suum iuxta tumbam super pavimentum ex parte australi, associato sibi priore [si…] (missing section owing to a hole in the ms) *vel alius prelatus non interfuerit. Et tunc incepto ab armario repsonsorio, 'Subvenite', integre fiet anime commendacio cum antiph*(onis)*, psalmis et collectis cum convento revestito. Novem regent chorum, responsorium a quatuor cantatur, tractus vero a sex.*

COMMENT

We have moved from Matins, to midday. Sext, the sixth hour, is at 12 noon. The main conventual Mass usually followed this canonical hour, as we read in the next section. This is a most significant passage as regards the exact location of Henry's tomb. The abbot's place in the choir is said to be on the south side of the chancel, and it is described as being *iuxta tumbam*. *Iuxta*, when used in a locational sense, is defined by all dictionaries as 'very close to' or 'alongside'.

Eve. Door lintel of the former north transept portal

Eve is moving through the Garden of Eden as if she were the serpent itself. She is talking to Adam, perhaps telling him what she has just done. Her left hand is reaching behind her, almost surreptitiously, as she plucks the apple from the branch, which is being bent towards her by the serpent.

The presence of her feminine nudity is further heightened by the anatomically exaggerated way in which her upper body is turned towards the observer.

SECTION 11

"All are to do the offertory chant, the verse of the offertory 'Redemptor' shall be sung by four between the tomb and the altar. All priests, both on the vigil and the day, shall celebrate masses for him, the remainder two sets of fifty psalms."

Omnes facient offerendam, versus offerende Redemptor a quatuor inter tumbam et altare canetur. Omnes Sacerdotes tam in vigilia quam in die missas pro eo celebrent, ceteri duas quinquagenas.

COMMENT

Reference to the 'Offertory' confirms that the instructions have moved on to the midday Mass which comes after Sext. Four monks are to sing the offertory verse. All brothers who are ordained priests are to say Masses on the vigil, and on the day itself. The Cluniac customaries likewise instruct that those brothers who are not ordained priests, and so are not able to say Mass, should chant psalms whist individual Masses are being said.

So once again, the Reading manuscript is in line with the Cluniac Customaries, which demand that everyone in the community should be fully involved in the ceremonial, rituals and life of the monastery. For instance, one instruction is that brothers who cannot sing should nevertheless play full roles in the liturgy, such as being candle and thurible bearers. The office of acolyte, is not merely being the bearer of candles. It is the highest of the four minor orders in the Catholic church; the others, in descending order, are exorcist, lector and porter. The Customaries also state that brothers who cannot offer Mass are to be otherwise occupied, or are to say fifty psalms and repeat these throughout the ceremonies.

There may also be some overlap or conflation of liturgical directions at this point. The Cluniac instructions for caring for the dead make frequent reference to the use of Psalm 50, *Miserere mei Deus secundum misericordiam tuam iuxta multitudinem miserationum tuarum dele iniquitates meas* ('Have mercy on me, O God, according to thy great mercy. And according to the multitude of thy tender mercies blot out my iniquity'). This psalm is recited on several occasions during the period of extreme illness of one of the brothers, again when he is being prepared for burial, and during the ceremonies that follow his burial. There may be a connection between the number fifty, referring to this psalm, and to the number of psalms to be said, as mentioned above.

SECTION 12

"They have full refection as on the Lord's Nativity with seven full extra dishes, because what is left over ought to go for the benefit of the poor, and a measure of wine both on the vigil and on the day. All the poor coming on that day will have bread and meat or fish, namely, each person having bread and a single portion of meat or fish."

Refectionem plenariam sicut in natale Domini habent cum vii. ferculis plenis, quia quod residuum fuerit in usus pauperum cedere debet, et caritatem de vino tam in vigilia quam in die. Omnes pauperes ipso die supervenientes habebunt panem et carnem vel piscem, scilicet singuli singulos panes et singulas porciones de carne vel pisce

COMMENT

The instructions tell us that the action has moved away from the church to the refectory. This is far from the only time that the manuscript details the duty to care for the poor and to give practical succour through providing food and drink. It is possible that this refers to the 'orts', that is, the food left at the abbey gateway. But, in the context of the next passage, (page 199), it is more than likely that the poor are to be fed in the hall, *aula.* No doubt the orts would have been left as usual. This passage provides further corroboration of the status of the occasion.

The Nativity. Westernmost capital. First pillar on the north wall of the north aisle.

Visitors and pilgrims would most probably have entered the church either by the north transept, or the north aisle doorway. If they came in from the main entrance, which in fact faces north-west, the first capital they would have seen would have been that of the Nativity of Jesus. The whole face of the capital is taken up with the bed on which Mary is resting. Unusual in western iconography, but to be found in Byzantine sources, Joseph is to her left, on the corner of another face of the capital. He appears to be in a pensive mood.

There has been comment as to the significance of the large spring flower that dominates the centre of the imagery. It has been suggested that this represents St Bernard's allegory of the Nativity: that Jesus was the flower, born of a flower, Mary, in a place that signifies 'flower', Nazareth, 'From (Jesse's) roots a Branch (*netzer*) will bear fruit' (Isiah 11:1). Whether Gislebertus really intended such an allegorical interpretation is open to question. But it is the sort of idea that a medieval monk may have contemplated.

SECTION 13

"Concerning the things that are done through the year in common for the soul of the same king

On the first of each month *(kalends)* as soon as possible there shall be the office for him immediately after chapter, with all the bells ringing outside and in and the morrow mass. On the next day, moreover, the responsory in albs, and on that day thirteen poor people are to be fed in the hall. He has the proper and particular collect for every office of the dead from Septuagesima to November 1; on the following day, after twelve lessons, he has the morrow mass. And at *Exultabunt* the first collect is said for him. On Rogation Days, at 'Exultabunt'and at 'Placebo he has the first collect. At the shaving of the tonsure, *Placebo* is always said for him. At all masses, both in the convent and private, he has the proper collect."

De his que per annum fiunt in communi pro anima eiusdem regis.

Kl' singulorum mensium quam cicius poeterit, sit pro eo officium statim post capitulum, pulsatis deforis et deintus omnibus signis, et missa matutinalis . In crastino tamen reponsorium in albis et eo die tredecim pauperes in aula pro eo reficientur. Collectam habet propriam et singularem ad omnia officia defunctorum a Septuagesima usque ad kl' Novembris, sequenti die post xii lectiones missam habet matutinalem. Et ad 'Exultabunt' prima collecta pro eo dicitur. In Rogacionibus, ad 'Exultabunt' at ad 'Placebo', primam habet collectam. Ad Rasuram semper 'Placebo' dicitur pro eo. Ad omnes missas tam in conventu quam privatas, collectam habet propriam.

COMMENT

What we read here is that the commemoration of Henry's death, the prayers for his soul, the liturgy and the distribution of food that accompanied this, took place not just on a yearly basis, but every month throughout the year.

The monthly ceremony was not as elaborate as on the actual anniversary day of December I[st]. The 'collect', or introductory prayer, literally meaning 'coming together prayer', was said at the beginning of each liturgical setting, such as the beginning of Mass. There are two types of 'collect': the general ones for the day of the year, and special collects known as 'proper collects' designed for a particular feast. In this case, it would appear that two collects are said, namely the collect for the dead and the proper collect of the day.

Reading Abbey - A pilgrim church

Later in the manuscript that contains the Annals, as published in Kemp's *Reading Abbey Records a new miscellany,* there are the following lists which give the types of feast and their number through the year.

9 Double feast days

9 Feast days (with processions through the cloisters)

16 Secondary double feast days (without processions)

28 Feast days in special copes

9 Feast days in simple copes

The total so far, and this excludes Sundays, is 71.

This is followed by a list of other days with special provisions

As Kemp notes, there are anomalies in the figures. However, the listings do give an indication of daily monastic life. As in the Cluniac and other Customaries, the orts, namely the left overs from the monks' celebratory meals, were distributed amongst the poor. In addition, the *Reading ms.* Section 14 shows that, every month, thirteen poor people were fed in the hall. In other words, what we see is not merely a distribution of 'left overs', but special meals being provided "under obligation of the Rule".

CONCLUSION

These details give us an insight into the elaborate ceremonial that accompanied the annual, and indeed monthly, commemoration of Henry's death.

They show us that, two hundred years after Henry had died, the monks were following the injunction to pray for his soul, as demanded in the founding charter. Is it possible to extrapolate from this document what other feast days must have been like?

THE LITURGY FOR THE COMMEMORATION OF THE FOUNDER

Above I gave a suggested timetable for the two days up to Matins on the 1st December. The following completes the horarium

30th November - (Eve of the day commemorating Henry's death)

1. Morning chapter - followed by the Matitudinal Mass.

2. Sext followed by the Main or High Conventual Mass. None said at 3pm.

4. The church is decorated. Vespers of the day

5. Vespers of the Office for the Dead,

6. Compline of the vigil or eve.

Ist December

1. Royal Matins. After this, and before Matins of the Office of the Dead, bells are rung throughout the monastery. This would have been sometime between midnight and approximately 3am .

   Matins for the Dead follows Royal Matins. The altar and the tomb are solemnly censed at several points in the service. No mention is made of lauds of the Office of the Dead but this would probably have followed on immediately after matins of the Office of the Dead. However, unusually, again, bells are rung after matins and before lauds. More usually, the two offices would have been said together without a break. The antiphon to the psalms *Exaltabant*, the canticle *Ego dixi* (sung as one of the psalms), and the composite concluding psalm *Laudate dominum,* are normal at lauds of the Office of the Dead. It should be noted that the so called 'little hours' of the Divine Office, namely prime, terce, sext, none and compline, are absent in the Office of the Dead. This consists of matins, lauds and vespers.

2. Prime (the first hour at 6am), terce (the third hour at 9am). The Morrow Mass, which, we read, was said after the morning chapter, most probably following prime and possibly terce. All these would have taken place according to the normal rubrics. As noted, the *Reading ms.* is only concerned with extra parts of the ceremonies.

Reading Abbey - A pilgrim church

3.   Sext at midday followed by the main Mass.

4.   At some point before compline there is a festive meal, and thirteen poor people are fed in the abbey hall.

5.   Compline. The four candles around Henry's tomb are extinguished after compline.
      This signals the end of the two days of commemoration.

Primary Sources for Commemoration of Henry I at Reading Abbey

1. *Summa de Dictamine* or *Summa Dictaminis,* Guido Fava (Faba) c 1190-1243

2. *Vetus Disciplina Monastica,* Marquard Hergott. This includes the Cluny customaries of Ulrich and Bernard.

3. *Constitutiones Hirsaugiensis* (Hirsau) S Wilhelm of Hirsau (aprox. 1030 –1091). *Vetus Disciplina* p 380.

Hoc ordine eadem tonsura agitur. Sacerdoti Missam celebraturo adest Armarius cum libro, Magister Novitiorum cum forpice & linteo, quae à Camerario data jugiter ad hoc opus servantur in Sacristia. Quod linteum idem Magister in manu tenens de manu Sacerdotis rescissum recipit capillum. Ergo in primis praemisso, Domtnus (Dominus) vobiscum, cum oratione dicitur, "Presta quaesumus". Deinde aqua benedicta eos aspergit & tondet , mox à juvene indirectum (id est , sine modulation vocis) incepta antiphona "Tu es Domine" & à Conventu finite adjuncto versu "Conserva cum Gloria", iterumque eadem antiphona canitur.

The English version in the text is a paraphrase, rather than a translation, of the above.

4. *Vetus Disciplina Canonicorum Regularium & Saecularium* (Also available online https://books.google.co.uk/books?id=qSU_AAAAcAAJ&printsec=frontcover&source=gbs_atb&redir_esc=y#v=onepage&q&f=false and also in *A medieval Latin Death Ritual,* Frederick Paxton which includes in translation the Cluniac customaries of the *Vetus disciplina monastica* and the *Consuetudines.*

5   Oderic Vitalis B X1   Ch XL111 Day after the Feast pf the Purification of Mary (Candlemas Feb 2) *Henry I admitted to the Community of St Evroult 1113 Feb 3* (Also available online https://archive.org/stream/ecclesiasticalhi03orde#page/438/mode/2up).

Other Sources

1. *Reading Abbey Records p 101f* B Kemp 2018
— original and commentary

2. *A medieval Latin Death Ritual* Frederick Paxton
— commentary

The Annunciation to St Anne

Capital, north nave, second pier from the main west doorway.

The story of the visit by an angel to St Anne, announcing that she would have a child, Mary, who was to be the mother of the Saviour, does not appear in the gospels. It only comes in the apocryphal gospel of James.

There are various versions of how Anne, beyond childbearing age, was told she would conceive.

Throughout the 12th century, popular devotion to this belief grew contemporaneously with that of the immaculate Conception of Mary.

It is interesting therefore, that at this early stage in the debate over both these devotions, this imagery should figure among the sculptures of the time, let alone in such a prominent position in the church at Autun.

St Anne's husband, Joachim, is shown on another face of the capital, carrying a bundle over his shoulder as he goes to guard his flock. On another face, not shown here, an angel tells him that his will bear a daughter who is to be called Mary.

The sculpture would have been brightly painted in the liturgical colours mentioned earlier.

CHAPTER 12

THE MUSIC OF A CLUNIAC BENEDICTINE MONASTERY

In the previous chapter, I related something of the liturgy of Reading Abbey, with special reference to the commemoration of its founder, Henry I. In this chapter, I will continue my analysis and look at what we know about the music the monks would have sung, and which the visitors and pilgrims would have heard.

The above illustration shows an excerpt from the *Codex Calixtinus.* Supposedly written by Pope Callixtus II, (c. 1065-1124) but most probably by Ayemeric Picaud, in the middle of the 12th century, this book is an anthology of hymns, sermons and travel advice for pilgrims making their way across Europe to the shrine of St James in Compostela in Spain. Most importantly for us, it contains both the Office and the Mass of St James: in other words, the Liturgy of St James. Many of the Cluniac monasteries were on the various routes to Compostela and became renowned as pilgrim churches. Reading was designed as a pilgrim church, and with the early acquisition of the Hand of St James, the abbey became the centre of devotion to St James in England, attracting many pilgrims.

The Liturgy of St James and the *Codex Calixtinus*

Once the relic of the Hand of St James had come to Reading, the liturgy of St James would have been celebrated at the abbey, especially on the 25th July, his feast day.

The way in which the music in the *Codex Calixtinus* is presented indicates that it was intended to be chanted aloud, and is an early example of polyphony. The hymn, or 'conductus', *Congaudeant catholici* ('Let all Catholics rejoice together'), may be the first known composition for three voices. As this has been disputed by some musicologists owing to the dissonance encountered when all three parts are sung together, it is useful to have some understanding of how 12th century music was performed.

Congaudeant Catholici, from the *Codex Calixtinus*

The general term for monastic multi-voice singing, is 'organum'. When many notes are sung to a single syllable, it is known as melismatic chant. Syllabic chant has one note, or neume, per syllable, though this may also refer to singing two to four notes to the same syllable. When between two to twelve notes are sung to one syllable, it is referred to as neumatic chant. Different musicologists apply slightly different numbers to those given here. The practice of layering voices one over the other, using a mix of the above, developed, so that the music became more complex, with voices moving in different directions, yet harmonising. This laid the foundation for the more florid sounds of later polyphony, where several voices are set against each other.

As we have seen, in the Cluniac Rule, the monks' main occupation was the *Opus Dei,* the 'Work of God'. The Office was divided into eight 'hours' starting with Matins (early morning), through the *First* to the *Ninth* hour (Prime to None), with *Vespers* as an evening prayer and *Compline* at the end of the day. The exact timings depended on the season of the year. Not only would the monks spend most of the day at liturgical services, but much of the rest of their time would have been dedicated to studying the Bible, and the psalms in particular. In the early centuries, they would have also transcribed them, creating illuminated manuscripts. The very act of writing was considered part of the prayer life. Painstaking thought would go into every pen-stroke, a prayer being offered for each act. Silence was observed throughout; indeed making too much noise whilst scratching out the letters could result in a reprimand, and even punishment.

Reading Abbey - A pilgrim church

Study of religious texts was rigorous, and many monks were not only versed in Latin but studied the Greek and Hebrew originals. The word 'abbot', or 'abbat', from the Aramaic *abba* (Hebrew אבא), means 'father'. As such, he was expected to give detailed explanations of the scriptures to the monks. This he would do, for instance, at the daily meeting in the chapter house.

Monasteries were at the epicentre of the great flowering of culture throughout Europe in the 11th and 12th centuries, and this included the development of musical theory and practice. One challenge was how to develop a way to standardise musical transcription. This was essential, as it was expected that a Cluniac monk from, for example, the south of France, could be sent to any other daughter monastery as far afield as England or Germany, and be able to fit into the regime of his new home. This would entail being able to join in singing the liturgy. It was essential, therefore, to have a universally recognisable system of musical notation. The development of this was crucial to the evolution of modern western music.

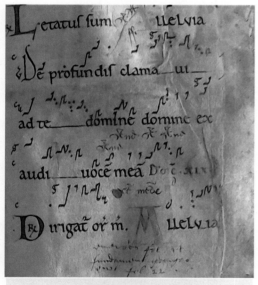

The *De profundis* from the
Douai Cantatorium
©Douai Abbey

The Douai *Cantatorium*

At Reading we know that, by the late 12th century, the monks were using a system of notation based on what is referred to as 'heightened neumes'. At Douai Abbey, the modern Benedictine monastery west of Reading, there is a cantor's book, a *Versarius* or *Cantatorium* (Gradual book), which uses this technique. It dates to c. 1200. The singer needs to have an idea of the tune; the notes only give a relative idea of breath and pitch, but are sufficient to act as an aide-memoir to one versed in the techniques required. The importance of this document is that it shows us the actual tunes used.

One such example is the *De profundis,* Psalm 130, (129 Septuagint version). Having the initial words *Out of the depths,* this psalm is associated with the Mass and Office of the Dead, and is to be found in the evening prayers, such as Vespers and Compline.

We can be sure that it was sung at Reading. Not only do we have the Cantatorium, which most probably came from Reading Abbey, but the rule of Saint Benedict, c. 530, stated that it should be sung at the beginning of Tuesday's vespers.

The Paris School of Perotin and Leonin

The art and skills of preparing the parchment and the inks, as well as the writing, were originally done by the monks in their monasteries. Later, specialist craftsmen and lay scribes were employed for these tasks.

The 12th century saw significant advances both in the methodology of transcribing music and in the theory and practice of polyphony. This latter may be described as the combination of two or more different parts, or melodic lines, into one sound. Two of the greatest and best known proponents of this style are Leonin and Perotin.

Their works have been preserved in the *Magnus liber organi,* (right), and consist of polyphonic settings of the liturgy. Both composers were well known throughout western Europe, and their music was doubtless used at Reading. However, these are but two of the best known names; it would be surprising if the monks at Reading did not also create their own musical settings. Innovations in notation, and other advances, allowed for the accurate reproduction of even the most complicated multi-part pieces.

The illustration on page 208, from Perotin's *Alleluia nativitas,* is for three parts, written on a four line stave. The music is complex, yet sufficient information is presented to allow for an accurate reproduction. Note how the singing parts at times follow one another, but elsewhere diverge. The lowest voice, acting almost as a drone, underpins the whole.

This was written as the new style of architecture, with its lofty pointed arches and intricate stained glass, was coming to fruition in the 12th century. Paris, St Denis in particular, was at the centre of this revolution, and its music was very much part of the great changes that were sweeping Europe and western European monasticism. Just as it has been suggested that Romanesque music reflected the rounded curves of its buildings, so in this new polyphony, we can hear, and see in its written notation, the intricate interplay of soaring pointed vaulting and the almost contrapuntal relationship between different features of the first Gothic structures. One only needs to think of Winchester Cathedral, and the complementary contrast of placing the soaring heights of its later architecture alongside the muscular pillars and arches of the north transept.

Alleluia nativitas Perotin c 1200

The illustration alongside shows a long melismatic *Alleluia* by Perotin. It is a magnificent example of both the academic theory, and the spiritual inspiration, that underpinned this whole movement, which we call 'the Gothic'. This was a conceptualisation of form that was to dominate western culture for the next four hundred years. The discovery of the plasticity afforded by music, allowed for a complexity and intricacy of sound that continued to evolve through the 13th century and beyond, culminating in the creation of motets, and later madrigals, for both religious and secular music.

Moreover, its relationship with architecture was not lost on these medieval scholars and builders. High stone vaulting, and its more delicate supporting stonework, in contrast to the dense pillars and robust supporting arches of the Romanesque, created a new resonance, compared with that heard under flat wooden ceilings.

Sumer is Icumen In (illustration page 209, opposite)

It is in this interplay between the 'secular' and the 'religious' art forms, that we encounter Reading's most famous contribution to the history of music: *Sumer is icumen in.* As this was most probably written at the abbey, it is reasonable to propose that it would also have been sung at Reading.

The British Library entry says: *"Sumer Is Icumen In* is a composition for several voices that was probably written at Reading Abbey in the mid-13th century. This song, written in Middle English, was composed to be sung in the round, with four voices singing the same melody one after the other, accompanied by two lower voices. The manuscript is the oldest known musical round with English words."

Singers, however, can choose between the decidedly secular, if not bawdy, Middle English lyrics, which celebrate the arrival of spring, and those in Latin: *Perspice Christicola (Look Christian),* which are religious. The manuscript is also the earliest known example in which both secular and sacred words are written down together to the same piece of music. The text towards the lower right of the page gives instructions in Latin for its performance as a round, the cross above the first line marking the point at which each of the four main voices enters.

The secular English words are written in black, whilst the Latin spiritual version, which has no bearing on the English words, is in red. Could it be that the choice of pigments is connected with the concept of colour as symbolising different aspects of creation, red and gold being associated with divinity?

It is generally agreed that this was a well known popular tune before it was adapted, or at least written down here as a round. It has also been suggested that the *pes,* for up to two singers, refers only to the English words. (In medieval music, the 'pes', meaning a 'foot' in Latin, was a short repeated phrase that provided the foundation supporting the other parts). This would lead one to conclude that the secular version came first. According to this theory, the religious Latin version followed, probably to convert it into a suitable piece of work, not just to be sung in church and included in the monastic collection, but also for pilgrims to sing on the road.

The 'Pes' written bottom left; the final 's' has the old ſ form

British Library, Harley MS 978© folio 11v
©The British Library Board

However, there are several inconsistencies in the manuscript. First of all, some commentators believe that the black writing is far more constricted than the red, indicating that it was squeezed in after the red had been written. Secondly, the Latin instructions in black for singing the English version, are squashed into what seems to be an available space, whilst the red Latin instructions are more widely spaced. Thirdly, if the black writing was done before the red, it is strange that, in the case of the word *Pes,* this is reversed. Problematically, the initial 'S' is in red for the upper 'Sing Cuccu' refrain, whereas the remaining English words are in black. These factors should at least be considered.

The British Library statement that it was probably written at Reading in the mid 13th century, is based on the evidence that the manuscript is to be found in in a bundle of documents known as Harley 978. This includes a monastic calendar giving the feasts for January and February similar to those of the calendar in the Reading cartulary (BL Vespasian Ev) The *Sumer* canon is on the first gathering of the folios, the calendar on the second. There is also a close similarity to the hand in which the "instructions" are written. Another indicator is that an obit in the calendar for 1261 is for a Reading monk, John Forn. This would give an earliest date when it is likely the canon was written, or at least included in the folio. Another section contains the *Song of the Barons,* which describes Simon de Montfort's victory at Lewes in 1264. As there is no mention of his death at the battle of Evesham the next year, it is reasonable to assume that this was the latest date when the Canon could have been written. There are, of course, other explanations how and why the Canon may have come to be included, but this is fairly compelling evidence to suggest that it was written in Reading between 1261 and 1264. If we accept the above, it is even possible to hazard a guess as to the role of two Reading monks in its composition, or at least its transcription. These are William of Wicumbe and William de Winton (Winchester).

Many Reading monks spent some years at the daughter house of Leominster. Wicumbe was there before the proposed composition dates, and Winton afterwards. In Harley 978 there is a *Contents* list of a book by Winton which contains several pieces of music, including the Canon. Since the list was most probably compiled before 1296, this give us another possible end-date for its composition. The reasoning behind proposing this date is that it refers to a monk called Robert de Burgate who became abbot at Reading in 1268/9. As he is not given the title 'Abbot', it is highly unlikely that the book was written later than 1268/9.

We know that Wicumbe was a critic and transcriber of existing musical works. He was also a prolific writer of liturgical music, as can be seen from his *compotum optimum,* a scholarly treatise on music in which he refers to transcribing two polyphonic works: one for two, the other for three parts. Winton was another polymath. Bodley MS 848 includes his works on arithmetic, geometry and astronomy. The grouping contains the texts for *Sumer* in both Middle English and Latin.

Despite the debate about the origins, and place, of *Sumer is icumen in* within the history of musicology, we should not lose sight of its popular appeal, which has lasted a millennium and still speaks to us today.

What should be noted is the contrast between this form of singing and the chants associated with the *Opus Dei.*

It is noteworthy that Harley 978 also contains the secular collection known as the *Lais* of Marie de France. These are short, narrative poems, written in late Anglo-Norman at the end of the 12th century. They glorify the concept of courtly love by relating the adventures of their main characters, and contrasting the positive and negative actions that can result from love. Though secular in content, they also served as metaphors for spiritual vices and virtues, and so it should not be surprising to find them in a monastic collection.

Sumer is Icumen In

English version, with translation   Latin version, with free translation

Sing cuccu …

	Sing cuckoo …
Sumer is icumen in	Summer (= spring) has arrived,
Lhude sing cuccu	Sing loudly, cuckoo!
Groweþ sed	The seed is growing
and bloweþ med	And the meadow is blooming,
and springþ þe wde nu	And the wood is coming into leaf now,
Sing cuccu	Sing, cuckoo!
Awe bleteþ after lomb	The ewe is bleating after her lamb,
lhouþ after calue cu	The cow is lowing after her calf;
Bulluc sterteþ	The bullock is prancing,
bucke uerteþ	The billy-goat farting,
murie sing cuccu	Sing merrily, cuckoo!
Cuccu cuccu	Cuckoo, cuckoo,
Wel singes þu cuccu	You sing well, cuckoo,
ne swik þu nauer nu	Never stop now.

Sing cuccu nu • Sing cuccu.   Sing, cuckoo, now; sing, cuckoo;
Sing cuccu • Sing cuccu nu   Sing, cuckoo; sing, cuckoo, now!

Perspice Christicola ('xp͞icola")	O Christian Man, behold God's love,
que dignacio	Seeing his blighted vines, the vineyard's Lord
Celicus agricola	Chose not to spare his only Son,
pro vitis vicio	But sent Him to endure the pains of death,
Filio non parcens	
exposuit mortis exicio	To save the suffering captives from their fate,
Qui captivos semivivos a supplicio	Giving them life and crowning them with Him
Vite donat et secum coronat	On heaven's throne.
in celi solio	

© Lindsay Mullaney 2017

Marian Music

According to the Foundation Charter, Reading Abbey was built in the name of the *Ever Virgin Mary, Mother of God and of St. John.* Although its most famous relic was of the Hand of St James, it is necessary not to lose sight of the abbey's main dedication.

The discovery of the stone of the Coronation of the Virgin is just one example of just how important this devotion was in the life of both the monks and visitors.

Reading Abbey - A pilgrim church

The Little Office of the Blessed Virgin Mary

All too often today, when looking at the spirituality of Reading Abbey, the focus is on the role of pilgrimage and the Hand of St James. However, devotion to Mary would have been a recurring theme in the liturgy. This was integral to the major feasts of the medieval church celebrating the role of Mary, such as the Annunciation and the Nativity of Christ. For instance, as noted in Chapter 9, Hugh, the first abbot of Reading and a Cluniac Benedictine, observed the feast of the Immaculate Conception at Henry's request.

The addition of the Lady Chapel in 1314, even shortly after a period when the Abbey found itself with financial difficulties, illustrates the importance of this aspect of monastic life, and the use of the monastery both for the monks and for pilgrims.

Late 13th century Lady Chapel,
Chichester Cathedral

The 13th century had seen a burgeoning in devotional practices to Mary. As with the Lady Chapel at Chichester, Reading's was built in the latest Decorated style of architecture. Note the elegant ribbed vaulted ceiling and the wide tracery windows. The walls would have been completely covered with painted images of the life of the Virgin. The stained glass likewise would have told the story of her life as co-redemptorix in Salvation History.

Groups of visitors to the chapel would have sung, chanted or said the *Little Office of the Blessed Virgin Mary*: a much abbreviated version of the Divine Office, with prayers focusing on Mary. Members of confraternities and guilds, both religious and craft, dedicated to Mary, may have visited the chapel to offer prayers of thanksgiving and petition. When discussing popular devotion in Reading, however, we should remember that St Lawrence's, the town parish church, was the focus of guild activity and devotion. Its church had been enlarged by Abbot Hugh II in 1196, for the townspeople.

The Salve Regina

One of the most popular Marian hymns, which would have been sung in the Lady Chapel, and which dates back at least to the 11th century, is the *Salve Regina,* known today as the *Hail Holy Queen.* The differs very slightly from the Latin.

Salve, Regina, (Mater) misericordiæ,	Hail, holy Queen, Mother of Mercy,
vita, dulcedo, et spes nostra, salve.	Hail, our life, our sweetness and our hope.
Ad te clamamus exsules filii Hevæ,	To thee do we cry, poor banished children of Eve;
Ad te suspiramus, gementes et flentes	To thee do we send up our sighs, mourning and weeping in this vale of tears.
in hac lacrimarum valle.	Turn then, most gracious advocate, thine eyes of mercy toward us;
Eia, ergo, advocata nostra, illos tuos	And after this our exile, show unto us the blessed fruit of thy womb, Jesus.
misericordes oculos ad nos converte;	O clement,
Et Jesum, benedictum fructum ventris tui,	O loving,
nobis post hoc exsilium ostende.	O sweet Virgin Mary.
O clemens, O pia, O dulcis Virgo Maria	

This was set down in its Latin form at the Abbey of **Cluny** in the 12th century, where it was used as a processional hymn on Marian feasts. **There are many musical settings, but two versions predominate. One is** ascribed to Hermann of Reichenau, though this is often disputed.

It is worth while reading the words, as they give us an insight, not just into the beliefs of the monks and pilgrims, but a feeling of how most people at the time would have viewed the world, their place in it and their final destiny.

Reading Abbey - A pilgrim church

The Regina Caeli

Another Marian hymn that was sung at Reading Abbey throughout its time as a monastery, is the *Regina Caeli* (O Queen of heaven). This hymn needs to be understood in the context of the doctrines both of the 'Dormition of Mary' and the 'Assumption', along with her Coronation by Jesus, as exemplified in the sculpture of the Coronation of the Virgin. It is a hymn normally associated with Eastertide, as testified by the word *Resurrexit,* referring to the belief that Jesus rose from the dead.

The music usually associated with it was reputedly written by Hermann of Reichenau in the 11th century. However, *The Golden Legend*, written in the 13th century by Jacobus de Voragine, tells us that, during an outbreak of pestilence at the time of Pope Gregory the Great, (590-601), an image of the Virgin Mary was carried in procession through the streets of Rome. As it passed by the mausoleum of Emperor Hadrian, angels could be heard singing this hymn, and a vision appeared of the angel of death sheathing his sword, so proclaiming the end of the plague. To commemorate this miracle, a statue of the angel was placed on top of the mausoleum, known today as Castel San Angelo.

Here we have an example of how different art forms: sculpture, music and poetry, inform one another. Remembering that, at Reading, these words would have been sung daily, certainly at Eastertide, and probably throughout the year, it is worth while paying close attention to their meaning and, if possible, listening to them being sung to the tune which we know that the monks and people of Reading would have used.

The *Regina Caeli* - *Queen of Heaven*

Regina cæli, lætare, alleluia:
Quia quem meruisti portare, alleluia,
Resurrexit, sicut dixit, alleluia,
Ora pro nobis Deum, alleluia.

O Queen of Heaven, rejoice, alleluia:
For He whom you did merit to bear, alleluia.
Has risen, as He said, alleluia.
Pray for us to God, alleluia.

COMMENT

Music was arguably the most important part in the daily life, spiritual and physical, of a monk. It must also have been at the heart of how visitors and pilgrims experienced the abbey. It is often claimed that, because the liturgy was in Latin, the majority of the people were excluded from understanding it, and the teachings of the Church that it presented. There is some justification for this statement, but this problem was recognised at the time, and it is not the whole story. As *Sumer is icumen in* demonstrates, integration of the vernacular into religious music, through song and drama, was a feature of medieval life. It would be a mistake to take just one medium in isolation. Architecture, and all other art forms, such as stained glass, music and drama, should be viewed in their entirety.

Can we today appreciate how it is possible to combine understanding a complex belief system with a foreign tongue? We do have a recent parallel. Those Catholics who are old enough to remember the days of the Latin Mass, and other parts of the Latin liturgy, will remember that many prayers and hymns were said and sung every week in Latin. Their sounds and meaning became familiar, and were repeated and understood. Though some of the theology behind them may initially have been obscure, this was compensated for through school learning, and explanations from the pulpit. Indeed the study, and contemplation, of the Latin words deepened the understanding of their spiritual significance. This is exactly what many a commentary claimed during the Middle Ages.

One modern commentator describes medieval chant as 'formalising the music of speech', by which he means the 'musicality' inherent in Latin words and their rhythm, both in prose and in poetry. Whether the listener understands, or not, the foreign words of a long melismatic chant, or of a brief antiphon, few who hear this music remain unmoved by the sounds that reach deep into the sensory and emotional essence that makes us human.

One such example is in Hermann's tune for the *Salve Regina*. The plummeting sound of the last syllable of its first word sets the tone for a psychological and spiritual journey: a pilgrimage of the mind and emotions. *Salve,* 'Hail', should be a triumphant shout of joy. But there is a tension between the word and the emotional fall in the music: a fall of a fifth, from 'A' to 'D'. This is repeated in the second word, *Regina,* but this time, we are led gently through a melisma of rising and falling notes which rests once more on the final 'D'. In contrast to its first use, this leads us straight into the calming reassuring word *mater* ('mother'); sung simply with a rising syllabic notation.

CHAPTER 13

PILGRIMAGE AND RELICS

On the 21st of September 1539, Sir William Penizon wrote to Thomas Cromwell saying, "I have received possession … of the Abbey of Reading". On the 14th or 15th of November, the last abbot of Reading, Hugh Cook, known as Faringdon, and two companions, John Eynon and John Rugg, were executed for treason. The abbey with all its lands and possessions passed into the hands of the Crown.

So ended, after 400 years, the great royal monastery that had been synonymous with the name Reading. To understand just how shattering this was, we have to look at the historical background. With the Reformation of the Church of England, the lives of the ordinary people of Reading, along with the rest of the country, were to change for ever. A revolution in much of the economy of the town had already been taking place. Outside forces were at work across Europe, let alone England, or Reading. A new commercial and industrial class was emerging, and with it came different attitudes to religion and to the relationship between a town's monastery and its inhabitants.

Reading Abbey had been founded as a place of prayer, for the salvation of the souls of Henry I, and of his ancestors and descendants. The church had been designed as a place of pilgrimage, and as a sanctuary, both spiritual and physical, for the poor, the infirm, the elderly and the pilgrim. The distinction between spiritual and physical wellbeing was often blurred.

Pilgrimage has been described as a spiritual journey through a physical landscape, to a holy space where heaven and earth become one.[1] As often as not, the destination would offer the pilgrim-traveller a tangible connection between the temporal and spiritual worlds. There, the pilgrim would encounter a 'relic': something left behind, something tangible that bestowed a physical connection with a mystical antecedent. It might be a bit of cloth belonging to someone special: a saint. It might even be a part of that person that had survived the centuries: a lock of hair or a bone. Abbeys, such as Reading, could boast impressive collections of relics, all designed to bridge the gap between the individual, living in this temporal 'vale of tears', and eternal bliss.

There is debate as to the extent to which the re-formation of the church in England and the dissolution of the monasteries by Henry VIII were initiated, and driven forward, as much by religious conviction as by economic considerations. As George Bernard has puts it, *much more than royal or ministerial greed was behind the dissolution: first, questions of authority, notably Henry's sense of his royal supremacy, and secondly, rival religious beliefs.*[2]

I would like to stress that, by focusing on this aspect of Henry's reforms I am not denying the existence, or belittling the importance, of other factors including economic and political considerations, such as *the question of authority,* in influencing Henry's actions. Supreme amongst these, of course, was the question of the *King's Great Matter*: the divorce of Queen Catherine.

With regards to the economic aspect of the reforms, there is debate as to the extent of the financial benefits to the exchequer. Suffice to note that Reading Abbey, with an annual income of around £2000, was one of the largest in the realm. Just how much of this saw its way into Henry's coffers is open to dispute. But I am going to focus on 'pilgrimage' as core to the spiritual re-formation of the church. Note that as this stage I am referring to the general 're-formation' of the Christian church in western Europe. This became the 'Reformation' with its separate movements and secessionist sects, which, though distinct, is not totally separate from, the wider re-formation of the Christian church, including the Church of Rome itself.

An important feature of the dissolution of the larger religious institutions, such as friaries, abbeys and convents, was the dismantling of pilgrimage shrines and the ending of the practice of pilgrimage. Time after time, the abuse of shrines and accusations of idolatry, were quoted as the reason for their closure. Henry VIII is too often presented as essentially conservative, and his break with Rome having simply produced 'Catholicism without the Pope of Rome'. That strikes me as quite inadequate. Henry's Catholicism was Catholicism without the Pope, without monasteries and without pilgrimages.

The medieval pilgrim, like today's pilgrim, was a traveller whose aim it was to visit a holy or meaningful place. But the act of travelling was, and is, almost as important as the sacred place itself. Both on the journey, and at the destination, the pilgrim hopes to find, achieve, or fulfil one or more of a variety of intentions. These may include to redeem a pledge, a sort of barter with the divine, or with God's representative such as a saint: *If you cure my son, I'll go on pilgrimage to Rome;* or of thanks: *You cured my son, so I'll make a pilgrimage to Rome.* It may be to show repentance for an ill done, possibly to gain some spiritual benefit associated with the act of pilgrimage, such as

The Pardoner
from *The Canterbury Tales*

forgiveness of a sin and remission of the punishment associated with that sin, which, though forgiven, might still merit the pains of purgatory: some sort of penalty, though not eternal, after death.[3]

Over the years, the concept of pilgrimage began to assume a metaphorical meaning, representing the journey through life. This theme appears in Langland's *Piers Plowman* and his *"journey through the wildernesse of this world"* and, nearly 300 years later, in the asceticism of Bunyan's *Pilgrim's Progress*. Its subtitle, *Delivered under the Similitude of a Dream,* reflects the motif of Langland's great poem.

And so Christian Pilgrimage implies some sort of reconciliation with God, a coming together of the Human and the Divine. The debate, about how this 'coming together' could be realised, revolved around the concept of 'justification'. In other words, the competing 'rival religious beliefs', about how man could gain eternal bliss, were at the very core of the great theological divide, resulting in the socio-political, as well as spiritual, movement which we call the Reformation, and which arguably shaped modern Europe.

At the centre of this debate was the question as to who could forgive sin. Could the Church lessen the punishment of purgatory by granting an indulgence to commute the effects of sin? And there we have it. The word "indulgence". The word that triggered Luther's reforms. The word that, it is often claimed, triggered 'The Reformation'.

It is easy to see why many 16th century reformers, especially those with humanist leanings, such as espoused by Erasmus, viewed pilgrimage, and practices associated with it, with such suspicion and distaste. Purveyors of superstition and simony found easy pickings, as we read in the *Canterbury Tales,* not just at the shrines themselves, but also along the pilgrimage routes. Moreover, many monasteries, including Reading, were centres of pilgrimage. For here were relics, such as the Hand of St James, promising untold rewards, indeed eternal reward, for those who made the journey and paid their respects, and most certainly paid much more, at the shrine.

It was this antipathy to these practices that was such an important religious motivation for the suppression of the monasteries. By the 16th century there was a popular move towards a greater emphasis on internal spirituality, rather than external manifestations of devotion. The 'Accounts of Visitations', and 'Injunctions'[4] concerning places of worship, in the 1530s, show an overwhelming concentration on condemning and forbidding such practices as lighting candles, censing, and, especially, crawling towards, kissing, and licking statues.[5]

The great theological questions of the day revolved around how man could know the Divine plan and how best to fulfil it. In simple terms, the Catholic church taught that Divine revelation was not achieved solely through the study of the scriptures. Their infallible interpretation, and consequently that of the 'Divine plan', had been given to the *magisterium:* the Bishops of the Church, and the most authoritative of these was the Bishop of Rome, the Pope. Against this was the other extreme, which preached that God's will could be discerned, if it could be discerned at all, through the Bible, the one and only reliable source of Divine revelation. In this Protestant 'weltanschauung', man's relationship with the Divine did not require any intermediary. As such, the more extreme a Protestant one became, the less one needed the services of priests, or the Mass. Nor was there any place for the forgiveness of sin by a human representative of the Almighty, let alone the intervention of saints, or their relics. Pilgrimage became redundant at best, and blasphemous at worst.

Priest with a Pardon
from Langland *Piers Plowman*

But was the populace really as gullible, ignorant and superstitious as the reforming zealots, and subsequently some historians, claimed? Was Reading Abbey in reality involved in a great Europe-wide conspiracy, led by the Papacy, to defraud the laity and even some of the clergy[6]

Let us look at some evidence as to how the medieval mind worked. In Chaucer's, *Canterbury Tales* and Langland's *Piers Plowman,* both written just over 100 years before the dissolution of Reading Abbey, it is clear that there was a certain scepticism about the power of relics and indulgences. This is not to deny that the norm was to believe in the efficacy of sainty intervention and, by association, the power of relics belonging to saints. We should remember that chroniclers such as William of Malmesbury, writing four hundred years before the Reformation, combined a mix of belief in Divine reward and retribution, with a strong element of pragmatism. In so doing, we can come closer to understanding how the 'common man', the ordinary person, felt about their relationship with the supernatural.

I will quote a couple of examples to illustrate this point. In 1107 the tower at Winchester collapsed. This was seen by many as 'Divine retribution' for the sins of William Rufus, who had been buried under this tower. William of Malmesbury duly reports this belief, but pragmatically states that *the tower might well have fallen anyway owing to its poor construction, even if William had not been buried there.*

Then again, when Henry I survived an assassination attempt, being hit by an arrow on the head, which should have resulted in his death, Malmesbury attributes this in part to 'Divine Providence'. But he also says that it was due to the strength of his protective armour. Malmesbury is not alone in demonstrating this causal link between the Divine and the natural.

Reading Abbey - A pilgrim church

Some chroniclers, in relating the sinking of the White Ship in 1120, when William Adelin, Henry I's son and heir, died, wrote that this was Divine punishment for the debauchery of the young knights and of William, but more practically, Malmesbury attributed the shipwreck to the fact that the ship was overloaded, that the sailors were drunk, and that the ship struck a rock.

There can be no doubt that some, indeed many, people (whether this was the majority or not we shall never know), acted either through fear, superstition, or trust in promises of redemption. Nor can there be any question that belief in Divine intervention, a belief in a direct relationship between human activity and the supernatural, was constantly present.[7]

Moreover, we should not fall for the fallacy of attributing modern thought processes to a past generation. We do well to remember that the Reformation was not the Enlightenment, let alone a proto-scientific movement based on reason, questioning the tenets of 'Salvation History'. Be it in the writings of that greatest of Renaissance humanists, Desiderius Erasmus, who sought a *via media,* or of Luther or even Zwingli, all believed in man as placed on earth as part of the 'Divine plan'.

Here is not the place to pursue this point but, at the time of the Reformation, there existed a belief in a strong link between natural events, both good and bad, and the supernatural. However, there also existed, alongside this belief, a certain degree of scepticism, and this scepticism was expressed not just by critics of the Church, but by the Church authorities themselves.

For example: in 1351 Bishop Grandison rebuked those engaged in superstitious and 'lascivious' activities at the Marian shrine of Frithelstock in Devon. In 1296, Bishop Sutton inveighed against those attending a chapel at Hambledon, driven, as they were, by 'certain superstitious and vain fantasies'.

We can read in the *Enchiridion*, the official summary of Church Councils and Papal decrees, repeated warnings against venerating images and other 'vain practices'. Moreover, neither the most extreme 'Catholic' nor the most zealous Christian Protestant Reformer disputed the existence of a personal God, and that same God's intimate relationship with the world and those living in it.[8]

The Reformation: Pilgrimage, Relics and Monasteries

Bearing all this in mind, it is clear to see why Henry VIII, Cromwell, Cranmer and other English reformers, targeted the veneration of relics as a way of underpinning their reforms. Whether this was the unfolding of a masterplan, or a series of responses to events, is open to interpretation.[9] Nevertheless, removing the focal point of pilgrimage, the relics and shrines, was an astute move. At a stroke, one of the major *raisons d'être* for many of the monasteries, namely pilgrimage to shrines, no longer existed. It is unlikely that Henry himself had a masterplan, yet the Visitations of 1534-1535, followed up by the *Valor Ecclesiasticus, 1535,* along with the *Injunctions* of 1536 and *The King's Primer* of that year, certainly give an appearance of a plan, if not a masterplan. Cromwell, Latimer and other reformers in Convocation, were consistent in their attack on the 'abuse' of relics and shrines.

Part of the process was not just to remove relics but also to destroy both them and their shrines: witness the vehemence of Dr. London's report when he dismantled the Marian shrine in Caversham.[10]

The main cause of the Pilgrimage of Grace in 1536, so Robert Aske its leader claimed, was opposition to the suppression of *the monasteries and the relics of the church of God unreverent used*. As Duffy points out, this rebellion, demanding a return to the 'old ways', underscored the suspicion, that those against reform were also to be numbered amongst those opposing Henry's authority. Whether there is a causal link, or not, between the failure of the 'Pilgrimage of Grace' and the wholesale suppression of monastic houses and the destruction of shrines, shortly afterwards, there is no doubting the fact that, within only a few years, the whole structure of friaries, monasteries, and most of the country's shrines and relics, had vanished, and with them the very reason for pilgrimage.[11]

Luther's challenge, in 1517, to the selling of indulgences to raise money for the building of St Peter's, is often cited as the beginning of the Protestant Reformation. In 1521, the Pope granted to Henry the title *Fidei Defensor,* 'defender of the faith', for his riposte *Assertio Septem Sacramentorum* (Defence of the Seven Sacraments), to Luther's attack on the sacraments. In this work, Henry argued against Luther's views about the sacraments, especially marriage, and he also defended the role of the Papacy. Henry's self-appointment, in 1534, as Head of the Church in England, effectively reversed this position. It is necessary to remember that, although Henry was a reformer, he was no Protestant, and considered himself a Catholic to his dying day. And so, by attacking the practice of pilgrimage, the role of relics, veneration at shrines, the concept and practice of indulgences, the very existence of religious houses, and by implementing these reforms, Henry created, a Catholic church without the Pope, without monasteries and without pilgrimages.

Reading Abbey - A pilgrim church

In fact Henry created a very different church, and one that opened the door to Protestantism. True, the new Anglican church could maintain its claim to be 'catholic', and still uses this word in the Creed. As the Book of Common Prayer says: *The Three Creeds: Nicene Creed, Athanasius's Creed, and that which is commonly called the Apostles' Creed, ought thoroughly to be received and believed: for they may be proved by most certain warrants of holy Scripture.* For those not familiar with the words in these creeds I will quote from one: *I believe in the Holy Spirit, the holy catholic Church, the communion of saints, the forgiveness of sins, the resurrection of the body, and the life everlasting.*

Reading Abbey: The Hand of St James—Pilgrimage and Miracles

The three greatest places of Christian pilgrimage in the middle ages were Rome, Jerusalem and Compostela. The last was renowned as having the body of the apostle James the Greater. Reading claimed to have the Hand of St James, and its abbey was considered one of the principal places of pilgrimage in England. The story of how Reading acquired the Hand is complex, and surrounded by somewhat contradictory evidence.

We do know that the Hand was brought to Reading Abbey when, on the death of the Holy Emperor Henry V, his wife Matilda, daughter of Henry I, returned to England with some of the Imperial crown jewels, including the Hand of St James. According to the chronicler Roger of Hoveden, Henry presented it to Reading Abbey in 1125, though another source, the *Flores Historiarum,* says that the Hand came to Reading in 1133. Whatever the date, Reading was soon renowned for the miracles wrought by devotion to this relic. In the late 12th century, a document was written describing some of the miracles. This is now in the archives of Gloucester Cathedral.[12]

One story, which tells us something about the architecture of the Abbey church, concerns *a certain rich man's keeper of hounds* from the North of England, who was struck blind as a punishment for hunting on St James' feast day, July 25th. He is said to have been cured, after a long period of blindness, when his wife brought him to Reading Abbey, at a time when Gilbert Foliot, who was Bishop of London between 1163 and 1187, transferred the relic from one bejewelled reliquary to a new one, and placed it back on the *pulpitum,* the screen between the nave and the chancel.

A page from the 'Miracles of the Hand of St James'.

By courtesy of Gloucester Cathedral

Many of the cures were effected through what was called 'the water of Saint James'. This was water into which the Hand, or more probably the reliquary containing the Hand, had been placed. It was then sprinkled on the sufferer, or used to bathe the affected part of the body, as in the case of a monk from the Abbey who suffered from a tumour on his head. We are told that *after the invalid's head had been signed with the apostle's hand, he moistened a linen cloth with water of the blessed apostle and bound up his head with it, covering it all round.* The cure began immediately and *after two days he was restored to perfect health and went in procession with the rest of the monks.*

Sometimes the relic would be taken out of the Abbey in procession. The fourth miracle story recounts how, after plague had broken out in Reading, killing large numbers of the population, including thirteen monks, a decision was taken to declare a fast, with special liturgies in the abbey church followed by *a well ordered general procession* around the town. The hand relic was borne aloft and the sick people were *laid out in the streets … so that they might look on the reliquary which contained the sacred hand and be delivered from their infirmities.*

The 'history' of the Hand of St James [13]

11th - 12th century apse mosaic, in the basilica church of S. Maria Assunta, Torcello

At this point, it would be useful to know something of the history of the Hand before it was brought to Reading. Among the archives of the Diocese of Portsmouth is a collection of notes, made by a Father Weale in the early 20th century, and based on an article in the Catholic magazine *The Month,* printed in 1882.

Father Weale tells us that in the seventh century the relic was held by the parish of Altino, in the Veneto region of Italy. It was believed that the arm of Saint James had been brought there by Heliodorus, a colleague of Saint Jerome, in the late fourth century. This was a time when many bones of the early Christian saints were being 'translated' from tombs in Jerusalem. It followed Constantine's Edict of Milan in 313 AD, which legalised Christianity, and Emperor Theodosius' proclamation, in the Edict of Thessalonica in 380 AD, that Christianity would, from that time, be the state religion.

According to Father Weale's notes, the relic, which is here described as the hand, not the arm, of Saint James, was taken from Altino around 640 AD, when the whole Christian community of Altino, along with its bishop, Paul, fled from the Lombard incursions and took refuge on the island of Torcello, in the Venetian lagoon, where Heliodorus himself had been buried.

Reading Abbey - A pilgrim church

In 1046, the island was visited by the Papal Legate, Adalbert, the Bishop of Bremen and Hamburg, who was accompanying the Emperor Heinrich III on his way to Rome to select the next pope, following a disputed election. Adalbert himself was offered the papacy but declined to accept it.

Adalbert was 'given' the relic by Bishop Vitale Unsiolo, perhaps not entirely voluntarily, according to the Portsmouth document, and brought it back with him to Germany. When he died, in 1072, the Emperor's son, Heinrich IV, seized it, and the Hand of Saint James became part of the imperial regalia. We do not know whether any miracles were attributed to the relic while it belonged to the Emperor, but it was clearly highly prized at a time when the cult of Saint James was at its zenith.

Many pilgrims travelled from Germany, and even from Scandinavia, on the *Jakobsweg* (Saint James' Way), to Santiago de Compostela, where it was believed that the remains of Saint James had been discovered in the ninth century. It is not clear whether the Hand in the Imperial treasury was believed to be from the same body as that venerated in Spain: the two legends are basically incompatible, as Baxter has pointed out.[14]

Seals and charters [15]

There can be no doubt that Reading was popular as a place of pilgrimage, and that St James was widely venerated. But how did the monks themselves view this relic? If we wish to find out how the monks and abbots looked upon their own monastery, and its relics, especially the Hand, we do well to examine the official seals appended to charters and other documents. These seals represented a solemn confirmation, similar to an oath, which bound the person, or institution, to the words of the document. Brian Kemp carried out extensive researches in this field, and what follows is a summary of his work, along with more recent study.

From the middle of the 12th century, both the King and the Church promoted the cause of St James . Seals often shed light on matters not directly connected with their legal function. As Kemp says: *the evolving iconography of the Reading seals between the twelfth and fourteenth centuries provides an interesting commentary on the growth of the cult of St James the Great in the abbey, based on its principal relic, a hand of the apostle.* Depictions of the Hand, and other references to St James, began to appear in the first half of the thirteenth century and became quite common by the end of it, as will be seen from the following list of seals and charters.

1121-1328. The first Common Seal of Reading Abbey (Fig.1)

The Common Seal was used for all official abbey business. The earliest for which impressions survive is known as the First Common Seal. This was almost certainly made not long after the founding of the monastery in 1121. It remained in use until 1328. Of pointed oval shape, somewhat resembling a mandorla,[16] and some 70·75 mm long when complete, it only has an obverse side, depicting the Virgin and Child. The Virgin Mary is seated frontally, wearing a crown. I looked at the significance of this iconography in Chapter 10. In her right hand she is holding a flowering rod on which a bird has perched, and in her left the model of a church. On her lap sits the Christ Child, also frontal, his right hand raised in blessing, his left holding an orb.

These symbols probably reference Isaiah 11:1: *And there shall come forth a rod out of the stem of Jesse, and a Branch shall grow out of his roots.* This was widely interpreted as a prophecy foretelling Mary and the birth of Jesus. The bird, as we saw when examining the Stone of the Coronation of the Virgin, is most likely the dove, representing the Holy Spirit, by whose power Mary conceived Jesus. The Christ Child is shown as a king, holding an orb in his left hand a and giving a blessing with his raised right hand.

Fig 1. First Common Seal of Reading Abbey c1120s-1328

Kemp, B. (1988) *The seals of Reading Abbey*. University of Reading, Centaur 85217 and by permission of the Trustees of the British Library

Fig 2

Fig 2. By permission of Salisbury Cathedral.

1139-1149. Abbot Adam of Lathbury's seal (Fig. 2)

This was appended to a 'grant of toll exemption' made to the bishop and chapter of Salisbury. It portrays the abbot in the same manner as in previous abbots' seals, but has a new counterseal, or reverse side, which depicts a hand with two fingers raised in blessing, accompanied by two scallop shells, all within a border bearing the legend: + ORA PRO NOB[IS] SANCTE IACOBE (+ Saint James, pray for us). The unequivocal references to St James on this counterseal clearly imply the full establishment of the cult of the Hand at Reading by the early thirteenth century.

Reading Abbey - A pilgrim church

1161-64 Charter and seal

Bartholomew, Bishop of Exeter, granted an *indulgence of twenty days to all those visiting the relics of St James at Reading Abbey, ... during, or within eight days, of the saint's festival.*

C. 1164 Indulgence

A very similar indulgence was granted by Bishop Jocelin of Salisbury on 19th April 1164. The indulgence was for twenty days to all who visited Reading on the anniversary of its dedication or within its octave.

This was the same day and year that Thomas Becket consecrated the abbey church. The abbey is described as built *in honore dei et beate dei virginis Marie et beatorum apostolorum Iohannis et Iacobi,* "in honour of God and the blessed Mother of God, the Virgin Mary, and the blessed apostles John and James". (*Reading Abbey Cartularies*, no 201, p156, edited Kemp, B.).

This attribution is incorrect, for as we have seen, St James was not mentioned in the Foundation Charter. What it does show is the extent to which, within half a century of its foundation, Reading Abbey was identified with the cult of St James, by bishops well beyond the immediate vicinity of the town of Reading.

1173 Pope Alexander III

By 1173, the association of Reading with St James reached as far afield as Rome and the very centre of Catholicism. Pope Alexander III officially sanctioned the pilgrimage to St James at Reading. Pilgrims from within the province of Canterbury could "avail themselves of the indulgence established by the glorious martyr, blessed Thomas, with the advice of his suffragans, when with them he dedicated the abbey". (*Reading Abbey Cartularies*, no 152, p133)

1173-1199 Abbatial seals

Whereas the above written references demonstrate the widely-held links between the abbey and St James, no signs of this connection had yet appeared on the seals of abbots Joseph (1173-c1180), and Hugh II (c1180-1200).

1192 Gift by John, Count of Mortain to Reading Abbey

In translation, Count John calls the abbey "the church of St James at Reading", without reference to Mary or St John.
"Let it be known that I gift to the **church ... of St James and to its monks ... at Reading** a **burgage** ... that belonged to William, son of William, son of Anand of Dunwich..." (*Sciatis me dedissee ... **ecclesie sancti Iacobi de Rading**(ia) **et monachis ibidem** ... quod fuit Willelmi filii Willelmi filii Anandi ... et in Dunewico. (Reading Abbey Cartularies*, no. 546, p. 412)

c1290-1305 The Seal of Abbot William de Sutton (Fig 3)

Fig 3

Abbot William de Sutton's seal, at the turn of the century, marks a new stage in design. It is carefully crafted, with more delicate detail. It may have been designed to re-assert the abbey's dignity and standing, after its recent rescue from insolvency under his predecessor. As I have said, a seal was not just a 'pretty' appendage: it was the sign of a bond made in heaven, as well as on earth.

In many ways its design follows previous patterns. It is approximately 70 mm in length, and portrayal of the abbot is still in the traditional form: standing frontally with a book in his left hand and a pastoral staff in his right. But there are significant differences. The abbot is now mitred, and stands in an ornately carved niche, with two small wyverns beneath his feet. The whole is set within a richly patterned background, upon which, to the left of the niche, there is the hand of St James, in the same form as appears on Abbot Adam of Lathbury's seal (Fig. 2). Likewise there is the image of the scallop shell: the emblem of St James.

Fig 3. By permission of Salisbury Cathedral.'

Fig 4

1305 -1328. Abbot Nicholas de Whaplode (Fig 4)

An impression of his seal appears on a charter dated 1st January, 1328. This was shortly before Abbot Nicholas' death on 11th January. It records his gifts of money and materials to the scholars of Balliol College, Oxford, towards the building of their chapel. The seal, in the shape of a mandorla, depicts the abbot, mitred and standing in a canopied niche in exactly the same manner as the previous abbatial seals; but now he is accompanied by a somewhat richer array of allusions to St James. To the left of the niche appear the hand of St James and a scallop, separated by a crosslet within a quatrefoil, while to the right are another scallop and what appears to be the head of a man (perhaps St James), wearing a pilgrim's hat, also separated by a crosslet in a quatrefoil.

Fig 4 Reproduced by kind permission of the Master and Fellows of Balliol College
Balliol catalogue reference: D.6.21

Fig 5

1341/42-1360/1. Abbot Henry de Appleford (Fig 5)

This seal is of the same type, though of an even richer elaboration, which includes for the first time allusions to St John the Evangelist. The abbot appears, like William de Sutton and Nicholas, standing in a canopied niche. However, he is now flanked by symbols both of St James and St John. On the left there is a chalice, for St John, though the emerging serpent is now missing,[17] the hand of St James, and two groups of scallops. On the right there is a pilgrim's scrip adorned with the scallop emblem of St James, an eagle (for St John), and two further groups of scallops. Despite the appearance of references to St John the Evangelist, one of the abbey's tutelary saints, the emblems of St James remain the most prominent features of the design.

Taxation Seals (Fig 6)

1319-1320

In the later Middle Ages, the abbot and monastery of Reading, or the abbot alone, were frequently appointed as sub-collectors of clerical taxation within the diocese of Salisbury, either for the whole diocese, or for the archdeaconries of Berkshire and Wiltshire, or for the archdeaconry of Berkshire alone. In this capacity, the abbey used a small circular seal, approximately 23 mm in diameter.

This seal was most commonly applied to receipts issued by the sub-collectors to ecclesiastics and religious houses for the payment of their contributions to the tax.

It consists simply of a shield bearing the abbey's crest of three scallops, suspended by a tie from the top of the seal and flanked by foliage trails to left and right, the whole being set within a circular border carrying an inscription, of which unfortunately only a few letters remain.

The scallops which appear on the abbey's crest were, and are, instantly recognizable as emblems of St James, and were clearly adopted by the monks because they possessed the Hand, and because his name was so closely associated with the monastery.

Fig 6

Copyright: Dean and Chapter of Westminster

Precisely when Reading Abbey assumed this crest is not known, but its occurrence on this small seal must be among the earliest surviving examples of its use.

1328 Second Common Seal (Fig 7 © Hereford Cathedral)

Fig 7

The abbey's Second Common Seal remained in use until the dissolution of the monastery in 1539. It is a large and splendid example of the Decorated style. It is different in many ways from the Romanesque First Common Seal, which it replaced. It was made shortly after the new Lady Chapel of 1314 was built in the same Decorated style.[18]

Whereas the First Seal was a single-sided, round-pointed oval shape, and depicted only the Virgin and Child, this seal is round and contains several figures.

The obverse (right) shows Mary crowned, and seated with the Christ Child on her left knee, carrying an orb in her right hand. She is flanked to her right by St James, with a pilgrim's hat, staff, book and scrip, and to her left by St John. He is standing on his symbol, an eagle. In his right hand is a scroll with the opening words of St John's gospel, *In principio* (In the beginning...), and he holds a palm branch in his left hand. The reverse (left) has Henry I, seated, with a sceptre fleury in his right hand, and a model of a church in his left. This shows a tower and spire. However, the building bears no relationship to what we known, from remains, was the plan of the abbey.[19] On his left stands St Peter holding the keys to the kingdom of heaven and a book. On his right is St Paul with a book and a sword: standard representations for both these saints.

In translation, the Latin inscription on the obverse states that this is the Common Seal of the "conventual church of Reading founded in honour of St Mary and of the apostles John and James". As pointed out above, we know, from the abbey's Foundation Charter, that this is not true as regards St James. The inscription, in translation, on the reverse reads: "King Henry, being a friend of the supreme Deity, lived in security: this man completed the possessions of the house."[20]

If placing St James at Mary's right hand is significant of hierarchical superiority, he has been given a place of greater honour than St John. But the Virgin Mary continues to occupy the most important position, in the centre of the seal.

The same cannot be said of the personal seals of the abbots. One of the most striking points to emerge is that the abbots chose to emphasise St James and, as far as we can tell, made no reference to the principal tutelary saint of their house, the Virgin Mary. This is equally true of those who devised the counterseal and the taxation seals on page 229.

By the time of its ending, the abbey was probably best known for its association with St James. In 1535, Henry ordered a valuation of church-owned properties, and their income. This is known as the *Valor Ecclesiasticus* (The Church Valuation). The entry for Reading describes the monastery as *The Abbey of St James.* It was valued as having an annual income of over £2000, which puts it certainly within the top ten, if not the top six, wealthiest monasteries in England.

Reading after the Reformation

So what was it that changed in Reading after 1539?

Dr London, the 'visitor' appointed by Cromwell and Henry VIII to report on the monastery of Reading, made an inventory of its relics. He listed over twenty and *many othere*.

These were mostly bones of saints, such as Mary Magdalene and Stephen, the first martyr. According to a cartulary belonging to the Earl of Fingall, there were over 234 relics in all.

Within a generation, most of the abbey buildings were reduced to ruins. Those that did survive were converted for other uses. The relics, library, even the dressed stones, were deliberately destroyed, lost or removed.[21] Soon, it would seem, the people of Reading had turned their back on this ancient religious site, and its association with St James.

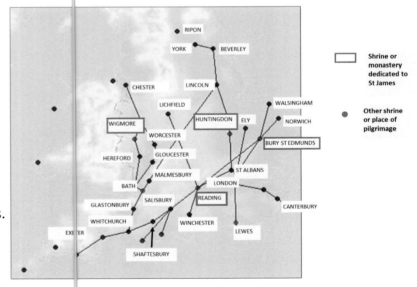

Shrines of St James in medieval England.

Reading Abbey - A pilgrim church

However, the early 17th century history of the Benedictine order, the *Apostolatus Benedictinorum in Anglia,* in naming the Benedictine monasteries in England, lists it at number seventeen, as the *Abbatia S. Iacobi in Radingis.*[21] In translation the entry reads:

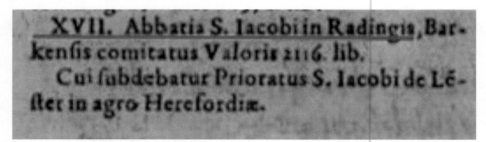

XVII The Abbey of St James in Reading, in the County of Berkshire. Value £2116. (This is based on the 'Valor Ecclesiasticus' of 1535.)

To which is subject the Priory of St James of Leominster in the agro (field, i.e. county), *of Hereford.*

A few pages later Reading Abbey's crest is reproduced, where again it is referred to as the *Abbatia S. Iacobi ...* ('The Abbey of St James ...')

Notice the letters 'A' for azure (heraldic blue), and 'OR' for gold, in the image of the monastery's shield with the three scallop shells.

COMMENT

The cult of St James, which had begun almost immediately the Hand was brought to Reading in the mid-12th century, continued to grow and became so popular that the abbey came to assume the apostle's name.

Today, many historians claim that the concept and practice of pilgrimage was waning, even before the Reformation. I dispute this. The 'Pilgrimage of Grace', a popular uprising defending pilgrimage, and the fanatical vehemence of the writings and actions of the reformers to supress pilgrimage, all point to its continued popularity.

The form that pilgrimage takes does vary. It also evolves over time. The way it manifests itself differs, depending on such factors as culture and climate. But the need to go on pilgrimage, the desire to travel beyond the present place or time, appears to be as much a part of what it means to be human, as speech or song or dance.

NOTES

1. Wynkyn de Worde, *The Art and Craft to Lyve Well*, 1505. Also quoted in Duffy, E. *The Stripping of the Altars.*

2. Bernard, G W. *The Dissolution of the Monasteries*. Lecture to The Friends of Reading Abbey, *The Late Medieval English Church,* 2014.

3. *Enchiridion Symbolorum*, Con. Lugdunensis (Council of Lyon), 1245 no 838, and in 1351 no 1066 Clement VI's encyclical. These are samples of many of the church documents summarising its teaching about purgatory and hell.

4. Duffy *ibid p. 407.*

5   Finucane, R. *Miracles and Pilgrims* Ch 11.

6. Philips, J. *The Reformation of Images* Ch 4, and see Walsham, A. *The Reformation of the Landscape,* page 83 quoting Thomas Bell *Survey of Popery (1596)* and other Protestant 16th century writers.

7. Walsham in *The Reformation of the Landscape* investigates this belief and how and if it manifested itself after the Reformation in Protestant theology and popular tradition. See especially Ch 5.

8. Calvin, J. *The Institutes of Christian Religion*. Calvin talks of the world as a 'most beautiful theatre' and as ' gorgeously constructed and exquisitely furnished' (cf Walsham p 331).

9. Finucane says it is misleading to talk of a government policy. He claims that Cromwell was the driving force, though of course supported by many others. This would account for Henry VIII's apparent vacillation at certain points in the process. In Elton's judgment, Cromwell was "the most remarkable revolutionary in English history", and his intellect "the most successfully radical instrument at any man's disposal in the 16th century". Geoffrey Rudolph Elton, *Thomas Cromwell: Secretary, Minister and Lord Privy Seal*, 2nd edition (Oxford, Davenant Press, 2008). James Clark continues this argument in *The Dissolution of the Monasteries,* agreeing with the modern consensus that there was no conspiracy or premeditated plan.

10 Letters from Dr London to Cromwell in *Suppression of the Monasteries,* The Camden Society, edited by Thomas Wright, 1843. Also Wriothesley, *Chronicle,* especially for the year 1538.

11 It should be noted that the assault on the fabric of the Abbey began in earnest in the reign of Edward VI.

12   The original Latin text and Kemp's translation of *The Miracles* are re-produced in *Reading Abbey Records a new miscellany.*

13   I am indebted to Lindsay Mullaney for much of the content of this section. Mullaney, L. *Henry I and his Abbey, Ch. 25.*

14   Baxter, R. *The Royal Abbey of Reading,* pp 48-56.

15   I am indebted to Brian Kemp for his work on the seals of Reading Abbey. Cf, Kemp, B. (1988) *The seals of Reading Abbey*. Reading Medieval Studies, XIV. pp. 139-162.

16   A mandorla, in medieval Christian iconography, is an almond-shaped frame surrounding the figures of Jesus, often as 'Christ in Majesty', or the Virgin Mary. It is the shape generally used for mediaeval ecclesiastical seals, secular seals generally being round. The figure itself consists of the intersection of two circles, and was thought to contain mystical properties related to the unchanging and unchangeable laws of mathematics: representing the Divine.

17   This refers to the legend that St John was put to the test by the high priest of the Temple of Diana at Ephesus, who challenged him saying, "if you want me to believe in your god, I will give you some poison to drink and, if it does not harm you, it means your god is the true God". John blessed the chalice and the poison turned into a two headed dragon which emerged from the chalice, allowing John to drink the wine without being poisoned.

18   See Chapter 5, Note 1 page 110.

19   For full Latin version and English transcription see Jamieson Boyd Hurry, *Reading Abbey (1901)* 95-97.

20   The illustration of the church on the seal clearly does not represent the appearance of the abbey. The building shown is not basilican in style, it has no transepts and no apse, but is a rectangular structure with a central tower. In brief it looks more like a generic image of a church, rather than an attempt at making an architectural portrayal of the Reading Abbey.

21   Most of the destruction of the abbey buildings did not begin until the reign of Edward VI, and not under that of Henry VIII.

22   The *Apostolatus Benedictinorum in Anglia,* 'The Benedictine Apostolate in England', was published in 1626. The Dictionary of National Biography says: *To Reyner bibliographers always attribute the authorship of the valuable historical work entitled 'Apostolatus Benedictinorum in Anglia,' Douay, 1626. The materials for this work were collected by Father David Baker. His friend, Father John Jones,*

D.D. (1575–1636) [alias Leander à S. Martino], reduced the mass of materials into respectable latinity, and they left Reyner to edit the work, so that it passes for being finished 'operâ et industriâ R. P. Clementis Reyneri.' In the dedication to Cardinal Bentivoglio, Reyner candidly says: 'Non author operis sum, sed jussu congregationis editor et dedicator' (I am not the author of this work, but by order of the congregation, its editor and dedicator). Dodd, Church Hist. ed. Tierney, iv. 97 n.

Title page of the *Apostolatus Benedictinorum in Anglia*

The *Apostolatus* is a long legal tract aimed at proving that the English Benedictine congregation had always been independent of any other Benedictine authority, especially the Spanish or French Benedictines.

Charles I had acceded to the throne in 1625, and in the same year had married Henrietta Maria, a Catholic and daughter of the King of France. In some Catholic quarters, there was the hope that this would lead to greater tolerance of Catholicism, and maybe even some restitution for the loss of the monasteries.

If this were to come about, the remnants of the English Benedictine congregation did not wish that any 'foreign' Benedictines should stake a claim. The term *adversarius* ('enemy', 'adversary', 'opponent'), is used throughout the *Apostolatus* not to refer to the English Crown or to Protestants, but to foreign Benedictines.

POSTSCRIPT

At the end of the 18th century, during the building of the County Gaol on the site of the abbey, a small iron chest was discovered hidden in the ruined walls. Inside was a mummified hand. Many people believed that this was the same hand that had been venerated, in earlier centuries in the abbey, as that of the apostle, St James the Greater. After many vicissitudes, the relic found its way to Saint Peter's Church in Marlow, where it remains today.

The 'Hand of Saint James', in St Peter's church, Marlow.

Radiocarbon dating, carried out in 2018 by the Oxford University Research Laboratory for Archaeology and the History of Art, strongly suggests that the hand does not date to the early years of Christianity, but from the late 10th to early 11th century AD.

It could be that the hand taken from Torcello to Germany, in 1046, may not have been the relic brought from Altino, in the seventh century. The original limb was described as an arm, whereas that seized by Adalbert was a hand. Could the Torcello community, anxious to retain their relic, have made a furtive substitution? Both arm and hand relics were widely venerated in medieval times, and the bishop may have been persuaded that he was acquiring a real 'piece' of the apostle James, when in reality he was being given what was, at the time, a recent forgery. Whichever story is true, it is possible that the mummified hand, now at Marlow, was that which was venerated for 400 years in the abbey.

Today, Reading is once again becoming a place of modern pilgrimage. As from 2022, signs with yellow arrows and the scallop shell, the symbol of St James, mark the route from Reading to Southampton, and so on to Compostela.

Is this just a re-enactment of a medieval practice? Or is it a new type of pilgrimage, providing an opportunity to reconnect with nature, with other people, or even just with ourselves? Could it be that pilgrimage today offers, just as it did to our medieval ancestors, an expression of hope for a better future?

In which case, our modern day relics, the skeletal ruins of Reading Abbey, fulfil a spiritual and psychological need, in much the same way that, a thousand years ago, holy bones gave comfort and hope to our antecedents.

Written eighty years after the Dissolution of Reading Abbey, and a lifetime after the attempt to eradicate in England even the very concept of pilgrimage, the final thoughts of Sir Walter Raleigh, that most Protestant of men, turned to pilgrimage and to St James.

Had he accompanied Queen Elizabeth I on one of her frequent visits to Reading?
Had he stayed at the ruined abbey, and had its spirit left a mark?

Below are the opening lines of the poem, *The Passionate Man's Pilgrimage,*
said to be have been written by Raleigh the night before his execution on the 29th October 1618.

> ***Give me my scallop-shell of quiet,***
> > ***My staff of faith to walk upon,***
> > ***My scrip of joy, immortal diet,***
> > ***My bottle of salvation,***
> > ***My gown of glory, hope's true gage;***
> > > ***And thus I'll take my pilgrimage.***

Pilgrim with staff, scrip (pouch) and scallop shell badge on his hat and on his scrip.
©The Luttrell Psalter (Brit. Lib. Add. 42130), c. 1325-1340

ACKNOWLEDGEMENTS

The contents of this book are a compendium of pieces of work spanning well over a decade. I am grateful for the advice, help and contributions of so many people. These range from maybe just an idea which I investigated, to substantial sections of the text. Throughout, I have endeavoured to credit such. I would like here to give a special 'thank you' to the following.

First and foremost is Dr Kevin Hayward. Indeed, much of the work concerning the stonework would have been impossible without his expertise. We also had great fun from climbing up the remains of the north transept, going round Windsor Castle, to enjoying several lunches where we mulled over our findings.

I would also like to thank Canon John O'Shea of St James' Church. Not only did his enthusiasm for discovering more about the ancient abbey result in important archaeological finds, but maybe more importantly, he brought together sections of our Reading community. This ranged from officials representing Reading Borough Council, such as Councillors Tony Page and Sarah Hacker, to members of the different communities, societies and associations across Reading, all of whom contributed something to the work. Tony, as Deputy Leader of Reading Borough Council and Sarah, when Mayor of Reading, gave me invaluable support.

Despite the difficulties of 'lockdown', another of the town's mayors, David Stevens, was not just a stalwart supporter, but undertook extensive research of his own. He not only promoted interest in the abbey, but instigated and hosted a series of online talks at Reading Museum, where he invited contributors to record interviews with him, covering differing aspects of the abbey.

The Friends of Reading Abbey have been most supportive. John Painter and Peter Durrant encouraged me in the work. The Friends kindly put my various pieces of research onto their website. It is these that form the backbone of this book.

Professor Anne Curry was kind enough to make several comments, which pointed me in the right direction. Thank you.

Geoffrey Scott, at that time Abbot of Douai, the modern Benedictine abbey west of Reading, encouraged our work. I say 'our' because my wife Lindsay, was very much part of the researches. We spent many hours in the abbey's stunning library, gave talks at the abbey and wrote articles for the Benedictine magazine.

And that brings me to my wife, Lindsay. Her gift, not just to analyse historical data but to communicate it in an accessible manner both in her writings and talks, was an invaluable aid. I also thank her for her assiduous reading of the final text and suggestions for its improvement.

Thanks are due to Ron Baxter and Stuart Harrison for all their work on Reading Abbey and for allowing me to use their material. Their practical as well as theoretical knowledge is second to none and helped inform me throughout.

I could not write an acknowledgment without mentioning Professor Brian Kemp. There isn't a single aspect of the abbey that doesn't have some connection with his work. This ranges from his early study of the abbey seals to his most recent book, *Reading Abbey a new miscellany.* This was published just before his death, and it includes a section on the liturgy which tells us so much about the life of the monastery and the monks. Brian's translation of the 12th century manuscript of the 'Miracles of the Hand of St James' is a work of art in itself. Over the years he gave me advice, came round to my house and helped in the design of the illustration of the abbey created by my son, John R. Mullaney.

And my final 'thank you' is to my son John, who is a Fellow of the Society of Architectural Illustrators, and apart from allowing the use of his abbey drawing also designed the jacket of this book.

Stone carving of the cross of St James of Compostela set within a mandorla

Carving John Mullaney, image ©John Mullaney

BIBLIOGRAPHY

The following is a very selective bibliography. Some of these are also mentioned in the body of the text. In addition to the following works, I have given references to other primary and secondary sources throughout the book. In neither case is this an exhaustive list, but rather are an indication of the wide range of material available.

Apel, W. *Gregorian Chant*

Baxter, R. *The Royal Abbey of Reading*

Bernard, G.W. *The Late Medieval English Church*

Bond, F. *Screens and Galleries in English Churches*

Conant, K. *Carolingian and Romanesque Architecture 800-1200*

Cramp, R. *Grammar of Anglo-Saxon Ornament*

Edson Armi, C. *Masons and Sculptors in Romanesque Burgundy*

Evans, J. *Cluniac Art of the Romanesque Period*

Evans, J. *The Romanesque Architecture of the Order of Cluny*

Finucane, R. *Miracles and Pilgrims*

Grivot, D. & Zarnecki, G. *Gislebertus, Sculptor of Autun*

Harrison, S. *Archaeological Survey Report on the Ruins of Reading Abbey, March 2015*

Hillaby, Joe & Caroline. *Leominster Minster, Priory and Borough c660-1539*

Hurry, B.J. *Reading Abbey (1901)*

Kemp, B. *Reading Abbey Cartularies*

Kemp, B. *Reading Abbey Records a new miscellany*

Kemp, B. *The seals of Reading Abbey. Reading Medieval Studies, XIV. pp. 139-162.*

Keyser, C. *Some Norman capitals from Sonning, Berkshire and some sculptured Stones at Shiplake and Windsor Castle* (Proceedings of the Society of Antiquaries, London 1915-1916)

Mullaney, J. *The Reading Abbey Stone*

Paxton, F. *A Medieval Latin Death Ritual*

Slade, C. *Reading Abbey excavations in The Berkshire Archaeological Journal, Vol 68*

Vetus Disciplina Monastica (ed Herrgott, M.)

SOME OF THE PRINCIPAL PEOPLE CONNECTED WITH THE STUDY OF READING ABBEY

ALBURY, FREDERICK WILLIAM (1845-1912) Albury was one of the original pupils at the Reading School of Art, founded in 1860. He went on to become a painter and prominent architect, designing many building in Reading.

BAXTER, RON Dr Baxter is a historian and author of many works on medieval sculpture and architecture. He is the Research Director of the *Corpus of Romanesque Sculpture in Britain and Ireland.* His book *The Royal Abbey of Reading*, published in 2016, is one of the most important studies of Reading Abbey

ENGLEFIELD, HENRY (1752-1852) Sir Henry Englefield was descended from a prominent Catholic family who had owned Englefield House. He lived at Whiteknights, now the University fo Reading. At only 26 he was elected a Fellow of the Royal Society and a year later Fellow of the Society of Antiquaries. Under his leadership the Society worked on producing engravings of several of England's cathedrals. He was awarded a gold medal by the Society of Arts for his "Discovery of a Lake from Madder". As a Catholic and antiquarian he was interested in the ruins of Reading Abbey and produced the report and plan of the site quoted extensively in this book.

HARRISON, STUART Dr Harrison is an archaeologist and architectural historian and a Yoirk Minster Fellow at the University of York. He produced and archaeological report on the ruins of Reading Abbey for Reading Borough Council in 2015. His work is quoted extensively in this book with special reference to the chapter house.

HURRY, JAMIESON BOYD (1857-1930). Dr Hurry was a medical doctor who settled in Reading with a specialist interest in botany. However, among local historian he is best known for his work on the history of Reading Abbey. he also commissioned such well knonw local landmarks, connected with the abbey, such as the memorial cross the Forbury Gardens and the plaques in the chapter house.

KEMP, BRIAN (1940-2019). Professor Kemp was educated at Woodley Hill House (now the Forest School) and at Reading University both as an undergraduate and then gaining his PhD. He worked under Dr Slade and in the mid 80's produced his study of the Reading Abbey Cartularies. This was followed by his pioneering book on English Church Monuments published by Batsford in 1980, and his Shire booklet on Church Monuments. These are still definitive guides to this subject. Brian was active for many years in the Church Monuments Society, serving as its President and remaining as a Vice-President until his death. He was also a much valued member of a number of other national academic committees concerning medieval church records; and was a Fellow of both the Society of Antiquaries and of the Royal Historical Society. Brian was a founder member of the Friends of Reading Abbey, in 1984, when the Abbey Ruins were closed to the public on safety grounds and in need of repair and conservation, and he served FORA continuously for the next 33 years, as Chairman and latterly as President.

KERRY, CHARLES (1858-1928). The Reverend Charles Kerry was vicar at St Lawrence's church. This is the spelling he used, though today it is often written as St Laurence's. He wrote several articles and undertook historical research. In 1883 he wrote a book *A history of the Municipla Church of St Lawrence, Reading.*

SLADE, CECIL Dr Slade was a local boy who became head of the History and Archaeology departments at the University of Reading. He was President of the Berkshire Archaeological Society from 1966 to 2001, and supported the founding of the Friends of Reading Abbey. He undertook several archaeological surveys of the, including the excavation of the apse and of the abbey mill.

WHEBLE, JAMES (c.1779-1840) Wheble was a wealth landowner, owner of Woodley Lodge. He belonged to a Catholic family which had made its fortune in the cable making business in the 18th century. He was married to Mary Talbot, niece of the 14th Earl of Shrewsbury. She died in 1814 and he married Mary O'Brien who died in 1834. He was a staunch Catholic. In 1833, the owner of the abbey ruins, Lord Bexley, decided to sell the ruins and what we now know as the Forbury Reading Corporation bought much of the land, but could afford no more. In 1834 Wheble bought the cloister area and the eastern section of the Forbury which included the chancel area and the Forbury Hill. Wheble was a passionate antiquarian and as a Catholic he wished to discover more about the abbey and excavated in the chancel area. It was here that he discovered the 'Reading Abbey Stone'. In 1837 he became High Sheriff of Berkshire and also engaged the young AWN Pugin to design the new Catholic church of St James alongside the abbey ruins. He died in the summer of 1840, just before the church was officially opened.

ZARNECKI, GEORGE (1915-2008). Professor Zarnecki fled Nazi Germany, and fought in a Polish regiment. He was taken prisoner but escaped and reached Britain via Spain, After the war he stayed in Britain, obtained his doctorate in 12th century sculpture whilst at the Courtauld. He became Deputy Director of the Courtauld and was appointed Oxford University Slade Professor of Fine Art. He did not wish to become Director of the Courtauld, preferring academic research and teaching. His most notable connection with Reading was the discovery of the stone capital of the Crowning of the Virgin at Borough Marsh.

INDEX

This is a selective index, mainly, though not exclusively, of places and people. For main and repeated topics such as the 'Chapter House' see 'Contents'. A few selected items of specialised interest, such as manuscript sources, are in italics.

Abbey Arms/Crest x, 17, 229, 232
Adeliza 33, 72,
Albury F.W. 7, 50, 58
Alfonso VI of Spain 94
Anglo-Saxon Chronicle 54, 61
Apostolatus Benedictinorum in Anglia 232, 234, 235,
Arundel 33
Aske, Robert 221
Autun 172, 173, 176, 182, 203, 240

Baxter, Ron 5, n43, 102, 106, 136, 142-144, 152, 156-158, 162, 224, 234, 239, 240
Benolt 31, 35, 36, 38, 42
Berkshire Archaeological Journal (BAJ) 12, 59, 60, 90, 240
Bernard, G. W 217, 233, 240
Board of Health Survey 54, 57,
Bond, F 43, 240
Bond, J vii
Brown, W 77,
Buckler, C. A 56, 58
Byzantine blossom 162, 163

Canterbury 68, 123, 226
Canterbury Tales/Chaucer 218, 219
Chichester 150, 151, 212
Cistercians 14, 43, 90
Clarenceux 35
Coates, Charles 54, 55, 71, 74, 76, 90, 91
Codex Calixtinus 204, 205
Conant, K 47, 97, 100, 108, 110, 240
Cramp, R 162, 163, 240
Cranmer, T 221

Cromwell, T 216, 221, 231, 233
Crowle lectern 160, 161
Curry, A 119, 238

Doran, J 66, 76, 90, 91
Dorchester Abbey 31, 32, 39
Douai viii, 131-133, 206, 238
Duffy, E 221, 233
Durham 48, 66, 69, 80, 86, 90, 99, 101, 102, 105, 111

Ely 102, 105-107, 111
Englefield, H and *Englefield's Survey,* 53, 55, 56, 58, 66, 72-74, 76, 80, 83, 84, 90, 91, 102, 114, 115, 117, 119, 125, 155,
Exeter 66
Exultet Rolls 169

Faringdon, Abbot Hugh Cook 216
Finucane, R 233, 240
Flores historiarum 34, 222
Foundation Charter 25, 165, 171, 175, 211, 226, 230

Gervase of Canterbury 6, 33
Gislebertus (Master of Autun) 94, 172, 184, 186, 198, 240
Gloucester 15, 16, 66, 222
Godfrey 73
Ground Penetrating Radar Survey (GPR) 12, 43, 44, 62, 100, 104
Guido Fava 19, 42, 172, 202
Gunzo 94

Hand of St James 11, 13, 96, 165, 204-205, 211-212, 218, 222-225, 229, 232, 236, 239

Harrison, S 64, 79, 81, 83, 85, 90, 91, 114, 119, 239, 240

Hayward, K   iii, viii, 1, 84, 112, 116, 120-122, 125, 127, 135, 138, 144, 146, 148, 156, 238

Henry of Blois 18

Henry VIII 217, 221, 231, 233, 234

Hézelon of Liège 46, 94

Hidden Abbey Project (HAP) vi, 44, 62, 100, 126

Hidden Abbey Stones Project (HASP) viii, 126

Holme Park 134, 136, 143, 165

Hugh of Amiens (First abbot of Reading) 137, 168, 212

Hugh II of Reading 212, 227

Hurry, Dr Jamieson x, 33, 43, 58, 59, 132, 234, 240

Kemp, B. vii, viii, 3, 13, 19, 20, 25, 27, 32, 35, 42, 43, 90-92, 137, 172, 175, 182, 185-188, 193, 200, 203, 224, 226, 234, 239, 240

Keyser, C 123, 134, 136, 142, 143, 152, 156, 162, 165, 240

King John 22, 24, 29, 38

King of Arms (See 'Clarenceux')

Lambeth Palace 31, 33

Langland 218, 219

Liber tramitis 42

Lincoln (Cathedral) 28

Luther, M 218, 220, 221

Malmesbury (William of) 219

Man, J 56

Mary Tudor viii, 130, 136

Matthew Paris v, 3, 34

Mellor, J 58

Miracles Of The Hand Of St James (See *Hand of St James*)

Monreale 82, 87

Monte Cassino 169,

Much Wenlock 80, 85, 160, 161

Norwich 103, 123

Origen 15

Penizon, William 216

Peter, Prior of Cluny 94, 137

Peter the Venerable 46

Peterborough 123

Physiologus (Pliny's) 15, 171

Pignot, J Henri 43

Poor Knights' Lodgings, Windsor viii, 130, 135, 136, 140, 141, 142, 144, 145, 149, 152

Pugin, AWN vi, 49, 108, 155

Quenington (St Swithin's) 166, 168, 171

Raleigh, Sir Walter 237,

Ravenscroft, W 59

Richard II 25, 26, 35

Ripon 96

Roger, Bishop of Salisbury 168,

Roger of Hoveden 222

Roger of Wendover 34

Salisbury 103, 106, 111, 124, 194, 225-227, 229

Silvacane Abbey 81

Silver Street (Reading) 16, 88, 90

Slade, Cecil vi, 7, 9, 12, 16, 40, 58-61, 63, 74, 79, 90, 91, 240

Sonning 120, 123, 125, 134, 165, 240

Speed J (Map) 51, 94, 106

St. Albans 96, 102, 105, 111

St Benedict of Nursia 14, 65, 87, 89, 98, 165, 206,

St James' church and school, Reading vi-viii, 17, 53, 59, 60, 107, 112, 117, 123-125, 128, 130, 143, 153, 155, 238

St Lazarus, Autun (See Autun)

St Swithin's church, Quenington (See Quenington)

Stokesey 66

Suger (Abbot) 95, 99, 101

Taylor, J. Okey 58
Taynton quarry 84, 94, 120, 122, 156, 168
Tewkesbury 93, 102, 103, 105, 109, 111
Tilehurst 16
Tomkins, C 75, 114

Ulrich 42, 90, 91, 184, 202

Valor Ecclesiasticus 221, 231, 232
Vetus disciplina 42, 90, 91, 178, 183, 184, 187, 194, 195, 202, 240
Vézelay 48, 82
Viking 54, 59, 61, 162
Villard de Honnecourt 126

Walkelyn 67
Waverleia 34
Werckmeister 173
Wessex Archaeology 62
Westminster viii, 19, 83, 103, 123-125, 172
Wheble, James 76, 153-155, 157-159
William Adeline 220
William d'Albini 33
William de Sutton (Abbot of Reading) 227, 228
William de Winton 210
William I 3, 137
William II (Rufus), 3, 18, 219
William of Poitiers 34
William of Wicumbe 210
Winchester 16-18, 29, 38, 39, 66, 67, 102, 105, 111, 156, 189, 190, 207, 210, 219
Windsor viii, 1, 18, 129, 130, 134-139, 142-144, 146, 149, 151, 152, 238, 240
Woodville, Elizabeth 71, 87
Worcester 22, 29, 38, 39, 102, 105, 108, 111
Worssam, B 156, 164
Wyatville 141, 142, 144

Zarnecki, G 162, 164, 165, 172, 240